Climbing Every Mountain

A Family's Journey
of Faith in South Asia

Jessie Glover

AF207326

All Scripture quotations, unless otherwise noted, are taken from the Holy Bible, New Living Translation © 1996, 2004, 2007 by Tyndale House Foundation.

Scripture quotations marked (GNT) are taken from the Good News Bible. Copyright © 1966, 1971, 1976, 1992 by American Bible Society.

Scripture quotations marked (NIV) are taken from the Holy Bible New International Version®. Copyright © 1973, 1978, 1984, 2011 by Biblica, Inc.™.

Scripture quotations marked (RSV) are taken from the Revised Standard Version of the Bible, copyright © 1946, 1952, and 1971 National Council of the Churches of Christ in the United States of America.

Poems by Eddie Askew, former General Director of The Leprosy Mission, on pp. 174 and 176 are quoted by permission.

Permission to quote Elizabeth Givens' poem *Ants in the Sugar Bowl* (pp. 139-40) and from *The Galilee Song* by Fr Frank Andersen (p. 147) has been sought.

ISBN   9780 6454 67208   Climbing Every Mountain

Cover design by Gordon Thompson

Cover photos by Gordon Russell, who says "Give credit to .the One who created it."

Follow a little girl from a tiny rural town in eastern Australia to the base of the towering Himalayas and beyond. See how she and her husband, persevering against great odds refused to give up. Leaning hard on God, they lived to see Him open doors closed for centuries to reach an isolated people group for whom He died.

GARY SHEPHERD
Bible translator and author of *Angel tracks in the Himalayas*

A captivating, biographical story that you cannot put down as you want to find what God will do next in Jessie's life. It is written with great sensitivity and demonstrates how God was watching over Jessie from the day she was born. Her dreams and hopes of seeing the world are fulfilled far beyond what she could ever imagine, as God leads her and Warren (her husband) to the mission field.

Throughout the book there are moments of humour, sadness, poetry, appropriate letters from friends, how God answers prayer for them and how they adjusted to a different culture.

JOCELYN FORMBY
President, Australian Church Library Association, Victorian Chapter

Stories of the faith have always been immensely enriching as people pass on their experience of God's love and "make [His] faithfulness known through all generations" (Ps 89:1). Jessie Glover's memoir is an enthusiastic testimony of deep lifelong faith, adventurous ministry and God's inescapable goodness.

OWEN SALTER
former editor *On Being* magazine

Reflections on God's loving presence and enabling power in the midst of life's challenges – we all need to let God work in our daily lives.

Canon Dr DAVID CLAYDON OAM
Former Federal Secretary of the Church Missionary Society

For our encouragement Jessie Glover has traced the hand of God in her life. Look what happens when she says "Yes!" to God and the adventure that he wants for her. Let us follow her example.

MICHAEL COLLIE
Former CMS missionary

I first met Jessie Glover as my lecturer in the SIL advanced Literacy Class in 1984. I was immediately struck by the fact she was both a teacher and a learner. I am therefore not surprised that in reading her story you will find someone who is always a learner. She is the adopted daughter fashioned by her parents of nurture, a mother who learns from her children, a teacher who learns from her students, a leader who learns from those she serves, an adventurer who embraces her misadventures. Most of all she is a follower of Jesus who learns not to fear but to lean on her heavenly father when times are uncertain. It leads Jessie on an extraordinary journey: a story all the more compelling by the honesty in which it is told. And right to the end she remains 'the learner' inviting the reader to learn along with her.

BARRY BORNEMAN
Former CEO Wycliffe Australia

Dedicated
to my family, who have shared much of this journey
with me, to my faithful friends and to the goodly
fellowship of prayer and finance partners, many of
whom have been part of the story for the whole nearly
six decades of our "going out and coming in".

An invitation!

Come journey with me in learning God's ways
through the challending climbs He set before me:—

discovering the unconditional love of foster parents,
struggling up sandstone gorges after summer swims,
overcoming grief in the loss of a brother,
overwhelmed by the comfort and love of God —
greater even than the affection of any other beloved one.
Called to cross cultures in sharing His great love,
challenged by unscaled language barriers,
facing unbelievably complex routes over illiteracy.
Discovering the Guide's care and protection for my children,
even in traversing the boarding school separations.
Discovering that transient housing
and constant travel are part of the climb.
Proving the importance of teamwork
and the joy of passing on to others
the skills learned in serving a loving God.

The LORD watches over you as you come and go. (Psalm 121:8a)

During 2020 when our world began to descend into the lockdown of the COVID-19 pandemic, Warren and I were often reminded in our morning devotions of the importance of passing on to the next generation a record of the Lord's power and goodness to us over many decades, during most of which we were constantly going and coming to and from parts of South Asia.

"Now that I am old and grey, do not abandon me, O God. Let me proclaim your power to this new generation, your mighty miracles to all who come after me" (Psalm 71:18).

With travel limited and public meetings prohibited, I realised that 2020 was the year when I should have plenty of time to record some of the story from my own life of how the Lord has led us all the way.

1

Warren and I have served with Wycliffe Bible Translators, Australia for over 50 years. Warren as a linguist and Bible translator and I in literacy and non-formal education. We have worked in several South Asian countries, initially amongst a people group in Nepal. Working with them, we helped to reduce their previously unwritten language to writing and to translate the New Testament. Subsequently, we focussed largely on training nationals of several South Asian countries in translation and language development.

In reviewing the history, I have been repeatedly reminded of the false starts, steep ascents, landslides, unexpected turns and unwelcome surprises. However, in all these challenges, I sensed the smile of God and had the assurance of His loving presence with me all the way.

For resources, I have drawn on our newsletters, "Glovers' Gazette", which served to inform and mobilize our wonderful team of prayer and finance supporters over the past 58 years. Collections of letters to and from family members have helped jog our memories, and I have drawn often on "Glovers' Pilgrimage", a chronological record Warren compiled in 1998, while recuperating from a heart attack. My own journals (1986 to present) reminded me of the deeper signals and nudges that clarified the next step on the trail.

I am truly thankful for Warren's keen editorial eye and attention to detail applied to my first draft and his countless hours in typesetting the whole document, and the kind advice, suggestions and insight from our author-daughter Merryn. I appreciate their time lovingly given. Owen Salter has given much valuable advice as a skilled and professional editor. The story has benefited immensely from all of this input.

The deficiencies and limitations in the story remain with me. I trust that our children, grandchildren and great grandchildren, along with any other brave readers, will come to a deeper understanding of the mighty wonders and grace our loving Lord works in the lives of anyone who sets their heart to follow Jesus on the pilgrim journey.

Jessie Glover, March 2022.

Dil Araam, Ringwood

PART 1 The first miles

1 Adopted

God decided in advance to adopt us into his own family by bringing us to himself through Jesus Christ This is what he wanted to do, and it gave him great pleasure. (Ephesians 1:5)

I must have been barely four years old. I awoke early one Christmas morning to the sight of a gorgeous china doll, nestled in a new dolly stroller by the side of my bed. She was dressed in an exquisite pink organdie baby dress, decorated with intricate smocked embroidery across the chest and with a matching pink bonnet on her head. My fondest hopes fulfilled! I ran excitedly into my adoptive parents' bedroom to show them the gorgeous gift left by Santa that night.

Today people don't look favourably on adoption. Will the child really fit into the adoptive family? Will they hanker to find their biological roots and feel resentful or shattered that they were given up as unwanted? Unloved? Psychological misfits?

Me as a toddler

In my case, my foster mum early on explained to me, as I stood by her busy treadle sewing machine, how I had become part of their family. My birth mother had died soon after my birth. My father, Cyril, in his grief, kept his two eldest children, Norman (13) and June (11), with him to help on the orchard and in the kitchen, but he needed to find homes for the other children: Jack (8), Gwen (6), Beth (3½), and baby me. Finding a home for the baby had proved problematic until close neighbours (of three kilometres distance), Nell and Fred Whitticase, offered to mind the baby "till Cyril could find a more permanent home for her."

Mum told me that within three weeks she and Dad both hoped that Cyril never would find me any other "permanent home". Unlike their three elder children, I was a baby who never had colic, was easy to get to sleep and of quite placid temperament. So, I never needed to hanker after who my biological family might be, nor puzzle why they'd left me for adoption. In later years, Mum and Dad hoped to go through the formal legal adoption process, but in apprehension that Cyril might decline, or request me back, they did not bring up the issue. But she said to me, "Jessie, you didn't grow under my heart, my love, but into it."

Occasionally both families travelled together for medical or dental treatments, available only in nearby towns or further afield in the city. Cyril often chided my adoptive parents that they were too soft on me. They needed to harden me up. "She's too much of a cry-baby!" he'd often say. So when the next visit to the dentist was upcoming, Dad had an idea for encouraging me in courageous behaviour. "If you don't cry at all at the dentist, I will build you a great big doll's house that you yourself and all your dolls can live in." This bribe worked wonders. I uttered not a whimper as the dentist noisily drilled away into my mouth. In contrast, my sister Beth roared the roof down. This certainly helped to highlight that the adoptive parents were not doing too bad a job of hardening Jessie up. And yes, the doll's house did quickly materialize.

My Dad was a craftsman specializing in leather. So all the hinges on the door and windows of the doll's house were leather. He lined the floor with pretty patterned linoleum and decorated the walls with framed prints of late 19th century domestic scenes. Dad built a lovely "piano" using a xylophone base inside a wooden piano-like outer shell. Dolls' beds, chairs, tables, and associated paraphernalia soon filled that wonderful space. In that two-metre square house of privacy, nicely removed from the main house, I lived in the imaginative world of my three children – who each had different names and personalities. I regularly lined them up to take solemn part in Morning or Evening Prayer services, which I conducted with an Anglican prayer book Mum had lent me. Did she know how I used it? Thus, from early on I was feeding on wonderful prayers and psalms about my heavenly adoptive Father.

My closest friend, Maria, lived two kilometres up the road, not quite near enough to visit. So Mum would often invite a second cousin once removed to come up from Sydney "so Jessie could have company during school holidays". But in fact, I already had three friends to play with, the three in my doll's house. I did not want cousin Rosemary intruding into my world. In fact, the poor cousin got quite a cold shoulder for at least the whole of Week 1 of the holidays, and by the time I realised she was really quite good company, it was time for her to return to Sydney.

Mum's loving persona was further shown by how she lived in the community. As a preschooler I would walk hand in hand with her through the thick Australian bush to one of the nearby neighbours. There was the lonely widow, Mrs Buxton, who always welcomed a visit. Mum would bring a gift of freshly baked scones or marmalade jam, while together we enjoyed the welcoming cuppa from our hostess and a catch up on local news. It always fascinated me how Mrs Buxton carved slices of bread from the loaf. She set the loaf upright and carved off each slice horizontally, in perfect thickness for the sandwiches she made.

Mum with 3-year-old Jessie

But I can't say I enjoyed the visit to the local medium a little further down the road. Mrs Waterson, with her wiry mop of unkempt grey hair and steely grey eyes, frightened me no end. She read people's teacups and was a fortune teller at the local annual fetes and agricultural shows. The house was always a shambles, smelt of urine, and the outside looked as though it had never, ever seen a coat of paint. But Mum kept including old Mrs Waterson in her pastoral visits.

Then there was the old hermit bachelor, Ces. He lived in a tin lean-to humpy in the nearby bush and was a regular visitor to our house, especially on the nights that his favourite TV soapie was on. The most demanding part for Mum of Ces's visit was the "letter box talk" at the end of the evening. Ces would stand, legs crossed and hand on hip, while he held the back door open and launched into a lengthy discourse on the affairs of his week. He seemed unaware of the night chill coming in, or of Dad's brusque signals to Mum, "Let him go!" But Mum unfailingly invited Ces back week by week, and fed him well with chocolate biscuits or whatever had been on special that week at the village store.

Ces was also a regular feature of my school holidays. I was very particular about keeping my doll's house clean and tidy, emulating my somewhat house-proud Mum, and so it worried me no end that Ces's corrugated iron lean-to was an absolute shambles, or a hoarder's paradise, according to your worldview. I would beg Mum to let me go across to Ces's place for a few hours during holidays to help him clean up. Amazingly, Ces never objected to this invasion of his privacy, and tried to cooperate with the blast of the "clean up, toss out" campaign associated with my visits. The main problem was that for several weeks (or months?) afterwards Ces would bring up a plaintive, almost apologetic query on his regular visits, inquiring about a particular document or letter that he "somehow hadn't been able to lay his hands on since Jessie's last visit. Might Jessie remember seeing it?"

In the bosom of this family I learned not only what compassion and kindness meant but also something about the character of my heavenly Father. God was everywhere, he could see all our behaviour, was pleased with the good, not so happy with the bad, they taught me. This truth got reinforced for me one day when I was watching Dad at his leather work bench. I marvelled at all the knives and awls that he used in his trade of making bridles, saddles and neck collars for draught and police horses. One day he drew my attention to a particularly sharp semi-circular bladed knife. "Now make sure you never touch this knife as it is very sharp and can do you great harm," he cautioned. As expected of a growing child, I needed to use that very knife when trying to cut some thick leather Dad had given me to play with. As Dad had warned, the knife slipped and gashed a deep cut between thumb and first finger. In shock and horror, I raced down to the bush where I could hold the gash tightly shut till the flow of blood had eased sufficiently for me to cover it with a large Band-Aid or two. I don't recall if Mum or Dad ever found out about why I had Band-Aids in abundance on my hand, but the sense of shame and guilt about the incident lasted – giving me an even deeper sense of how important it was to heed what Father God might want to teach me.

On a more positive note, my earliest God memory was, at about three years of age, of lying down on the grass on a lovely sunny afternoon, marvelling at how clever God must be to draw such amazing cloud pictures in the sky. I imagined woolly lambs, white bushes, and flowers flying across the sky.

A more significant God memory goes back to the time in primary school when the aged lady who taught us weekly boring Bible lessons brought along a tall young trainee minister. Instead of the usual monotonous drone, he spent the time teaching us an action song that went:

> Wide, wide as the ocean,
> High as the heavens above,
> Deep, deep as the deepest sea,
> Is my Saviour's love.

> I, though so unworthy, still am a child of His care,
> For His word teaches me,
> that His love reaches me,
> Everywhere!

That is my first remembered awareness that I had a loving heavenly Father, who loved me even more deeply than my earthly adoptive one could.

Wilton Public School 1946—I'm leftmost in the back row ,
my sister Beth is 3rd from left and Maria rightmost in the front row

I mostly enjoyed the five years at the little one-teacher primary school at Wilton. It was just one long room, with a closed-in verandah where we hung jackets and bags, and an all-weather shed across from the school for use on rainy or boiling hot days. I don't recall there being any play equipment at all in the yard. The teacher divided us into classes by assigning the eleven to thirteen pupils to different long desks.

Maria from up the road was my only friend and classmate. She came from an Italian migrant family and was nervous that she might speak with a laughable accent like her parents, so refused to address the teacher. She had me translate for her after whispering her responses in my ear. Out in the playground she didn't even try to communicate orally, but still entered fully into playground games. One game which engaged us girls for months on end, and needed little talking, was to use the exposed root system of an ancient pine tree to make little segregated dolls' houses with bits of glass, shiny material, pebbles and sticks. From time to time, the teacher offered a small prize for the best "house". A small price to pay for the self-contained entertainment for half of his pupils during every snack and lunch break.

I remember little of the academic matters, except that Maria always beat me in just about every subject. Miss Smith, one of my earliest teachers, signed us all up as members of the *Gould League of Bird Lovers* and so we accumulated a growing set of cards to help us identify Australian birds. Sadly, I don't recall that she ever took us outside to help us identify the birds in our own locality. But I subsequently did develop a strong interest in the world of birds.

There was a glass fronted library cupboard at one end of the room. I don't recall the teacher ever introducing us to any of the books from that cupboard, either to read them ourselves, or to have them read to us. Perhaps having to manage about four or five distinct classes in the one room meant she didn't have time for any such "frills" as reading for leisure. Even in the Whitticase home, there were very few books. An annual anthology of stories, poems and songs published by Coles was about my only resource for reading for pleasure.

"It is a public holiday, and you are all free to go home!" It was 10 August 1945 and I was in Grade 2 when the teacher suddenly informed us that the war was over. On the way home, we detoured to the shade of Allens Creek bridge to eat our lunches. That added to the excitement and fun which the older students felt. They understood more of the significance of the day. My other memory of postwar pleasure, after rationing was lifted, is of gently gliding on the swing in our backyard to enjoy the first sweet biscuit I had ever tasted – nibbling as slowly as I could to prolong the pleasure! It was a delicious Iced Vovo, still one of Arnott's favourites in supermarkets today.

Summer holidays were a highlight of the year. During that time Dad's work partner, "Mr Smith" as we respectfully called him, would take a bunch of kids from nearby families down to the Cataract River that bordered our property, for a welcome swim.

The river meandered through a deeply stratified sandstone gorge for several kilometres until it joined the larger Nepean River on its way to the Sydney water supply reservoirs. The sandstone gorges were challenging to scramble down, and even more challenging to climb back up at the end of the afternoon. However, from much use, climbing trails were quite clear and once we took a breather at the top, we were soon home again after an easier walk through the bush, with eyes glued to the path ahead in case of snakes. All this effort was worth it for the pleasure of the swim in the crystal clear gently flowing river. Large slabs of sandstone lined the bottom and at certain clearly visible places there were deeper holes. The braver older lads would climb up huge riverside rocks to show off by diving into these holes. But I just enjoyed the challenge of learning to swim further and further as I grew older. I loved the backstroke laps across the river, from which I would leisurely look up to the lovely red Christmas bushes clinging high up the sides of the gorge, amazingly thriving in crevices seeming to lack any soil. The calls of whipbirds, magpies and kookaburras seemed to laugh at the antics of those humans frolicking in the waters below.

But there were also dark sides to this bush paradise. One had to always beware of the not so friendly wildlife. Dad shot the goannas (which were eager to get into the chook pen for eggs and fowl), and we avoided snakes wherever they might appear, especially the deadly ones such as the red-bellied black and the brown. To me, they all seemed deadly and were my chief fear, or at least apprehension, while walking through the bush.

But the deadliest enemy in the environment were the bush fires that inevitably flared up each summer. I have early memories of watching the glow of the approaching fire during the night, and trying to estimate how close the fire might come to our house before dawn. Would it be safe to go to sleep or should we keep watch just in case? Nowadays in a world warmed by climate change, waiting till dawn is never possible. Then also memories of preparing scones and thermoses of tea for the weary local volunteer firefighters who came to help. Thanks to the vigilance of the local Bush Fire Brigade, and the thoroughness of Dad's never-ending mowing of the grass for about 300 metres all around the house, the fires never did burn the house down. However, the house did burn down several years later, because of a faulty electrical fitting. Thankfully, Dad had already moved to an aged care home, and mercifully did not understand the sad news of the destruction of the house he had so lovingly built for his family. The fire-ravaged sandstone walls are free standing on the property but of no structural use after the fire damage.

A highlight of many a summer night was the dance in the village hall. Dad loved music and was the popular disc jockey for most of these occasions. He had a great store of vinyl records that were played over a loudspeaker for the Pride of Erin, foxtrot, and quickstep. In the all-time favourite progressive barn dance you changed partners throughout the dance, and could thus prove your stuff as a skilled dancer, hoping to extend future dancing options. There was many a romantic match hatched during these dances, much to the speculation and interest of the local matriarchs watching (and gossiping) from their seats around the dance floor. The delicious supper of elegant sandwiches, slices, scones and sponges was worth dying for.

My early childhood was thus filled with a joyful sense of life being good and of my natural environment being both beautiful and awesome. But there were family tensions ahead which, in my naivety, I did not foresee. Being the child of two families in the one district presented some challenges! (See the family tree on page 210.)

2 A child of two families

A gentle answer deflects anger, but harsh words make tempers flare. (Proverbs 15:1)

When I became part of the Whitticase family there were three elder siblings, Norma (14), Alan (9) and Shirley (7). My earliest memory of sibling care is of Norma's effort to bring some wave into my thick straight hair by carefully rolling it around about 20 strips of cotton cloth before I went to bed. She guaranteed this process would transform my hair into pretty ringlets. I remember crying in horror and disbelief as I glimpsed into the mirror the next

Alan, Shirley and Norma in 1932

morning, a transformation I decidedly did not like. Thankfully, I don't remember any repeats of that procedure.

I remember how fastidious Norma was in carefully ironing clothes with the solid flatiron, which she heated on our black topped wrought iron stove. She placed a damp cloth and brown paper over the garment to guarantee a creaseless finish. I was still small when she moved to Sydney, where she became an apprentice milliner, a skill she mastered well. Before long, she set up her own business, which flourished in the years when hats were mandatory for any properly dressed lady, and not just for race attendees. Norma was clearly gifted with her Mum's creative genes.

Alan was the practical one of the family, keenly interested in birds. He had many exotic breeds caged in our backyard aviary. As he got older, he became devoted to motor bikes and was pleased to get an apprenticeship as a motor mechanic in his teen years. I loved riding pillion with him, despite once getting a nasty burn on the inside of my ankle from the exhaust pipe when trying to get off the bike.

Shirley was closest to my age, but with seven years between us, we had little in common. We both learned to knit on cold winter evenings as the family huddled around the open fire in the loungeroom. Shirley was not as creatively talented as Norma, but became a well valued "lady in black" as a shop assistant in Mark Foys, one of Sydney's most prestigious stores. One day when I was still quite young, she severely rebuked me for some advice or criticism I gave her. "Who do you think you are? The Queen of Sheba?" I didn't have any idea who the Queen of Sheba was, but assumed she must have been quite a powerful lady. Apart from this put down, I have no memory of the Whitticase siblings resenting the unexpected sister arriving in their family.

In her generous kindness, Mum felt sorry for my biological father, the widower Cyril, and his remaining children, and often invited the Segal family for Saturday evening meals and/or games nights. Grandpa Louis, Cyril's Jewish father, also lived at the orchard and was thus a regular part of the family visit. Louis had escaped from the Lithuanian pogroms of the late 19th century and eventually settled in Australia. He had spent a brief time in England, where he had met my Welsh grandmother, Gwendolyn Thomas. My memory of Grandpa Segal was of his strange thick accent, white beard and incredibly long white eyebrows which seemed to hang out like a verandah over his eyes. There would also have been my eldest brother Norman (until he joined the Army in 1942), June, and the two other sisters, Gwen and Beth, who by then were living back with Cyril.

Brother Jack lived with another local family and so was not included in the Saturday night family get-togethers, much to his regret.

To me, it was a night of invasion that I dreaded all week. I didn't want to be hugged and kissed by the unwelcome intruders. Their presence reminded me that there was a conflict of allegiance, and my emotional allegiance was, quite early on, firmly with the family of nurture. In addition, these siblings were often shabbily dressed, with dishevelled hair, noisy in behaviour, and they all smelt unpleasantly strange to me. It might have been just the smell of the orchard life, but it was strange to my nostrils. (I am ashamed to recollect these unkind negative attitudes. Cyril was obviously finding it hard to be both Dad and Mum to his bereft children.)

At one point, the sister next elder to me, Beth, joined me in Camden hospital when we each had a tonsillectomy. I think I was about four years old, and Beth seven or eight. (Doctors recommended the operation if sore throats or upper respiratory tract infections persisted.) I imagine that Cyril and Mum agreed it would be nice for the siblings to share this enforced absence from their homes to help in the bonding. However, that loving thought backfired when some kindly friend came to visit Beth, bringing her a lovely tub of icecream which she devoured *alone*! Neither family visited during the week of hospitalization, perhaps rightly assuming that a midweek visit might cause a midweek mutiny by the patients to return home. Beth did dink me on the back of her pushbike to the little Wilton public school, but chatting along the way was not a feature of the trip since the effort required on the undulating roads kept her entirely focussed on getting to school on time. Bicycles of that era had no gears to help manage hills. However, through her I had a daily connection with the orchard family.

For my eldest sister June, Saturday nights were a welcome break from cooking. Forced to become housekeeper at twelve within a year of her mother's death, she was deeply disappointed to miss high school and she struggled under Cyril's harsh expectations. June told me she timed boiling eggs by songs on the radio, but when one song was longer than usual and the egg she served to her Dad was hard, he threw it at her. Similarly, Cyril expected Norman, fifteen, to help on the orchard, but Norman clashed too much with Cyril, so he left home as soon as he could, soon to enlist in WW2.

Elder brother Jack's foster parents were Maggie and Ted Thornton, a childless couple living high above the little village school and church. Jack could easily get to school from their home. The Thorntons meant well, but didn't understand the needs of a lively boy. He had to spend his free time studying, and they did not allow him to play with other children. They enforced this restriction, even watching with a telescope his progress up to their hilltop home after school. Six-year-old Gwen went to a loving family and even moved with them to another town, until Cyril worried he might lose her and fetched her home.

Three-year-old Beth probably suffered the most from her mother's premature demise. She was old enough to miss her mother badly, but too young to understand. No longer a cute baby, she didn't get the affection and attention that I did. She went to relatives for a little while, but was unhappy and came home, where she was left to her own devices and somewhat neglected (sister June's comment). She was seven before she started school, because no-one had thought about it till my Mum had a word to Cyril.

A few years later, Cyril remarried. Pearl was a Sydneysider who brought some emotional support to Gwen and Beth, but was quite adamant that

she felt she couldn't cope with the teenage son, Jack. Years later, Jack spoke to me of the deep hurt he felt in not being able to return to life in the family home on the orchard.

The Saturday nights at the Whitticase home, with slap-up meals and table games, were precious to everyone. Except for me. Once I was old enough to work things out, I found the gatherings uncomfortable. Mum and Dad Whit loved and looked after me as one of their own and I was happy with the people I believed were my family. But then this wild bunch of ragamuffins would turn up, squeeze and cuddle me, and say, "You're *our* little sister." So these visits made me anxious

Cyril and his 6 children on Jessie's first birthday, at Whitticases' place

that I might one day have to go back to the Segals. I felt very different from them. While they were unkempt, I was always beautifully turned out in the dresses Mum, a professional seamstress, made for me. While Cyril seemed cold and hard, Dad Whit was a great lover of music and dance; a skilled craftsman, making me gifts like the walk-in doll's house.

When I was 9, the matter was forcefully settled. In a bitter village dispute over the closing of the local one-teacher school, my two fathers were on opposite sides and never spoke to one another again. Mum was mortified and afraid that Cyril, by then re-married to Pearl, might ask for me back. He didn't, but he also wouldn't let the family come around anymore. No more Saturday nights of fun and games for the Segal siblings. This was devastating for Mum, who missed them and worried

14

about them. One time she said, "Surely Cyril won't be so pig-headed that he refuses the catch-up with his own daughter."

I responded instantly, "Well, I don't care if they never come down again. I've never liked those Saturday nights." Mum's face showed she had had no idea how difficult I'd found those gatherings.

In fact, I don't recall meeting Cyril again, nor the other siblings apart from Beth. We both travelled on the school bus to Picton when we were in High School together for a short time. However, being three and a half years apart, we had very little to do with one another.

When June married in 1953, she asked me to join Gwen and Beth as a bridesmaid and thus complete the complement of her three sisters as her attendants. I remember little about this event, though it must have

Beth, Gwen, June and me

been exciting to be a bridesmaid at just fifteen, and the photographs show my Mum's skill in the making of the beautiful salmon-coloured chiffon dress. Since Cyril didn't die till 1955, I must have seen him at the wedding, but I have no memory of our meeting or speaking together. Perhaps I was still avoiding him, or he was avoiding me so as not to embarrass me?

In 1955, during my first year away at Wagga Wagga Teachers' College, I received word that Cyril had died suddenly. From that distance, it was not possible for me to return for the funeral. But during my next vacation back home, Mum and I visited Pearl to offer our condolences. She clearly welcomed this gesture, and it opened the pathway for reconciliation between the two families.

Being then older and more mature, I could welcome more interactions with my biological siblings. Jack and his new wife Esther spent some time helping at the orchard after Cyril's death and often came down to visit the Whitticase home. In time, just before their first child's birth, Jack and Esther went to live in Perth, Esther's home place. There, Jack and Esther built up a very successful business in the sale of outdoor furnishings. *Segal's Furnishings* became such a well-known shop that when Jack eventually sold it to new owners, the goodwill of the name went with the sale.

Gwen and Beth did the usual thing for young people of the time and travelled throughout Europe. Beth returned and took up training as a nurse. She worked for some years in Mt Hagen hospital in PNG where she met a builder, Owen. They married and raised their two children, Andrew and Wanda, in Townsville. They both felt climatically more at home there than further south.

Gwen stayed on in London. Because of a good reference from a well-known fashion house where she had trained in Sydney, she got a position as a seamstress with Norman Hartnell, dressmaker for the queen. She had the thrill of an invitation from the Queen Mother to tea at Clarence House along with other Hartnell seamstresses in appreciation for their work on the wedding gown of Princess Margaret. Gwen also had a part in working on the Queen's wardrobe for overseas tours. She still has a scrapbook of pieces of cloth and pictures of the Queen on her trip to Canada, in the garments Gwen had helped make.

On her way home to Australia, Gwen detoured via Canada and while in Quebec joined a class for learning French. In the class was a rather ebullient, handsome fellow student, learning French to relate well to the clientele in his hairdressing business. In quick time, Norman Zimring persuaded Gwen to change her travel plans and her surname! They soon moved down to Los Angeles where Norman built up a very successful swimming pool manufacturing business in which Gwen partnered with him for many years. After Norman's passing in October 2017, their elder son, Bernard manages the thriving business.

My eldest brother Norman Segal spent four years as a POW. According to the "Calendar of Events" he wrote up after the war, his unit arrived in Timor from Darwin 11 December 1941, and surrendered to the Japanese Army 23 February 1942. He was in Timor for a further seven months before being sent to Java in September 1942, where he worked in three or four labour camps until May 1944. He was then sent to Singapore, from where he was immediately shipped to Japan via the Philippines and Taiwan. The ship carrying the POWs was torpedoed by American forces near midnight on 24 June 1944, and Norman was rescued after ten hours in the sea by a Japanese vessel. He was taken to Nagasaki in Japan. The war with Japan ended on 15 August 1945 (Victory over Japan, VJ day) and Norman was released 22 September 1945. After ten days of physical rebuilding in Manila, Philippines, Norman was returned to Australia 16 October 1945. The war experience took a huge toll on his physique and mental health.

He had written me a postcard from Manila, introducing himself as the brother I probably couldn't remember but who was looking forward to meeting me again on his return. With the emotional immaturity of eight years, I dreaded that reunion. In my adult years, I recognised Norman as a very successful salesman of farm tractors in the Nambour region, north of Brisbane, but somewhat overtaken by a preoccupation with Old Testament views of God, the Ten Commandments and God's judgement upon the world and most everyone in it. Not a peaceful man to reason with, perhaps like his father. No wonder they quarrelled in the orchard.

June was the academic of the family, but sadly had little opportunity to shine due to not attending high school. She got training in Sydney in office skills and subsequently married Ken Aylward, who was an army man, then and for most of his adult life. June was a lifelong reader and learner. When her son Bruce showed evidence of reading and spelling difficulty, June linked up with Speld QLD and researched causes of his challenge and ways to help dyslexic people with reading. She was also a very creative person, flower decorator, artist and writer. She was a keen actress and became known as the Queenie Ashton of the North during her many years with the Townsville Little Theatre company.

My husband frequently comments, "You certainly come from a very interesting family!" Perhaps their initiative and success might stem from the fact that their tough Dad, Cyril, more or less pushed them out of the orchard home as soon as they were 15 in order to find their own feet and stand up for themselves in the city. This they all did. However, in Norman's path to adulthood through the POW experience, he endured trauma that no young man should ever have to bear – and the lifelong scars he bore as a result affected not only himself, but alienated his wife and two children from him for the rest of his life.

Sad though Norman's story became, it was a traumatic incident within my family of nurture that impacted me much more.

3 Where is God when it hurts?

The eternal God is your refuge, and his everlasting arms are under you. (Deuteronomy 33:27)

On 21 February 1950, I was sitting on a front seat of the school bus on the way to the High School in nearby Picton. As we approached a crest of the road, I noticed an upturned motor bike. I knew instantly that it belonged to my elder brother, Alan. The wreckage sprawled awkwardly on the edge of the road. A group of tow trucks and police cars were already crowding the road, making it difficult for our bus to get through.

"That's Alan's bike. Where is he?" I screamed out in fear and horror as the bus inched its way past the accident site. One of the school teachers on the bus quickly came forward to sit with me and comfort me. She tried to assure me he was probably OK and not to worry. But I did worry, because I couldn't see him at the crash site. At school another teacher offered me shelter in the staff room where I spent a very anxious three hours. At around 12 noon, I was taken to the office of the school principal. There Dad was waiting for me and told me the dreaded news. A utility truck had come over the crest on the wrong side of the road and crashed into Alan's bike. In those days protective helmets for bike riders had never been invented, let alone made mandatory. He died of head injuries. I remember screaming at the news and Dad trying to comfort me.

We were in a small country community and so for many days and weeks friends and family flooded our home, coming to grieve and share in our loss. The story of the accident got repeated over and over, increasing the sense of tragedy that one so young should have his life so violently snuffed out. Was the ute driver, known as given to alcohol, already drunk so early in the morning?

Amid this unending grief, there came also a sense of being held and comforted. Jesus said, "Blessed are those who mourn, for they will be comforted" (Matthew 5:4 NIV). It felt as though there were arms around us, as though God was crying too at this senseless loss. On the lounge room wall was a framed scripture verse which read, "The eternal God is your refuge, and his everlasting arms are under you" (Deuteronomy 33:27). That promise took on palpable reality for us despite the ongoing floods of tears which often burst forth even when trying to sing hymns of faith and hope in our little country church Sunday by Sunday. Mum was a strong soprano and her voice was often the one leading the little group of worshipers in singing. But more often than not during the months of grieving, halfway through the song, her lead would fall away.

My "brother" Allan Laing

Soon after Alan's loss, another Allan entered our world. He was of a similar age, same name and had a similar love of motorbikes. Each Sunday he rode his bike out from Moore College in Sydney to fulfil his church assignment as part of his training to be a minister in the Anglican church. We always had the preacher come to our house after church for lunch. Thus, Allan became a regular Sunday visitor, always bringing humour and laughter to our saddened hearts.

However, one Sunday he seemed somewhat more sober than usual. Eventually he broached a subject which was obviously difficult for him to talk about.

"Dad," he said, using the intimate term which was now customary for one who'd also been fostered into our family, "I've been thinking about you all week and something quite amazing has come to my mind."

"What's that?" asked Dad tentatively.

"Well, Dad, it occurred to me that you, more than any other person I know, can probably understand how strong is God's love for us."

"How's that?" was the gruff response.

"Well, you understand very well how deeply traumatic it is to have your only son torn from the bosom of heart and family. But you know God actually FREELY GAVE his ONLY son for us worthless humans. Seeing what a mess we find ourselves in, he sent Jesus away from the perfect unity they shared in heaven to come and walk this earth just like us. Jesus not only limited himself to human form, but even offered up his own life on the cross so that we might have all our sins forgiven and a clean slate before God. Then we could have the heart-to-heart fellowship with Him that He had always planned for us to have."

I don't recall any response from Dad. But I do recall this conversation as though it happened yesterday. It certainly touched my heart at the time and set me seeking to know more of this loving God who not only comforts the mourner but also would pay such a painful price to bring us into a living relationship with himself.

Little did I guess what challenges awaited me in the world beyond Wilton.

4 Hopes and ambitions

My purpose is to give them a rich and satisfying life. (John 10:10)

In my early days after transferring to Picton school in Year 6, I experienced what might have been a catty attack typical of preteen girls. I had foolishly told some friends that my real name was Edith Roseanne Ada (quite old-fashioned names, after ancient aunts), not Jessie. During recess one day, one of the bully types rounded up all the girls in the class, formed a ring around me and danced around the circle chanting "Edith Roseanne Ada, Edith Roseanne Ada…" in loud unceasing ridicule. This incident reinforced my view that, given my academic mediocrity, I was vulnerable to such ridicule.

My High School years are a bit of a blur. Not being academically gifted, I found most subjects, especially maths, quite challenging, requiring hours of additional homework to maintain the hoped-for level – never first in the class, but sometimes second or third. No subjects stood out as particularly interesting or satisfying.

However, one day in Year 11 the headmaster tapped me on the shoulder to offer me nomination as school captain. Why me? Well, by then I had gained a reputation for being quick to speak up in the classroom if the teachers lacked clarity in what they said. (I needed all the clarity I could get and figured there were probably other struggling students who were reluctant to display their ignorance.) As school captain I would have many opportunities to speak on behalf of the students, either to thank visiting speakers, or to work as a team with other prefects.

In my senior High School years, my career ambitions fluctuated between becoming an air hostess (free travel all over the world) or of being a teacher (lots of holidays during which one could travel widely). What made me want to travel? I hardly know, but perhaps I knew there must be a bigger, more exciting life outside the confines of our rural district.

The other significant person in my teenage life was the beloved new brother, Allan. He began a youth club in the district, which included lots of social activities along with good teaching about how we could experience and nurture friendship with God. Through Allan's teaching, I understood more about why Jesus had to die to reconcile us to the Father, and how we must acknowledge our need to receive personally that gift of forgiveness and life in Christ. I don't recall just when I did that, but in 1953, at 15 years of age, I was glad to declare publicly my trust in God by receiving confirmation at our then parish centre of St Peter's Campbelltown. I certainly do remember praying during my last year of High School, "Lord, if You want me to be a teacher, please help me pass the Leaving Certificate at an adequate level to be accepted into Teachers College."

God answered my prayer in January 1955 when I got a Commonwealth Scholarship to Wagga Wagga Teachers College, a two-year residential course in a rural city about 400 kilometres from home. In February I boarded the train with Liz Cox, a High School friend, and soon found myself surrounded by a carriage full of excited new and returning students. We were heading to a new year of adventure and excitement and, yes, probably of learning too.

I immediately fell madly in love with one of the fellow passengers, a handsome blue-eyed second year student, Michael. I hoped he might return the feeling. But I don't think he ever noticed this first-year fresher, having eyes only for a second-year beauty, Pam, whom he subsequently married. For an innocent country girl who'd never had a boyfriend, the vista of possibilities was exciting.

Life in college was exhilarating! Not only the possibility of boyfriends, but getting to know other students from all over NSW and learning new subjects that as primary school teachers we would need to know at a level sufficient to teach.

I was helped along by my roommate, Pam Schofield. Pam and I met on our first day at the college. Pam remembers us having different shifts of swotting for exams. I took the night shift, sitting in the deserted shower recesses until 1 am or so, and then woke Pam for her early morning study shift. Her method seemed always more effective than mine. In most subjects I continued my B grade mediocrity.

Eventually, though, I found a few areas where I could shine – Art and Drama. I never had them at Picton High School! Parts in Gilbert and Sullivan productions and also in more serious one-act plays helped me feel comfortable on the stage, and learn to empathise with, or at least feel for, the character I was playing on stage.

My country accent needed remediation and I had to show up for several sessions to practise better pronunciation, particularly of vowels, trying to get the *ai* out of my Strine. (It was much later, in phonetics classes at linguistics school, that I learned to identify the problem and address it.)

Amidst all this activity, letters turned up weekly in my mailbox from dear brother Allan Laing. He kept asking how I was finding the Christian Union meetings. He urged me to not let the lure of co-educational residential living sweep me away, but to realise that it was in Jesus that I would find life more "rich and satisfying". So, at his urging, I began attending the various Christian activities on campus. And several of us went to the youth-oriented Sunday evening services at the local Baptist church. I found there many of the college students who had experienced the excitement of being a follower of Jesus that Allan had told me about.

One leader in that church was a lecturer at our college, Gordon Young. About once a quarter, the church put on a public youth rally in a city hall, under the auspices of Youth for Christ. Mr Young asked me if I'd be willing to share a component during an upcoming event. This would be the first time I had shown my colours in such a public forum. I hardly remember what I said, but it gave me confidence to speak for Jesus – even in public places. (My future husband thinks he was in the audience on that occasion, but he also cannot recall anything of what I said. Mediocrity at large!) Later, some of us got involved in the Anglican church near the college. We used the Baptist model of more contemporary and personalised presentations to encourage folk to a more living relationship with Jesus.

I also enjoyed very much the twice-yearly opportunities to practise teaching skills in various schools throughout the wider Riverina area. I really loved teaching and found the mentoring and supervised practicums very helpful and satisfying.

It was during my second year that a promising relationship developed with a new first year student, Terry. Although only in first year, Terry was a mature age student who had recently left a Catholic seminary where he had been preparing for priesthood. He was not only vibrant, a wonderful dancer and communicator, but also serious about God. I welcomed the relationship, and we quickly grew close. After each

My practice teaching class at South Wagga demonstration school

evening meal, especially in summer, we walked the back paths of the campus, talking about the Lord and studying the Bible together.

This was before the reforms within the Catholic church started by the Vatican II Council (1962–65). Terry believed the teaching that our right standing with God depended on keeping the rituals and traditions of the Church. However, as we studied Paul's letters to the Galatians and Romans together over several months, he came to understand more about the gift of God through Jesus Christ, which one can receive through simply trusting Him. Terry seemed ready to make his own leap of faith. However, each time he returned to Sydney during vacation times, he discussed these new understandings with his parish priest. The priest warned him of the moral and spiritual dangers inherent in a relationship with a Protestant woman. Rather, Terry should encourage her to attend the Catholic services in Wagga to learn more of the true path. I did this for some time, mostly just the Sunday evening Benediction services. I enjoyed the beauty and sanctity of the services, but I did not see this as my pathway to growth in God. It soon became clear that we were on parallel spiritual journeys that were not likely to meet.

Mid-January 1957, two months after graduation, many of the college students who lived in or around Sydney planned a reunion so that we could meet, perhaps the last time before scattering all across NSW to take up our teaching appointments. I travelled down by train from the country to attend. The night before the reunion, Terry and I met. It was now clear to us both that we should split up. An emotional evening, since we remained very attracted to each other! I returned to my sister's place in Lane Cove, expecting a sleepless, tearful night. I remember kneeling beside my bed, just waiting for the tears to come. But I found myself surrounded by an illumination which seemed to fill the entire room. Along with that came an overwhelming sense of peace and joy. I can't remember when I actually climbed into bed, but I slept well.

The next morning, I turned up at the reunion with a broad grin across my face and a spring in my step that gave the false impression that Terry and I had become officially engaged. "Where's the ring?" several asked. It was hard to describe to those looking for the engagement ring that, on the contrary, Terry and I had broken up! I'd now found in Jesus a life even more satisfying than any human relationship could bring. Most of my fellow students looked mystified and sceptical. Little did they, or I, imagine what even more life-changing events were soon to follow.

With my best friend Pam at our graduation

5 Other sheep also

I have other sheep, too, that are not in this sheepfold. I must bring them also. (John 10:16)

My first teaching appointment was at Hammondville, an outer suburb southwest of Sydney. The school served nearby migrant hostels which housed newly arrived English folk. These immigrants were colloquially called "Ten Pound Poms" as ten pounds sterling was all they had needed to pay for their sea voyage out to Australia. Most were from lower middle-class families. Living in close, rather primitive quarters through probably their first hot summer was a culture shock they'd not envisaged. Their children soon filled our school, and my Grade 1 classroom held many more than are in classes today! Having such a large class of uprooted children brought plenty of challenges, but as a newly trained and spiritually energised graduate teacher I was ready for it all.

About a month after the first term began, our country parish church at Picton, under the leadership of Barry Schofield, facilitated a first ever missionary expo as a united effort with other denominational leaders in the town. It was a new display filling the large Agricultural Hall of the showground. The ten-day event housed exhibitions from about 20 different mission agencies whose vision and activities were there for all to see. Since it was the first such event ever in the district, hundreds of local people turned up every night – including me, at least on the weekends. I was particularly interested to find agencies looking for teachers for their areas of service. The options seemed limitless! But I doubted God would want an inexperienced teacher in such challenging places.

Many of the speakers were Christian leaders from overseas mission fields. Bishop Festo Kivengere from Uganda, who later served through the tyrannical rule of Idi Amin, was a charismatic figure, "The Billy Graham of East Africa". His oratory captivated me. And his challenge gripped me, of why anyone should hear the Gospel twice when so many throughout the world have never heard it once. On the last night of the convention he preached from 2 Corinthians 5:14,15, "Since we believe that Christ died for all, we also believe that we have all died to our old life. He died for everyone so that those who receive his new life will no longer live for themselves. Instead, they will live for Christ, who died and was raised for them."

I realised that night that if God should want me to serve overseas, then I must follow that call. When Bp Festo gave an invitation for those who would go anywhere Jesus might lead them, I don't recall leaving my seat, but suddenly found myself amongst the goodly number of young folk at the front, filled with joy and expectation!

But harsh reality soon dawned on me. In the first place, my teaching bond still required three years of service to the Dept. of Education in return for the scholarship for teacher training. Second, I was still a very inexperienced teacher and needed each of those three years of men-tored experience. Third, I should now give back to my adoptive parents some support and presence in appreciation for all that they had given me throughout my life.

So, while the timing for pursuing overseas service was certainly not imminent, I could use the next three years to gain more teaching experience, to learn more about mission, to pray and to give financial support. I joined the youth wing of our denominational mission society,

CMS League of Youth. At monthly meetings in Sydney, I heard stories from mission workers on home visits and learned to pray for their work. Through these contacts, I was increasingly open to where the Lord might want me to serve overseas as a teacher.

Meanwhile I found "other sheep" much closer to home. CMS had a children's ministry and I began an after-school club for the Hammond-ville kids. These kids were all from challenging socioeconomic backgrounds and were a mission field in their own right! I had much to learn here. One problem teenage nuisance at that club, Nev, drove me to distraction (and much prayer) week after week. I often dreaded his arrival, but came to understand his antics as attention-getting tactics which probably reflected an emotionally needy young lad. In time his emotions were healed in the love of Jesus and he grew to be not only a highly respected servant in his local church but also a faithful supporter of my eventual missionary endeavours in subsequent years, and indeed he and his lovely wife Maureen remain so till now.

The Lord opened up many other opportunities to tell children of His love and purpose for their lives. My headmistress gave me permission to begin each school day with my class of 50 with Scripture Union materials, including a short Bible reading, song, and prayer. For these kids whose lives had been so impacted by the uncertainties of migrant life, it was very comforting to know that the loving Lord was with them – even in their new surroundings. I took some particularly needy ones home to "the bush" for some weekend respite times, which they enjoyed and which gave me a stronger relationship with them. Mum and Dad's generous hospitality to the fore again! (Sadly, these days most State schools forbid such activities.)

I took up a request to be on staff at beach missions and Scripture Union girls camps held in the summer holidays. So I learned how to communicate at a spiritual level with older children, as well as with my six-year-olds in school. All helpful prefield experiences.

At the end of my requisite three years of teaching experience, I felt I could now pursue formal application to CMS Australia to serve overseas as a teacher. However, in repeated ways, and particularly through my daily Bible readings and devotions, I felt a strong conviction that I needed to wait. One verse (actually quite out of context!) said, "This vision is for a future time. It describes the end and it will be fulfilled. If it seems slow in coming, wait patiently. For it will surely take place. It will not be delayed." (Habakkuk 2:3).

During these years, I read the story of the five American missionaries martyred on the banks of a river in Ecuador while seeking to reach the Waraoni people (sometimes called Auca) with the Gospel. Their sacrifice stirred me deeply. They died on my 18th birthday, 6 January 1956, but their story only came to the attention of the wider Christian public later through the book *Through Gates of Splendor* written by Jim Elliott's widow, Elizabeth. In her description of her brilliant husband's call to "lose his life" (Mark 8:35) in missionary service, I marked and memorised one of Jim's life mottos, "He is no fool who gives what he cannot keep, to gain what he cannot lose." I became increasingly moved to also lose my life in some part of God's world where the Gospel was not known.

My home church, St Luke's Wilton

One exciting remote part of the world which I learned of during this time was Nepal. Barry Schofield had invited Dr Graham Scott-Brown from the Nepal Evangelistic Band to come and share his story with our church. Graham and his team had pioneered a medical ministry to very isolated communities of people living in the foothills of the mighty Annapurna range of central Nepal. His slide presentation was stunning and evoked a strong desire and hope to be involved in such an outreach.

A challenge that came to our parish through the now annual Missionary Conventions was that we as a church commit to pray for some un-reached people group, asking God that someone might go and make Christ known to these people. Our church signed up for the project and began praying for the Wiru people group in Papua New Guinea. They lived in a quite inaccessible and dangerous part, which up to that time the Australian administration had not opened up for any outside visits or development. Before too long we were encouraged by the news that an Australian couple, Dr Harland and Mrs Marie Kerr of Wycliffe Bible

Translators, had received permission to live amongst the previously uncontacted group.

Even more encouraging was a visit from the Kerrs when they were next in Australia. Harland came out to speak at our little branch church at Wilton during the week they were visiting the Picton parish. He told how the Lord had not only opened the way, but given them a welcome in the village and good language helpers to help them learn the previously unwritten language.

I marvelled not only at Harland's story but also at how the Lord had answered our prayers of previous years. I often wondered if it might have disappointed Harland to see only about six people at the service at St Luke's Wilton that day. But he would realise before too long why the Lord had sent him to that little remote church that day.

More opportunities were coming to broaden my teaching experience: I was asked to teach for a semester in a rural two-teacher school, which I absolutely loved. The head teacher's wife cooked up delicious cookies and slices for our shared morning teas, which greatly enhances my memory of that place.

Not such a positive memory is of a term of teaching at a school that served a new housing development for people from a lower socioeconomic background. The school was a blackboard jungle with little respect given to the teachers. On reflection, I suspect the leadership from the top was weak, but all I remember thinking was, "No school on the mission field could be as difficult as this one is. Perhaps this is what they call Good Missionary Training."

After five years at Hammondville, I felt I should apply for a transfer to a school where I could learn more in a different social environment and from a new head teacher. I can't remember specifying where I wanted to go, but delighted in the assignment to West Wollongong Infants School for the beginning of 1962. It was to be my most important school for gaining invaluable professional experience, and Wollongong would turn out to be the right place for a change of mission call!

6 Professional paradise

God is the true source of any gift; all success comes from him. (2 Corinthians 3:5)

The city of Wollongong nestles on the slopes of beautiful Mt Kiera, an outcrop of the escarpment towering over the NSW South Coast.

West Wollongong was quite an affluent part of the city where many professionals from the nearby steelworks, business people and teachers lived. There were several strong, spiritually live churches in the town and the pupils of West Wollongong Primary School (WWPS) mostly came from wealthy, secure and upwardly mobile families. The leadership of the school was superb. Both the Headmistress and her Deputy knew the clientele of their school looked for excellent educational outcomes for their children. If not achieved at WWPS, they would enroll their children in the private schools in the area.

From Day 1, I knew I would be under quite strict professional supervision and mentoring even though I was already a five-year experienced teacher. Under their tutelage, I learned the theory and best practice of teaching children how to read and how to write creatively, along with other curricular expectations. The children were attentive and eager to learn. I felt I was in an educational paradise. In addition, I was boarding

in another paradise – with Jean Whitfield, a friend from teachers' college days, now married and settled into a lovely new home in West Wollongong. I was truly blessed.

I saw that in this city of many churches, there was an opportunity to present the challenge of serving the Lord overseas. So I asked permission from CMS Sydney to begin a branch of League of Youth in Wollongong. Through Jean and her husband Colin, I came to know several folk in youth fellowships in local churches and this gave me a good network of contacts to begin the work.

CMS Sydney sent down to Wollongong some of their best people for the monthly meetings. The General Secretary of the time, Geoff Fletcher, a gifted evangelist and missions motivator, came in May 1962. The League of Youth meetings became a popular meeting place for young Christian teachers and engineers (mostly from the heavy industries of nearby Port Kembla) to meet together for fellowship and spiritual challenge. I found myself as the sole leader, secretary, and treasurer for several months. The responsibilities grew increasingly hard to manage since I still returned home 30 kilometres to "the bush" every Friday evening for my Sunday School classes at Wilton and time with Mum and Dad, which they really appreciated.

One month a crisis arose when I mislaid a very generous cheque, signed by a "Warren W Glover", which had been in the offertory bag at the previous meeting. I had put it in a safe place where I wouldn't lose it. (I later found out that the cheque represented a healthy portion of his tithe from working solidly as an electrical engineer for three months in commissioning a new processing line at the steelworks. No wonder I wanted to keep it safe.) I searched for days! But it was fruitless, and I had no option but to find out who this Warren Glover was and seek him out to "fess up" and ask him to cancel the cheque.

I still remember the knot in my stomach as I approached the front door of the house he was sharing with a couple of other Christian young men. He would no doubt correctly assess that I was a clueless woman, hopeless in handling money, and wonder why CMS would let me loose in Wollongong with such responsibility. However, he seemed remarkably unfazed and forgiving and assured me he would go into the bank Saturday morning and "do the needful" (a phrase common in Indian English). A day or two later, I *found the cheque* and immediately sent it off to CMS in Sydney with great relief. I wanted to inform Warren of what had happened, but how could I contact him – no mobile phones in those days! So, when he went into the bank the following Saturday, he was told that the cheque had already been cashed!

At the very next League of Youth meeting, I not only clarified with Warren the resolution of the problem and why I hadn't been able to inform him, but also gathered together a few of the now regular attendees to ask their advice. "These League of Youth events are growing and the activities are increasing. I really need some of you folk to consider if you could help me either as secretary or as treasurer for the future."

Without a second's hesitation, Warren said, "I'll be your treasurer."

Little did he, or I, realise then just how prophetic those words would be.

My diligent "treasurer", Warren,
a graduate engineer

PART 2 Beginning the long partnership

7 Paradise threatened

Right behind you a voice will say, "This is the way you should go," whether to the right or to the left. (Isaiah 30:21)

Over the following months in 1962, Warren and I increasingly worked together in planning and facilitating the League of Youth activities in Wollongong. He was not only deft in handling the finances, but helpful in doing whatever else was needed to keep the League of Youth folk informed and followed up after each meeting.

Warren's vision for overseas service had also been birthed through CMS, in 1958, four years before he and I met. A year after he began Engineering at Sydney University on a generous scholarship from Australian Iron and Steel (AIS), Port Kembla, Warren was called up for three months of National Service. The night of his discharge in March, before catching the night train home to Wagga, he decided to kill time by dropping into a back-row seat in the Sydney Town Hall. It was a rally organized by CMS. At the door he picked up a leaflet and popped it into the pocket of his army greatcoat for reading later. He says he remembers nothing of the rally, nor the eminent speaker "brought from overseas at great expense", but he left in time to catch his train at Sydney's Central Station.

Next day, at home, he discovered the leaflet in his pocket, and he found it quite disturbing. It set out the challenge of a world without Christ and declared the Lord Jesus' commission, "Go and make disciples of all nations." The leaflet finished with a reply form which read:

Are you willing:
- to learn about mission?
- To pray for mission?
- To give to support missionary endeavour?
- *If God calls, to go?*

Warren felt that, as a follower of the Lord Jesus, there was only one logical answer that he could give to all of those questions. So, he wrote YES four times on the form and posted it back to the CMS Sydney office.

CMS responded with an invitation to attend a Missionary Fellowship of NSW house party over the Anzac Day long weekend which provided lots of opportunity to learn and to pray. With this added information, Warren felt the Holy Spirit was impressing on his heart and mind the challenge, "Why should anyone hear the Gospel twice before everyone has had the chance to hear it once?" and he responded with a commitment to serve the Lord Jesus in overseas mission.

At Sydney University Warren regularly went to Evangelical Union meetings, both the huge weekly Bible studies and the smaller Engineering faculty meetings. On one occasion at the latter, Bruce Hooley came to share his mission story. An engineer himself, Bruce told how he was led to Bible translation with Wycliffe Bible Translators in Papua New Guinea. Another translator had challenged him with the relevance of an engineer's skills in analysis and synthesis (design) to the work of reducing a language to writing. Analysing phonetic and grammar patterns comes more easily to the mathematician or engineer. Bruce described how the Lord had used this challenge to direct him towards linguistics and translation. That made Warren think deeply. Over subsequent years he had separate contacts with Bruce through Wycliffe and through Ridley College, and he started corresponding with Bruce in PNG.

The scholarship from AIS in Port Kembla did not involve a bond, but Warren felt that two years of service there (1962–63) was a minimum response in thanks for the company's generous scholarship support. So, he began attending the Wollongong League of Youth meetings and he gave top priority to them as an opportunity to learn more and pray for mission. They were also an avenue for him to "give to support missionary endeavour". Hence the generous cheque which had initially brought him across my path.

From time to time, opportunities arose to attend deputation meetings organized by other missions. In June 1963, my parish church in Picton invited a lady from Wycliffe Bible Translators, Martha Phillips, to come and tell how important Bible translation was to the growth of any newly founded church. "How could they hear unless they heard the Gospel in their own language?" A very compelling challenge.

Warren and a mate of his, Ray, joined me on the hour's trip from Wollongong up the escarpment to hear Martha's presentation. We all felt very stimulated by her story. For me, this was a revisit to other challenges I'd been hearing about the work of Wycliffe, firstly from the story of Jim Elliott's martyrdom in Ecuador in January 1956, and also from the deputation visit of Dr Harland Kerr to our little Wilton church just three years before. I knew how the Lord had, through pioneer missionaries, opened closed doors to reach isolated people groups, the "other sheep" who were not part of His fold.

It was after this visit that Warren shared with me that, given his feeling of unsuitability to be a preacher, he wanted to consider a role in Bible translation – a more scientific and academic challenge. But CMS at that stage was not sending workers out as specialist translators and advised, "Talk to the specialists in this ministry, Wycliffe Bible Translators." This was further encouragement to consider serving with Wycliffe. He was planning to attend the summer training school (the Summer Institute of Linguistics, SIL) in Brisbane at the end of the year, to join Wycliffe.

He then asked me, "Jessie, would you consider coming into SIL with me?"

"Not at all. The Lord is calling me to be a missionary teacher. There's no way I would have the academic skills to be a translator."

Warren then explained that Wycliffe's mandate included teaching people how to read, since the mere presence of a Bible in someone's language was useless unless people could read it. That made sense to me and caused me to have a more open mind to service with Wycliffe.

However, the very next evening he came back to me with an apology. "Jessie, I'm very sorry that I didn't make clear my intentions last night. What I was rather clumsily trying to ask was whether you would consider marrying me and **us** joining SIL together?"

Warren's proposal, although not totally surprising, was a challenge .

Firstly, I still believed that God's call to me was as a **missionary teacher** under CMS, where I had been nurtured and encouraged on my missionary journey.

Second, I didn't really know Warren very well at all. We had interacted only in planning and facilitating the League of Youth meetings, except for the occasional classical concert that Warren had invited me to attend with him, and which I had thoroughly enjoyed. (The concerts certainly highlighted my culturally deprived country background.)

Third, and more fundamentally, since the close of the Terry relationship seven years before, I had prayed that God would spare me any emotional attachment not of His leading, and that in any potential relationship we would be of one mind in our spiritual journey. I had avoided any close relationships with members of the opposite sex. My standard evasion was, "Sorry, but I'm not free at all over the weekends. I go up to Wilton for Sunday School and other commitments there." This put most fellows off, as they interpreted correctly that I just wasn't interested. But when I tried the same tack with Warren about a concert or such like, it was to him just a challenge. He always found an option for doing something during the week, to which I could hardly keep objecting. The engineer at work again.

On the third point, I was absolutely sure that Warren and I were of one mind and heart in our spiritual vision for sharing the Gospel, particularly to unreached peoples.

The Glovers in 1954 at Lake Albert: Philip, Warren, Margaret, Richard, Mother and Alice

On the second issue, I did not know Warren's family or background. His family by this time had moved from Wagga to Melbourne and I'd had no opportunity to meet them, or for them to meet me. I think Warren had told me that the family were active members of their local Anglican church, that his Dad was a high school teacher of Maths and Science, and his Mum a former primary school teacher. He was the eldest of five siblings, with two sisters and two brothers. And that was about it.

On the first point, area of ministry, I needed time to pray and consider more what the Lord's will was for me. Warren was just about to go off on a bus trip to the Red Centre for a couple of weeks' holiday, so I suggested he give me those weeks to think more about his proposal, and I would give him my response on his return. I felt his absence would give me the space I needed to think, and pray, more clearly. However, over the next two weeks, daily I received long letters in fat envelopes from Warren, sent from each stage of the coach journey.

Mum kept asking, "Who are these fat letters from? Why does he write every day?"

Warren was not actually pleading his cause, but sharing much about the journey and the various fellow travellers, asking for prayer that he would be a good witness to them, many of whom were non-Christians. He also shared his disquiet about the conditions of the indigenous peoples they met along the way. This was in line with his advocacy through the ABSCHOL support group at Melbourne University for scholarships for Aboriginal students to study in universities. Through these letters I was indeed getting to know the real Warren more and more, and I liked the view.

I also sought the advice of my friend and CMS mentor, Geoff Fletcher. He surprised me when he encouraged me to follow God's leading into Wycliffe with Warren, even though it wasn't the CMS path I'd originally planned. So, on Warren's return I was ready with an affirmative answer, the first of many leaps of faith in our journey together.

Mum and Dad welcomed Warren's request for the hand of their daughter since I think they believed I was well and truly on the shelf. If I hadn't found a husband by 25 years of age, my chances were few. The reality of Warren taking me off to another country on mission service had not really sunk in. They gave their blessing even though Warren had already shown on an earlier visit that unlike brother Allan Laing, he was pretty hopeless in practical skills. (He'd begged on that visit that his experience as an electrical engineer did not cover washing machine repair!)

Further, my Dad refused to ever go anywhere with us if Warren was the driver. One experience had confirmed that he didn't want to repeat a joy ride with Mr Toad at the wheel!

We announced our engagement on 4 October 1963. For the occasion we visited Melbourne for me to meet Warren's family, the first time they had met their future daughter-in-law. Their warm and unanimous welcome was very encouraging to me.

All too soon I would learn what "coming into SIL with me" would involve!

8 The joint journey begins

The LORD watches over your life. (Psalm 121:7)

In December 1963 we began our study of linguistics in Brisbane. I flew to Brisbane a week after the course began, as I had to finish my semester of teaching. Whether because of this delayed beginning, or just that linguistics was *not* my cup of tea, I found the course very difficult and irksome. I often felt that it was just as well that we were formally engaged; otherwise I would have bolted and returned home.

However, there were two very significant factors which assured us both that this was indeed the Lord's direction for us. The Principal of that summer's linguistic course was none other than Dr Harland Kerr, the very person who'd come out to my little country church five years earlier with the story of the Wiru and of God's open door to that community through Bible translation. And the Deputy Principal was Warren's lodestar from Sydney University days, Bruce Hooley. We were pretty gob -smacked by the double coincidence.

As a further confirmation of call toward Asia, Dr Richard (Dick) Pittman, SIL's Area Director for Asia, was on staff and had much to share about new opportunities in India. We remember so clearly Dick's humility, and the richness of his devotional life and spiritual leadership.

Also, Dr Jim Dean, the newly appointed director of the Wycliffe advance to India, visited the course. He told of doors opening in that linguistic paradise. However, he warned that, because of India's hostility to Christian missions, we would have to present our Christian identity with caution, and observe strictly SIL's secular approach to language analysis and documentation in cooperation with local universities. He highlighted the challenges of developing writing systems in a country which used 15 unique scripts for their major languages alone. We were glad to meet Jim and learn more.

Icing on the cake was that my "brother" Allan Laing and his wife Barbara were fellow sufferers of this intensive linguistic torture as part of their preparation for service with Sudan United Mission in Chad. Many an

Allan and Barbara Laing and family

afternoon found us three taking advantage of Warren's informal tutorial help to grasp something of the day's lectures, or the homework required before the next day. A clear sign of how much easier it was for my engineer fiancé's analytical mind to penetrate the mysteries of linguistics.

Another positive feature about the Brisbane venue for the course was that at weekends we could visit members of my biological family who lived there. In getting to know these Segal relatives more closely, I learned of their talents and interesting history. As I noted earlier, eldest brother Norman had been a POW in Changi and Nagasaki during WW2 and had suffered much privation there. He was well read and had the larger-than-life mentality of a survivor. Eldest sister, June, married to an army man, was a very creative, artistic woman and generous and talented cook. We enjoyed getting to know them and their children, and enjoyed June's tropical salads on hot, steamy Brisbane days.

In March 1964, after we had completed the three-month course, the Wycliffe Australia Council formally accepted us as Wycliffe members. In prefield preparation, we each began a year of Bible college. Warren went to Ridley College in Melbourne (and lived back at home with his family) focusing on Biblical languages, while I took a more general Missions course at Sydney Missionary and Bible College (SMBC). During the year we met twice during vacations to plan our November wedding while Warren says he kept Australia Post in business for the rest of that time. Emailing, skyping, texting and even phoning were out of the question in those days. From time to time we even used reel-to-reel magnetic tapes for a longer chat.

One positive factor during this forced separation was that I could give more quality time not only to my studies, but also to Mum and Dad. I realized it would be my last opportunity to do so. I was always aware of the great debt that I owed Mum and Dad Whitticase, for the love, nurture, and educational opportunity they had given me. Although Dad disapproved of our plans for overseas service, I knew that he was in some sense proud of me undertaking such a challenging life work, one that would continue to use my professional training and experience.

SMBC's residential experience was more "good missionary training". The living conditions were VERY basic. Each room comprised a simple narrow single bed, a small desk and chair, plus a small wardrobe. Only thin ¾ height Masonite walls divided the rooms and noise travelled well from one room to another. One could hear conversations or singing all along the dormitory. The arrangement had its inherent stresses and embarrassing moments.

The college instilled table manners and courtesy according to old world traditions. For example, one wasn't to ask one's table mate to pass the marmalade, but could hint by saying, "Are you wanting to have marmalade on your toast?" at which your friend should get the hint that in fact **you** wanted her to pass you the marmalade!

After each lunch, while we all sat demurely at the table, the women's matron read us a chapter from a book that was deemed suitable for our spiritual growth. I remember her reading *Hind's Feet on High Places* by Hannah Hurnard. It is a deeply spiritual allegory but I sadly admit that I

Our wedding party—Ray, Pam, Warren, Jessie, and Warren's sister Alice and brother Richard

don't appreciate allegory, and have only recently come to enjoy the classic Narnia tales by CS Lewis. I'm sure though that others, more academically literate, benefited from the daily readings.

I did appreciate and enjoy the weekly missions-focused guest speakers. One stimulating presentation was by Alan Healey, another Wycliffe translator who described sentence by sentence the challenges of translating Mark 1:1–4 in the Telefomin language of PNG. I felt proud to be joining such a strategically and spiritually important mission. Several others in the student body at college were also new Wycliffe recruits, who we related with later, both in our SIL training, and also in field work. They included Alec Magill in India, and Chris Kilham and Marjorie Marsh, who both worked amongst Australian indigenous peoples.

Mr & Mrs Glover

We were married just two days after my finishing the year at SMBC, at my parish central church, St. Mark's Picton, on 28 November 1964. The celebrant was Barry Schofield, who had played such a big part in facilitating the mission vision in the parish eight years earlier. I had the joy of wearing a wedding dress made by Mum, and she had also made the dresses of the two bridesmaids. My maid of honour was Pam Rendell, my longtime friend from Wagga Wagga Teachers' College days. I had been her chief bridesmaid just three months earlier. In fact, Pam and I swapped the wedding dress and bridesmaid dress for the two occasions! Warren's best man was his Wollongong mate, Ray Christmas. The same Ray who had been with Warren on the initial visit to Mum and Dad's place just 18 months before on our way to Martha Phillips' Wycliffe deputation meeting at St. Mark's.

One scripture passage we selected for the wedding service was Psalm 121. Little did we realize then just how repeatedly significant verses 7 and 8 would become throughout our shared journey together:

> The LORD keeps you from all harm and watches over your life.
> The LORD keeps watch over you as you come and go, both now and forever.

9 Hassles along the way

We can rejoice, too, when we run into problems and trials, for we know that they help us develop endurance. (Romans 5:3)

1965 saw us seriously preparing for the next step of our journey. But where? From 1958 Warren had felt a particular interest and call to serve in Afghanistan. So, when filling out application forms for Wycliffe in 1963 –64, he answered the question on fields of interest with Afghanistan, but wrote, "I realise Wycliffe is not yet working in Afghanistan. However, since you are preparing a team to begin work in India, may we join that team as a step in that direction?" And so Wycliffe assigned us to India.

The Hobart accident

But there was a lot of preparation needed before leaving for India! Wycliffe encouraged members to visit churches and friends who would pray for them and, as led by God, support them financially also. We visited potential supporting churches in Picton, Wollongong, the Riverina of NSW and Melbourne, and in May 1965 we made an extensive tour of Tasmania to encourage support for WBT in that State.

We had what could have been a fatal car accident in Hobart. On our way from a night meeting, with rain battering down on our windscreen, we approached a city intersection. Instinctively, as a NSW driver, Warren checked to the right that there was no oncoming traffic and then proceeded into the main road. We were instantly hit by a speeding car coming downhill from our left. (NSW did not use Give Way signs then, but rigorously applied a "give way to the right" rule, and Warren had failed to register that there was a Give Way sign in the Hobart side street.) The impact pushed our car about 50 metres down the road. Apart from head bumps on my left temple, no one was injured – how grateful we were for wet roads and old tyres that allowed our car to slide with the impact, rather than roll over.

We wrote to supporters after that trip, "Why were we delivered so wonderfully from what could have been a serious injury in a car smash in Hobart? We are encouraged to believe that God still has a purpose for our lives and this, we trust, is the translation of His life-giving Word for some tribe which as yet does not have that lamp for their feet or light for their path."

Church acceptance

During our second summer of linguistic training in Brisbane, in January/ February 1965, we received letters from my home church in Picton reporting an unexpected experience of the infilling of the Holy Spirit. For some years, Barry Schofield had been preaching the need for spiritual renewal and had held special prayer meetings for renewal the first Friday of each month. We had attended these meetings while at home in Wilton, before heading up to Brisbane, and indeed wanted whatever empowering from the Holy Spirit that God had for us. It was at the monthly renewal prayer meeting on 1 January 1965 that Molly Fergusson received the gift of speaking in tongues, in a language unknown to Molly or to her hearers. Other members of the parish in due course also received a similar gift and folk were now writing to us in Brisbane, "This is what the Lord has done. You also need this."

Returning to the fellowship at Picton, we sought from the Lord this same gift but, despite considerable prayer, effort, and earnestness on our part, and coaching from Barry, we did not receive it. As the months of 1965 went by with preparations for departure proceeding, our failure to speak in tongues presented a real problem for our primary sending church of St Mark's Picton. They regarded this gift as a seal of God's approval and empowering. How could they endorse and support us as missionaries sent out from their parish when we had not received God's seal, confirming His call on our lives?

Finally, in February 1966, we requested a special prayer meeting with the church leadership to discern whether they could commission and support us. We met in my little branch church, St Luke's Wilton, the very place where Harland Kerr had first sparked the Wycliffe flame in my heart. As these devout and prayerful folk gathered, Barry said to us all, "I believe God is going to do something special for us this evening." And so it was! As they were praying, Molly Fergusson received a further New Testament gift – prophecy. She spoke out an amazingly encouraging word to this effect, "You are my servants. I have chosen you and I will strengthen you." As we walked out of the church after the gathering, someone commented to Molly about how fitting her message had been.

She said, "Why, what did I say?" The message she had spoken was truly supernatural, and not merely of human design.

Encouraged by this message the good folk in the parish blessed and commissioned us for the ministry of Bible translation and literacy and they continued to support us faithfully over many years.

Jungle Camp

Wycliffe required members to attend "Jungle Camp", a four-month stint of prefield orientation, before taking up their field assignments. For

Australians going to India, the only Jungle Camp option then was in Papua New Guinea and so in August 1965 we flew to PNG. Although the culture, climate and lifestyles of PNG and India share little in common, still we found the four months very helpful in learning the ways of Wycliffe in at least one field environment.

Crossing a river in Jungle Camp, with help!

Perhaps the experience most valuable in preparation for later allocation in mountainous Nepal was the five-day trek over the mountains of PNG doing a language survey.

During that time, we wrote our prayer team a summary of our experience, using the model of CS Lewis's well-known book *Screwtape Letters*:

> 2 October 1965
>
> My dear Wormwood,
>
> I have just examined your interim report on your two subjects during their time at Jungle Camp. It represents a disgraceful failure on your part despite the golden opportunities presented you.
>
> The climate itself, with its oppressive humidity, should have helped you, but you erred in letting them be forewarned of this so that they simply praised the Enemy that it wasn't as bad as they'd expected. Of course, the mould and immovable dirt in clothes was an irritation, and the infestation of ants, and the resultant variety of holes eaten in clothes, tried the woman's good housekeeping

instincts, but the Enemy helped them with a sense of humour which evidently made your efforts worthless!

The failure of their packed drum of equipment to arrive had great promise, but the generosity of the Enemy's friends in lending them gear nullified its effect. Similarly, the failure of all their torch bulbs became a point of praise for the friends who lent them torches! Likewise, the trouble you instigated with the failure of their pressure lantern became another occasion to praise the Enemy for the timely purchase in Lae of a reliable hurricane lamp!

You came nearest success in the personal attacks, especially in making them irritable and thoughtless of others so that arguments developed. I hope you have noted for future reference that these attacks are most successful if you can hinder the subjects from fellowship with the Enemy, and to a lesser extent, the friends of the Enemy. Make even greater efforts, therefore, to keep them so busy (trying to get a fire going with wet wood, or washing clothes in cold water, or any other necessary tasks) that their Quiet Time is squeezed right out, or at worst, is very rushed and short.

For the future, see what you can do along the line of frustration at delays in going to India (the war with Pakistan may help in this) and of hindrances in gathering together their field equipment. Try interrupting mail deliveries, letters from friends of the Enemy at home with all those assurances of prayer.

If you don't do better in the future, I foresee you will be relieved of your assignment and I look forward to taking part in your chastisement.

Your diabolically affectionate uncle,

Screwtape.

We survived Jungle Camp, but could I survive the painful rejection awaiting me back home at Wilton?

10 Nature or nurture?

Even if my father and mother abandon me, the LORD will hold me close. (Psalm 27:10)

We returned from PNG in November 1965 in time for our first wedding anniversary. Living in a small flat in North Wollongong provided a splendid opportunity to reconnect with Wollongong and Picton supporters and to return hospitality that we'd enjoyed from many of them over the years before. Dad particularly enjoyed being able to visit us "in your own place". He hoped still that Warren would lower his sights and be content with establishing a home back in Australia, which is what he considered the fundamental responsibility of any good husband. "An Englishman's house is his castle!" was a value he held strongly.

In fact, my Dad's true feeling about our life decisions came to the surface just a few weeks before we left for India. "Well, all I can say is you're no child of mine to be taking off like this to a far country, leaving behind your family and loved ones."

I don't think that Dad actually realised how hurtful this comment was for me, since biologically, I wasn't a child of his at all. Mum and Dad treated me in every way as a child in parallel with my three Whitticase "siblings" but I always had a feeling of vulnerability about whether I was fulfilling the expectations, hopes, and dreams of my family of nurture. I appreciated very much the huge commitment they had made, in not only providing a beautiful home for me as a child but also in enabling me to gain an education that my birth siblings had not. Therefore, in appreciation and love, I wanted to please them. But this last stab just before our departure for India sounded the failure knell of any hopes I might have had of winning Dad's affirmation for my life choices and vocation.

Being a bear of very little brain, it took me about six months to remember that this parting shot of his was actually completely untrue! Why had I not remembered at the time that Fredrick George Whitticase had himself in 1911 left family and loved ones in England to make a life for himself as a manufacturing saddler in far off Australia?

Dad had been an apprentice to Butler and Co. of Walsall, Staffordshire, as a saddler and worked there until he was 24 years old. The management of Butler and Co. had opened a saddlery business in Australia and asked Fred if he would go to Sydney and work in their new branch. He accepted the challenge and arrived in Sydney a couple of months later, taking up a good job with the company.

Within a year he'd earned enough to purchase a 60-acre block of land in the Southern Highlands of NSW, between Douglas Park and Wilton. However, he had bad dermatitis on his hands and arms from the pigment coming out of the leather, so he took a brief break from the city to work on a building project out west, at the Mungeribar Station between Narromine and Trangie. The owners were the Thomas Bragg family. His health condition cleared up, and he returned to Sydney.

In 1916 Fred enlisted in the 1st AIF, serving in Flanders as a horse handler in the artillery. He was miraculously spared in several skirmishes,

George Frederick WHITTICASE

Regimental number	29382
Religion	Church of England
Occupation	Saddler
Address	427 Riley Street, Surry Hills, New South Wales
Marital status	Single
Age at embarkation	28
Next of kin	Mother, Mrs M Whitticase, Primrose Cottage, Turvey, Bedfordshire, England
Enlistment date	8 May 1916
Rank on enlistment	Saddler
Unit name	Howitzer Brigade 117
AWM Embarkation Roll number	13/136/1
Embarkation details	Unit embarked from Sydney, New South Wales, on board HMAT A60 *Aeneas* on 30 September 1916
Rank from Nominal Roll	SDLR
Unit from Nominal Roll	2nd Division Ammunition Column
Fate	Returned to Australia 24 December 1918
Miscellaneous details (Nominal Roll)	*Given name George

© 2011

but was eventually invalided to a hospital in England with a shrapnel wound to his forearm. He could reconnect there with his family and his mother begged him to take his discharge in England and resettle there. He replied, "I've made my home in Australia, purchased land, and that's where I see my future," returned to Australia 24 December 1918 and was demobbed in April 1919.

Nearly five years after discharge, in 1923, he married Helen (Nell) Lambert, who had actually seen him off to the war several years before.

Nativity play in Ultimo, with Nell far right in the front row

Nell was born in 1895 in Ultimo, an inner suburb of Sydney. Her life centred around the Congregational Church, where she was part of the Sunday School and girls' club activities. At an early age, she showed talent in singing and in handcrafts. Her faith grew through evangelistic meetings in Sydney which used the hymns of Alexander and Sankey. She still loved to sing at her sewing machine many years later. *"Man of Sorrows, what a name, for the son of God who came, ruined sinners to reclaim, Hallelujah, what a saviour!"* was one of her favourites.

As a young woman she had been apprenticed as a tailoress within the prestigious firm David Jones and throughout her life in Wilton she shared her handcraft skill with her well-dressed family, and she blessed many a local bride, newly arrived babe or struggling clergyman in need of new black cassock or white surplice. The beautifully dressed doll for my fourth Christmas gift was typical of her expertise and love.

As newlyweds Nell and Fred settled in Flemington, a suburb of Sydney, where Fred, with partner Atlee (Ted) Smith, continued their leather trade in making saddles, horse collars and other bridling equipment. Fred founded his own business, Sydney Bridle Company, employing some 30 craftsmen. With the hard days of the depression in the early

1930s, Fred couldn't continue to pay rent and wages in the city. He felt it might be more possible to make a living if he worked from his country property in Wilton. So Fred and Ted took the risk of uprooting business and family and moved to the Southern Highlands of NSW in 1932. They were pioneers, setting up a saddlery business in the rural area, and had the telephone connected – being subscriber #1 on the exchange, with phone number Wilton 1!

Fred had already worked on the construction of a stone house; the stone for which was quarried from the sandstone bedrock on his property. It was to this simple but beautiful home that Fred brought Nell, who'd never lived outside Sydney, along with three youngsters (Norma, 8, Alan, 3, and Shirley, 1) and Nell's invalid mother. I was to be embraced into that family some six years later, just a few months after the death of Nell's mother.

The house that Fred built, in Wilton

My belated remembering of Fred's own history of leaving family and loved ones gave me no small comfort and a touch of amusement. At least in that respect, I was indeed a child of his.

Over the years, through weekly airmail letters and our regular returns to Australia for home assignment, we could assure Mum and Dad that we still loved and valued them immensely. And we convinced them that our choices had not been altogether irresponsible. We were actually thriving and being well cared for in the countries the Lord had led us to.

With Mum and Dad at Wilton

In retrospect, I have also wondered whether his earlier protest may have been a cry of regret or even pain on his part for losing the "child" who had become very much part of his heart and home for over 26 years.

PART 3 Distant Horizons

11 Passage to India

He will cover you with his feathers. He will shelter you with his wings. His faithful promises are your armour and protection. (Psalm 91:4)

After another repacking of the Jungle Camp 44-gallon drums, we set sail for India on the *Galileo Galilei* (an Italian cruise ship) on 10 March 1966 from Melbourne. I was pregnant with delivery expected in September.

I seem to lack any ability to consider ahead of time what dangers or difficulties might follow a course of action. Apart from letting our parents know of the impending event, we set off with no further forethought, planning, or packing of baby paraphernalia in the said drums. Our parents were concerned about my giving birth in India, but I figured that since there were millions of women successfully delivering babies there, I didn't see why I should be any different. We wrote to Dr Jim Dean, the SIL India director, of this slight complication for the Glovers, and he greatly encouraged us with his positive reply quoting the promises from Isaiah 40:11 (KJV).

> He shall feed his flock like a shepherd:
> he shall gather the lambs with his arm,
> and carry them in his bosom,
> and shall gently lead those that are with young.

The two-week voyage included a day stopover in Fremantle where I could meet up with second eldest biological brother Jack, who lived in a Perth suburb. Jack and his family warmly welcomed us at the dock. The day included a luncheon with some other relatives, of whom I had no previous knowledge! We set sail that evening, leaving Australia on 14 March 1966.

Life on board the *Galileo Galilei* was a welcome touch of luxury, certainly a big contrast with the Jungle Camp experience of the year before. An early introduction to the frequent swings between luxury and loss in missionary life. We enjoyed dressing up for dinner and the Italian cuisine, which was served up in abundance! We even went to Italian language classes to learn the phrase "poco, poco" (just a little please),

The liner Galileo Galilei

hoping to persuade the waiters to reduce the huge piles of pasta they loaded onto our dinner plates with unrelenting regularity. Either our pronunciation was deficient, or the request was unbelievable. Whatever the reason, the piles of pasta continued.

We enjoyed regular swims in the pool, and it was after one swim I threw up – the only occurrence I ever had of any pregnancy discomfort. We played bridge with another couple who were delighted to find someone to make up a four. Warren several times tried to motivate me to learn some Hindi from a textbook he'd got before leaving Melbourne. I found the first chapters so unintelligible that I managed to convince him I'd probably do better with a teacher and the spoken language all around me. An early indicator of our completely different adult learning styles!

As we came closer to Bombay, Warren became quite unwell with headaches, body pain, and fevers and chills every second day. The day we reached Bombay (now called Mumbai), 24 March 1966, he was particularly ill. We were grateful for mission friends who met us at the dock. Our drums were eventually unloaded and cleared through customs, and then we could rest in the fan-cooled waiting room of Bombay's Victoria Terminus railway station all afternoon. By then Warren's fever had passed. The Deccan Queen was the pretentious name of the evening express train which took us up to the hill station of Poona (now called Pune). The first of our many journeys on India trains. Over the next forty years Warren calculated he had travelled over 150,000 kilometres on Indian trains. But that's another story!

We reached Poona after dark, and Jim Dean met us at the station. He'd managed to hire a very large taxi (the like of which we never again saw) to take the large party and our mountains of baggage to our accommodation. I thought that the taxi must have had an electrical fault as the horn blared out incessantly throughout the entire trip. I was soon to find out that all vehicle drivers just rammed on their horns nonstop to ensure that the throng of pedestrians were aware of the oncoming danger – or perhaps it was to intimidate other vehicles and animals to get out of the way! At the guesthouse we joined an American Wycliffe couple, Dick and Edie Hugoniot. They had arrived in Poona a couple of weeks before us and were already settled in a small bungalow on the campus of Deccan College, a postgraduate research institute of the University of Poona.

Dick and Edith were the first ones to begin our orientation to India. They soon discovered they in their turn needed some orientation to Australian English. It puzzled Edie when on the first morning Warren came out to the living room asking for a "bicycle". It took several repetitions to clarify that it was actually a basin (which he pronounced *bison*!) that he needed. We have enjoyed a long friendship and collegial association with Dick and Edie, in India and in Nepal, despite the occasional dialect challenges.

Warren's mystery illness continued. But the pattern of alternating days of fever and chills immediately alerted Jim Dean. He had served for ten years previously in PNG. "It's malaria!" he said. No doubt Warren picked up the bug while we were in PNG the previous year for Jungle Camp, and it had lain dormant despite our taking all the prescribed prophylactic medications during and after our time in PNG. The cure for malaria was straightforward and easily available in Poona, though it alarmed our Indian friends that Warren might be reintroducing to Poona a scourge that had been eradicated!

We arrived in Poona's hot season and Dick Hugoniot quickly introduced us to a very special delight of Indian cuisine. Sweet lime soda, a carbonated drink made from lime juice with sugar, really hit the spot on a hot day! "Yes, I'll have another one, please!" Quite a contrast was the luncheon menus prepared by our local cook – his spicy curry laced with copious chilli and many unfamiliar spices, burnt our tongues and triggered our nasal passages such that we spent the meal wiping flowing noses and eyes and drinking lots of water. We soon learnt to bring a packet of tissues, and to add yogurt and/or banana to the dish to neutralise the fire somewhat.

While living with Dick and Edie, we used the cool of the evening for a stroll around the rural setting of the college campus. We loved its beautiful scarlet-flowered golmol trees and the tall slender ashoka tree avenues. But we were not the only inhabitants. Warren well remembers my fright at encountering a "herd" of buffalo – my first experience of this ubiquitous Asian animal with wide-spreading horns and glaring eyes. Warren tried to reassure me that there were only three and they would not harm us if we ignored them as we passed by. All very well for him! We kept our distance and did get home safely.

Not long after recovering from the malaria, Warren had another mystery debilitating illness. At the time we were trying to keep up a fairly solid routine of Hindi language learning, aided by resources available through Deccan College staff and library facilities. But Warren's stamina declined to the point of needing hospitalisation. The doctor there quickly diagnosed the problem. "Hepatitis!" he declared, observing the yellowish colour of Warren's eyes. It was good to have a diagnosis, and I knew hepatitis is treatable given good rest. The doctors were concerned about me, as a pregnant woman, getting infected, but were glad to learn that I had immunity, having had hepatitis when teaching at Hammondville some five years earlier. So Warren could convalesce at home, but he took many months to recover full strength.

I was maintaining excellent health. That was indeed fortunate, not only for helping in Warren's convalescence but also for reassuring our families that all was going well for me in the pregnancy. The gynaecologist had earlier given me a two-page foolscap listing of her CV. It included lots of post grad courses and gynaecological degrees that she had done both in India and in prestigious UK universities. We sent copies of this document home to help assuage our parents' concerns, though the academic detail was probably just as obscure to them as it was to us.

During the months of Hindi study and country orientation, we were part of a largish group of new Wycliffe members starting work in India. We all looked forward to allocating amongst some Indian tribal community, probably in eastern India. But government permission for foreigners to live in such remote areas was not forthcoming. After yet another fruitless and frustrating visit to offices in New Delhi in May 1966, our SIL directors followed up a letter of invitation from Tribhuvan University in Kathmandu, Nepal, and found there a warm welcome to describe and document the minority languages of Nepal.

On his return to Poona, Jim Dean called us over for a chat: "Would you two consider transferring to Nepal, rather than waiting for an Indian assignment? This could be another step towards your stated goal of serving in Afghanistan."

I jumped at the possibility, remembering the stunning slide presentation given by Dr Graham Scott-Brown at St Mark's, Picton, some seven years before. Was this another thread in the Lord's plan being revealed? But all plans were on hold till after my delivery, due in late September.

12 Then we were three

Children are a gift from the LORD. (Psalm 127:3)

The long hot season in India seemed to show no promise of easing. September was said to mark its end, with the cessation of daily downpours, and the onset of cooler weather. I couldn't wait. I was tiring of carrying around an ever-increasing load, hot day by even hotter day and was counting the days till the end of September when our first baby was due to arrive. But the cooler weather showed no sign of arriving, even though the rains had ceased. There seemed to be no relief from the ongoing heat. In fact, it was getting hotter – we were discovering the so-called Indian summer, the return of the heat after the rains. It usually lasts a month. Our wait and my increasing tiredness went on. Years later, I wrote to our grandchildren about their father's late arrival in Poona:

> Midnight on 5 October 1966 was when it all began – at least the warning pangs. So Grandpa found an auto-rickshaw "wallah" willing to take us along to the hospital in the depth of the night. The ancient three-wheeler rattled along with apparently no springs to ease the trauma. I feared our firstborn might just arrive in this ignoble vehicle. But your lazy dad enjoyed the comfort of my tummy for longer than needed, so after 20 hours of Grandpa's rubbing of my painful back, your dad had to be pulled loose with a vacuum extractor. It alarmed me to see the little scrawny figure, quite blue all over, lying on the side table across from me.

> "Is that our baby? Is he still alive? Has the cord caught around his neck?" But, thankfully, he was OK and the next thing I remember was being given a warm, red-faced, but still scrawny little baby to cuddle. He looked perfectly normal and well, except for a rather large lump at the top of his head – from being vacuumed out. Check him out and see if there's any remaining scar!

> Because of the heat, your dad was always thirsty! My milk supply was not enough. How to keep him filled up? We tried a milk supplement, but even that didn't seem to satisfy. He seemed to beg for milk every few hours. An experienced mother staying with

us, Kay Pittman, suggested I mash him some banana with Farex and milk and see if that kept him happy. It did, and so from one month of age, your dad thrived on porridge and at last enjoyed some tummy satisfaction. Something still important to him now indeed, and he still loves porridge!

While still in Poona, we asked for his baptism at the local church where we worshipped. My mother, the talented seamstress, had made him a beautiful baptismal gown, all delicately smocked and frilled. This was all state-of-the-art baby gear for the mid–60s.

So we had him appropriately dressed for the occasion, and went off to the service in the relative cool of the evening,

Mark dressed for baptism

chauffeured by our good friends, Margaret and Milton Cashman. They also stood in as proxy godparents. We fed Mark well beforehand. Still, he liked to have a dummy between feeds, perhaps helping him to feel that food would not be too far away.

When the minister called for the baby, parents, and godparents to come forward for the ceremony, I felt it might be inappropriate for the baby to be baptised with a dummy in his mouth, so I withdrew the comforter. This evoked a deep lunged, prolonged protest from your dad which resonated through the vaulted cathedral throughout the ceremony and until I restored the dummy to its rightful place on our return to the pew! You can imagine what Grandpa thought about Nana's false pride in removing the dummy.

I missed not being able to share the joy of this new phase of life with my Mum. But in those days, international travel was only for the wealthy (and for Ten Pound Poms, the assisted immigrants from the UK). So apart from weekly letters, many black-and-white photos of the new arrival, and the celebratory telegram, I had to accept the reality of life without my parents. Another colleague and friend, Sandy Gordon, had delivered her firstborn, Becca, just three months before Mark's arrival, so it was good to have her company and to share notes of baby challenges and progress.

A month earlier, about 20 colleagues, brothers and sisters, had blessed me with a surprise baby shower of gifts for the soon to be born one, as they had done for Sandy earlier. This American custom was quite unfamiliar to us Australians, but very welcome and encouraging. Included in the gifts was a stuffed Humpty Dumpty soft toy, hand made by Beth Morton, one of our fellow Australian passengers on the *Galileo Galilei* and a lifelong friend.

There were also in Poona several proxy Mum and Dads – wonderful senior couples who took us under their wings in support and care. Milton Cashman managed the Philips Electrical Industries factories in Poona. He and Margaret had a generous heart for mission in India and regularly invited our Wycliffe group round to their lovely spacious home on a Sunday evening for a delicious meal and fellowship together – a welcome break from campus food. Indeed, the Lord promised those who leave mother and father for His sake, "a hundredfold" in return (Mark 10:29,30). "All the way, God is good," I was learning.

Mark was only 10 weeks old when we left Poona, heading for the much cooler city of Kathmandu in Nepal – one of the many travels which became a regular part of his and our lives. Perhaps my childhood dream of becoming a world traveller was indeed to be fulfilled, though not free of cost as for air hostesses!

13 Nepal at last!

I look up to the mountains – does my help come from these? My help comes from the LORD, who made heaven and earth! (Psalm 121:1)

The country I glimpsed in Dr Graham Scott-Brown's slides some seven years earlier had now become a reality.

On Christmas morning, in our meagre winter clothing, we shivered along on a bicycle rickshaw to join with Nepali Christians in the larger of the only two Christian churches, Gyaneshwar Church, then in Kathmandu. (There are now over a hundred!) While we understood little of the content of the service, the love feast that followed warmed our hearts (and bodies) as we appreciated their welcome. I well remember my first taste of the moderately spiced Nepali cuisine and of the delicious home-made lapsi chutney served with it. We were grateful to learn soon that most Nepali cuisine, although similar to Indian, was milder in its use of chilli seasoning.

Our major assignment in Kathmandu was to gain good orientation into this country, only recently opened to Western visitors, and to learn the national language well enough for shopping, polite conversation and negotiating with domestic helpers.

Nepal is a tiny country wedged between the two giants of India and China. It stretches about 800 kilometres northwest to southeast and varies in width from around 90 kilometres to 230 kilometres. Within that

"Bhaktapur, near kathmandu"

small area is the greatest range of altitude to be seen on the planet, from the Gangetic plains in the south to the world's tallest mountains in the north. Mt Everest's Nepali name, Sagarmatha (= above all), affirms its status as the tallest mountain in the world.

Thomas Hale (1993), a pioneer missionary doctor, described Nepal as "an enchanted land", indeed a unique and intriguing land, a story-book kingdom of royal palaces, exotic temples, breathtaking scenery, fearless Gurkha soldiers, tiger hunts in sweltering jungles, bleak desert highlands, and even, it is said, the Abominable Snowman. Many people think of Nepal mainly as a land of ice, snow and lofty mountain peaks, but in fact, most of its people live below 1,500 metres of altitude. Large parts of the country are barely above sea level. At a point 25 kilometres from central Nepal within the space of only two miles, the elevation changes from the valley floor 600 metres above sea level, right up to 8,000 metres – the sharpest change of elevation found anywhere on earth. The variation in climate is equally extreme, ranging from torrid heat to biting cold. "Indeed, the Nepalis' whole manner of living varies according to the altitude at which they live," wrote Tom Hale.

Kathmandu is in a rare geographic feature of mountainous Nepal, a broad expansive valley. The valley floor is at an altitude of 1,500 metres while the encircling mountains reach up to around 3,000 metres. Aeroplanes must carefully navigate their descent through these peaks, while departing flights circle around the valley to gain altitude.

Learning the Nepali language was not such a challenge for us as the months of intensive Hindi learning in Poona proved very helpful. Nepali is from the same language family, with many words of similar origin. But there were inevitable glitches along the way. For example, our language teacher looked nonplussed at Warren's asking in Nepali, "Do you drink buffalo milk?" and then laughed. He had not known there are different words for female buffalo and male buffalo and had actually asked "Do you drink bull's milk?" When I tried to ask the same question more accurately, the poor girl collapsed in uncontrollable laughs. This time the omission of one syllable meant I had asked whether she drank younger brother's milk!

The university gave us a list of languages they felt priority for research – Newar, Tamang and Gurung were near the top of their list. After prayer and some counsel from colleagues Colin and Jean Day, we decided on Gurung. Only six weeks into our Nepali study our Area Director, Dr Richard Pittman, visited Nepal and said, "Let's get a letter of introduction from the university to the top Government official in the Gurung area, and go have a look-see."

There were no roads to the Gurung area, and so he and Colin flew out with Warren to Pokhara, the geographical centre of Gurung territory (some 200 kilometres west of Kathmandu) in February 1967. They asked the *anchaladhish* (the governor of the province) for advice on the best village for a family with a small baby to live in for the study of the Gurung language – no further than a day's walk from the nearest hospital and market town, Pokhara. Without hesitation the governor gave his recommendation, Ghachok (gah-chook), and a letter to village elders asking for their support and help.

After Dr Pittman's return to Kathmandu, Warren and Colin walked the five hours up to Ghachok. They met the Pradhan Panch (village mayor) and discovered that Ghachok was a large village built on a geographical rarity in the hills of Nepal – a long plateau. The lower part of the village was Nepali-speaking, and the upper part predominantly Gurung. As they left Ghachok to return to Pokhara, they were delighted to meet on the road the deputy mayor, Ser Bahadur Gurung, and asked his help to find a house for our return, hopefully in May before arrival of the next monsoon in June. Ser Bahadur promised to arrange that.

I had given Warren a list of edibles for him to check out whether they were available in the village, so that I'd know what foodstuffs to take out with us from Kathmandu. Things such as rice, lentils, green vegetables, milk, eggs, flour, fruit, and cooking oil. Ser Bahadur assured Warren, to his delight, that all the above were available. But I'd neglected to add to the list a second column headed, "which months are they available?"

In May 1967, Warren went again to Pokhara and Ghachok before me to confirm accommodation, buy up some basic things that would not be available in the village such as potatoes, onions, kerosene and cooking oil, and tee up the porters needed to carry our goods up to Ghachok. I'd already purchased in Kathmandu a goodly supply of pasta, tomato sauce, tinned tuna, powdered milk, and cheese and I had some dehydrated vegetables and soup powders which I'd brought from Australia many months before! Household goods were minimal, but included a folding cot/playpen to serve Mark not only as a safe bed, but also as a clean space for him to move about in safely.

And so it was that on 5 May 1967, after a very early flight in a small Dakota plane out from Kathmandu, Mark and I joined Warren in Pokhara. The majestic Annapurna Himalayas dominated the landscape above the small Pokhara bazaar, so I hardly noticed the rustic nature of

Mt Machhapuchhare from Pokhara

the airport facilities or that the strip was just grass – hence the bumpy landing!

Within an hour our little party of three, plus four or five porters, was trudging through the narrow streets of the ancient town lined with small shops belonging to a traditional merchant community, the Newars. By about 10 am we gratefully reached the compound of Dr Graham Scott-Brown's Shining Hospital at the top of the bazaar. Warren had arranged with them to have a cuppa there before taking off for the longer trek up to Ghachok. Never had a cuppa tasted so good, nor the crunchy cookies prepared by their Gurung cook!

By 11 am we gathered our porters together again, strapped seven-month-old Mark to my back in a cloth carrier, and took off following the banks of the White River which would lead us eventually up to the Ghachok plateau. The first two hours were fairly easy going, as the river wound its way through the relatively flat Pokhara valley. But as the sun moved higher in the sky its heat, reflected off the white stones of the river gorge, left us hot and sweaty. We stopped frequently at the ever-welcome little tea shops along the way for more milky sweet tea and biscuits and to replenish fluid supplies for Mark. He, thankfully, was an easy traveller, and showed little sign of discomfort.

A typical Gurung village

Before long the trail turned north, going up and up towards the village which nestled close into the folds of the foothills of Mt Machhapuchhare (Fishtail Mountain). Thankfully, the temperature moderated as we reached the higher plateaus, but by mid-afternoon Mark was obviously feeling too cramped in the cloth bag, so Warren carried him in his arms for the latter stages of the climb. It was about 5 pm when we finally reached the village and trudged toward the upper Gurung section. The narrow village paths there had picturesque tall rock walls capped with crown-of-thorns succulents with brilliant small red flowers. But as we entered the tunnel-like path, we met a herd of water buffalo coming home from their grazing. I was petrified! I couldn't climb the rock walls, so pressed myself into a crevice until the herd passed, making sure I didn't make eye contact with any of the huge animals.

We met up with our sponsor, Ser Bahadur, and he showed us to the empty tea shop he had arranged for us to rent. I collapsed onto the verandah, keen to get the porters' basket loads unpacked and find the cot/playpen for Mark and some food to eat. But Ser Bahadur insisted we have a meal with them – typical Gurung hospitality! I couldn't eat anything because I was so utterly exhausted. So, after Warren did justice to his large platter of rice and curry, we returned to our first night in the village with an absolutely bare minimum of stuff unpacked from the baskets. In the days that followed, we unpacked all the baskets and set up our "bedroom" on the upper floor. We were glad of tin trunks for storing food supplies to frustrate rodent visitors.

We soon learned that the food supplies that we expected would be available in the village turned out to be not available in the pre-monsoon hot months. The previous season's harvest was exhausted. Food was scarce and the female water buffalos were dry.

After this difficult experience we developed a shopping list for supplies for our three-month stays in the village and I had good success in baking bread which was *never* available in the village.

On day 4 of that initial village stay, Warren returned to Pokhara to stock up on the basics on my "available in the village" list. But Mark needed eggs and I took off around the village to meet with

7	kg sugar
13	kg wholemeal flour
4	kg rice flakes
7	kg rice
4	kg onions
24	D size batteries
8	kg potatoes
20	tins tuna or sardines
15	blocks laundry soap
12	cakes toilet soap
3	pr sandshoes for each child
10	kg cheese
12	bottles jam
13	packets dried vegetables
20	packets pasta
3	tins Nescafe
	Shopping for three months

some neighbours, hoping that someone would have eggs they might sell me. No success! I prayed, "You know our need, Lord, and our situation. You have promised to be especially near those who are with young. And our young one here is in special need right now." As I returned home, on our little verandah was a person wanting some medical help. (She assumed all foreigners would be competent medicos!) I gave her some basic treatment – and as she left, she held out an egg in gratitude for my help! I received it with overflowing thanks.

For my 60th birthday our daughter Merryn wrote a poem that captures a lot of our life. I quote here a selection relevant to early days in Nepal.

My Mother's Hands

My mother's hands are large
with life and love;
stretched by all they've held,
swollen into the tight rings
of promises kept.

Cracked and cut from the
heat, chopping,
dishwater, dough kneading
of thousands upon
thousands of meals.

My mother's hands are creased
with the life lines of us all;
the worry, clenching fists,
wiping tears, wringing,
rescuing, praying,

Warm with hot water bottles,
running baths, rubbing
Vicks into crackly chests,
pouring tea.

"Dough kneading"
success!

14 And then we were four

He will carry the lambs in his arms, holding them close to his heart. (Isaiah 40:11b)

Our daughter Merryn was born 12 April 1969, one month beyond her due date!

Two months before her expected arrival we took a holiday, travelling around India to catch up with former Poona colleagues now working in various tribal areas of eastern India, and to meet up in Poona with our long-time friend Ray Christmas, now married to Elisabeth.

We flew from Kathmandu to Calcutta and took a taxi to Howrah station to get the train to Visakh where we were to meet Dick and Edith Hugoniot, friends from Poona days. As always, Howrah was absolutely jam-packed with people. To make things worse, severe flooding on the east coast of India had disrupted the train services and many, including the one we had bookings on, were cancelled. Our carefully booked train tickets were quite useless! But the amazing red-jacketed train porters, with our luggage atop their heads, got us through the teeming multitude and found another train they could put us on – also going south. With no valid reservation, we had to find a spot in the unreserved section along with what seemed millions of other passengers deprived of their reservations. A Caucasian family comprising a little boy with his Dad and pregnant Mum stood out like sore thumbs in the packed carriage of Indian travellers.

With their sympathy we found a seat and an empty luggage rack above our heads where we settled Mark for the night. He was well beyond the travelling cot by then! After 18 hours we eventually reached Visakh around midday, and found ourselves amidst a throng of passengers. Some were scrambling to exit the train and others, packed three or four deep, shoving to get on. How do we get out of here? Dick Hugoniot was on the station, awaiting our arrival. When he saw our plight he called out, "Pass Mark out overhead." Warren's height enabled him to hand toddler and also our luggage across to Dick. But what about the pregnant Mum? Was I also to be passed out overhead! We just pushed our way through the throng, seconds before the train set off again, going on south toward Madras (Chennai). Our placid 27-month-old Mark happily held Uncle Dick's hand till we could join him again.

From Visakh Dick drove us up the Eastern Ghats (escarpments) of Andhra Pradesh to their village home in Araku Valley. What a happy reunion with Edith, and meeting their little Ken, just 17 months old! It was while we were staying with the Hugoniots that Ken encouraged Mark finally to say his first words, "Yes" and "No", at somewhat over two years of age! Ken was 10 months younger than Mark, but already a fluent chatterbox.

Another good friend from Poona days, Kent Gordon, came to Araku Valley to collect us in his jeep and take us across the State border to Jagdalpur, where we met up again with Sandy, Becca and now baby Nate.

We joined other friends from Poona days, Beth and Nancy, in their Parji village, where they arranged for us to stay in the Government rest house! We enjoyed a swim in the clear forest river on the border of Bastar District and Orissa. They only mentioned the crocodiles later!

We then went west across India, two days by train, back to Poona, Mark's birth place. Another joyful reunion, with Ray and Elisabeth, plus an introduction to their firstborn, David. Finally, the train to Kalyan, near Bombay, and then all the way (36 hours by train) to Patna, whence we were to complete the circle by flying back to Kathmandu.

But about one hour short of arriving in Patna, early morning, Warren came to me in great distress. His wallet, with all our Indian money, had fallen down the toilet hole of the speeding train! What to do? We got to the Patna airport (probably paid the rickshaw puller with Nepali rupees) and sank exhausted into our seats on the Dakota DC3 back to Nepal, to await the birth of our second child due in March.

Soon after our return, all three of us succumbed to a virulent Asian flu, which caused uncontrollable dry hacking and general weakness. At that very time, when neither Warren nor I were well enough to get up and cook anything, we were awed by the Lord's provision of our need in the timely arrival of a large parcel. Gordon and Kay Hutton, good friends at St Mark's West Wollongong, one of our faithful link churches, had mailed large tins of Maggi soups several months earlier. Another wonderful timely provision from our Father God! The soups became our staple diet for the next four weeks, till our coughs subsided. Coughing as I was, I dreaded the forthcoming birth if I couldn't breathe deeply and well.

I'm so thankful that the Lord spared me the physical challenge for two more months, a month longer than the doctor expected. Many years later, I wrote to Merryn's boys about the drama of their Mum's late arrival:

"You'd better go home and pack your bag, Mrs Glover. The baby's head is already in position so it could come any time." I excitedly returned to tell Grandpa the news and to get a bag of baby clothes ready to take to the hospital. We were both a bit puzzled because we felt that our second child should not come for yet another month – due in March. And I had a terrible cough at the time which would have made the big push very difficult.

Two months on, the cough was gone. The bag was still packed, but the baby had not come. Your Mum, like her brother, was also reluctant to leave the comfort of Mummy's tummy. There was no vacuum extractor in Kathmandu, but there was another trick. Spring in Kathmandu is a wonderful time for tropical fruit, and one of my favourites was pawpaw. One night I just felt like having a little piece of pawpaw before going to bed. After the first piece, I felt another piece would be good too. It was so delicious, cool and mouth-watering that, piece by piece, I finished the whole big pawpaw all by myself in the one sitting! Then I remembered something. Pawpaw makes things in your tummy move along fast! And the very next morning, your Mummy also decided to move along.

I had to get up to the hospital quickly to await her arrival. But she still seemed to be reluctant to come. So the doctor said I should just keep walking around and she would eventually be born. Grandpa, Uncle Mark, and I walked, and walked, and walked around the rose gardens at the hospital, till we felt we knew every rose by sight and smell. But there was no progress, and I was exhausted. I asked if I could go home and join a potluck dinner with friends, planned for that evening. The doctor agreed, but asked if we had a car for a quick return to the hospital.

"Well, ye-es." We thought of the old Volkswagen Kombi van which rattled us around the Kathmandu streets when we were desperate for transport.

Within an hour back home, I knew that there was serious movement happening at last, so I got Grandpa to drive me quickly back to the hospital – in the shaky old Kombi van.

But the road was unsealed and pot-holed: "Warren, please slow down!"

Then the movements in my tummy were getting sharper: "Warren, hurry up!"

The van was too bouncy: "Warren! Slow down!"

The movements got worse: "Hurry, hurry!"

Grandpa was sure that he was going to have to deliver baby #2 in the Kombi. But we did get to the hospital, only to find the entry gates shut and locked. Where was the chowkidar (gatekeeper)? Apparently asleep. Grandpa anxiously blew the horn and shouted, "Chowkidar! Chowkidar! Come quickly!" At last the sleepy chowkidar came slowly forth to open the gates at 8.30 pm, allowing us to speed on and up to the hospital's front door. A group of nurses hurriedly came out and helped me up the stairs and onto the delivery table. And just 15 minutes later, before the Scottish obstetrician could arrive, your Mummy was born – warm, nicely rosy-cheeked, with a mop of black hair sticking straight up. Just like you had, Sam, when you were born.

As I lay in the hospital resting after her delivery, a gift parcel arrived from Australia - a full set of lovely baby clothes, from my wonderful Mum in Australia. Our Father God's timely provision once again!

Uncle Mark was excited to have his new baby sister to cuddle, and Nana and Grandpa gave thanks to God for this gift of another life to cherish, love, and care for. Spring was a lovely time to bring a new little one into the world. I could hear the birds chirping away in the trees. Perfume from blossom

trees somewhat countered the less pleasant Kathmandu street smells, where cows had priority right to wander and drop their poo. The weather was pleasant, and the baby seemed happy with her Mummy's milk, at least at the beginning.

The feeding nightmare was yet to come.

15 Close to His heart

The LORD keeps you from all harm and watches over your life. (Psalm 121:7)

The baby born in Kathmandu's spring soon became a thirsty summer baby. I seemed to spend all of my days sitting breast feeding her. I grew exhausted, but Merryn still seemed thirsty and hungry, even when I added banana and Farex to supplement her diet as I had with her brother Mark in Poona. After three months I realised that my own milk supply would never be enough to fill her up, so I switched her completely to a milk formula.

This change she liked even less, and for the next two years she suffered from almost constant diarrhea, of which neither we nor the paediatrician could ever diagnose the cause or treatment. However, she did put on weight and developed in every other way.

One time during a stay in Ghachok, she became so ill with this problem that we decided to take her down to the mission hospital for help. Warren put her into the baby backpack and walked the three hours down the valley for help. (Walking down was always quicker than the journey home!) At home I prayed that the doctors would have wisdom to know how to help her. But they assured him we were doing all we could, gave him some different medicines, and told him there was no need for hospital admission. So he began his journey back home. Since it was already late in the afternoon, he decided to take a shorter, but more precipitous, route up a high cliff to get to our village plateau. (This was the very cliff route that the shepherds had prevented toddler Mark from going down two years earlier—see the story on p. 71.) Half way up, he needed to change her nappy again. With no alternative but to lay her down on the narrow cliff trail, he took her off his back, got the change of nappy out of his bag, and cleaned her up for the rest of the trip home, now in almost total darkness. I still vividly recall my relief and thankfulness as they came in through the door that evening, tired from the long day's trekking, but safe.

Some months later we made a return trip to Australia. The paediatrician in Kathmandu had suggested a diet of mashed banana and carrots to help stabilize Merryn's tummy. My mother was horrified!

Guarding the winter crops from monkey Invasion!

"No wonder the poor child cries so much. So would you if all you had to eat was bananas and carrots!" Mum despaired at the unexpected incompetence of her own daughter to be a good mother.

I well remember the relief when, at about two years of age, our grumpy cry-baby suddenly became a happy, healthy toddler. We still didn't know what caused her problems, nor what made her better, but we thanked God very much for the answer to our desperate prayers over the previous two years.

Mark and Merryn entered fully into village life, with lots of playmates. One escapade when Mark was but a toddler was quite alarming. I described it to his own children many years later:

When we were living in Ghachok, your Dad, locally called Surje, loved playing out in the courtyard with all the village children, and also with all the farm animals, most of which were to be found in the house's courtyard or in adjacent barns. Goats, buffalo, hens, chicks and puppies were all of huge fascination for a little boy. But one day sheep also came through the village.

In the winter months, the Gurung shepherds used to bring their flocks down from the high pastures (then under snow!) to be grazed in the village and in the river valley below. They often passed by our house on their way to the lower village grazing fields early in the mornings. In front were the shepherds, whistling and calling to keep the sheep moving on, while behind the sheep came the big ferocious sheep dogs keeping the stragglers in line and protecting them from harm. Everyone told us, "Don't go near the sheepdogs! They bite."

One morning we heard someone shouting out to us from a nearby field. "Father of Surje, Father of Surje! Come! Come quickly and get Surje. He's gone down through the village with the sheep, and the shepherds now want to go down the cliff to the grazing fields. He could easily fall down the cliff." This was the first we knew of Surje's absence from the courtyard. Grandpa raced down the path to find the shepherds and found them sitting with your Dad. They were holding the little boy to stop him from going on down the steep cliff descent, following the sheep and the dogs! And Grandpa persuaded your Dad to come home for lunch.

But of course, that wasn't the only incident which reminded us that the Lord was indeed "watching over our life" (Psalm 121:7 NIV). I later wrote to Mark's children about another time that Mark's curiosity and love of animals led him to wander away into a potentially dangerous situation:

Little Boy Lost!

I think your dad was about three years old when Grandpa had to go to Kathmandu for meetings and so your dad, auntie Merryn, and I took a break from village living, to spend a few days with our good friends Graham and Margaret Scott-Brown at the Shining Hospital in Pokhara.

Graham and Margaret had children about the same age as your dad, so we weren't always keeping a check on their whereabouts in the apparently safe environment of the Scott-Browns' big house and yard. It was about 3 pm when we realised that our three-year-old was not with the other children. We hunted high and low through all the rooms of the big house and garden, to no avail. Then we ran out into the surrounding roads, asking people if they'd seen a little white boy walking anywhere.

With no successful leads, I was now really worrying about where he could have wandered off to. Just along the path from the house was the White River, which narrows through a deep gorge as it tumbles through caverns under Pokhara. The wild rapids create such a crescendo of sound that if you live nearby, you can hardly get to sleep at night for the noise. If your dad had got caught up in those waters, there was no hope for him. I shuddered at the thought and cried out again to the Lord to help us find him.

By 5 pm we were all panicking and I was praying desperately for God's protection over our little boy, and that someone might have seen and rescued him. Hadn't anybody seen a little three-year-old white boy anywhere? He would surely stand out in the crowd of little brown Nepali children around him, and Nepalis have always shown themselves lovingly protective and caring of children, especially foreigners' children.

Eventually, we got a message from a neighbour saying that they'd heard about Tibetan salt traders discovering a little white boy running along with their caravan of grey donkeys as they trotted through the bazaar.

"Where are they now?" I asked frantically.

"They are all down at the Mahendra bridge (some four kilometres down through the bazaar). You should go down there and see if he's your boy."

Graham grabbed a taxi going down to the bridge and, sure enough, there he found your dad sitting quite happily with the Tibetan traders and listening with interest to the tinkling of the bells on the necks of the donkeys as they grazed on their evening meal. They had clearly fed him a generous evening meal of Tibetan

bread, judging by the grease marks all over his mouth and cheeks, and he showed no consternation about his new surroundings.

Was it the bell sounds, or the colourful head decorations on the pack donkeys which attracted him to join the jogging caravan as it came jingling past our front gate? We'll never know, as your dad wasn't old enough to tell us, but you can be sure we all went to bed that night with deep thankfulness to God for His protection and care, and for the friendly Tibetan traders who found the little white boy jogging along amongst their donkeys.

This fearless, adventurous spirit was clear throughout his following years, reflecting our firstborn's phlegmatic and inquisitive approach to many of life's challenges. Our daughter-in-law Jenika, hearing of these escapades, asked me once, "Jessie, are you sure you only had two children, or is it that only two survived?"

PART 4 Translators' Tales

16 Unwelcome surprises

Let those with understanding receive guidance. (Proverbs 1:5)

The front door of our village house opened directly into our kitchen-cum -living room. The door was actually a totally open wall. We could close the wall completely by placing some thick planks horizontally down a slot. But during the day we removed the top lot of planks so light could come into our living area. It wasn't long before we had a constant stream of visitors draping themselves over our half door and marvelling at all the stuff we had. "*kati leh saamaan!*" was an oft-repeated phrase we heard early on, but only later learned that it meant, "What a lot of stuff they have!" Our stuff comprised a set of two enamel plates, bowls and mugs, plus two picnic cutlery sets, a pressure cooker, frying pan and some basic cooking utensils. We also had a couple of plastic bowls and spoons for Mark's food. And in addition, we had a couple of Australia-themed tea towels decorating the walls to maintain a touch of nostalgia for home.

I took delight from then on when visiting their homes, with shelves laden with large, small, and decorated vessels made of copper, brass, and stainless steel to exclaim, "*kati leh saamaan!*" – and not always under my breath. In the early days I wondered whether we would have a problem with theft, since access to our "stuff" would be simple for someone to simply just jump over the half door. But nobody ever took even a single spoon. We soon learned of the widely recognised honesty and reliability of Nepalis, chosen by preference above locals as guards of residences and office facilities across India and abroad. Further, com-pared with their copious display of copper, brass and stainless steel, our aluminium camping spoons were not likely to be attractive.

Perhaps the most challenging aspect of our former tea shop was its height or, more accurately, lack of height. There was only one area in which we could stand upright and that was under the gable of the roof upstairs in our bedroom. We had to keep ourselves bent over in all other parts of the building, and a constantly bent posture is not good for the back, or the digestion! The house was so low Warren, standing below floor level, could easily seat Mark on the roof.

Putting Mark on the dolls' house roof

Warren routinely took his notebook outside for noting down any Gurung words he could catch as people talked with him. One day, he was chatting in our front yard with some schoolboys returning from school, while I was busy with meal preparation inside the little house. Suddenly I heard a deep groan and rushed out to check what had happened to Warren. "Oh, no!" he groaned. "Just listen to these lads as they tell me the numbers 2 and 7."

I could immediately hear that the only difference was in the pitch with which they pronounced the two words. I shared Warren's dismay. During our prefield linguistic training in Brisbane, both of us failed miserably in dictation exercises that had anything related to pitch differences in words. "Oh well," we comforted ourselves then, "I'm sure the Lord won't send *us* to a tone language."

Why were we unaware that the language we had chosen to study was indeed a dreaded tone language? Months earlier in Kathmandu, when presented by the University with a list of potential languages to study, we had tried to find out about them but there was very little we could lay hands on and nothing mentioned the importance of tone in Gurung. So, in our ignorance, it did come as a surprise, and an unwelcome complication to our language learning.

Over the next two years we slaved over countless varieties of words which seemed to be different only because of the pitch at which they were spoken. For example,

74

Tone level	Gurung	English	Gurung	English
High	*mi*	eye	*tsa*	he/she/it
Mid	*mi*	name	*tsa*	vein
Low–mid glide	*mwi*	money	*tsa*	tea
low	*mi*	person	*tsa*	son

Within a couple of years, it became clear to many of our colleagues working in Nepal that these kinds of tone contrasts occurred also in their languages. We needed to have some professional help in unravelling this linguistic problem. In 1968, our beloved Area Director, Dr Richard Pittman, came through Vietnam on his way to Nepal and brought us a practical tip of how to harness the intuitions of our native speaker language helper to sort words he felt similar in pitch into different lists, and then use those lists to train our own ears. We were well on the way.

In 1969, two years after that painful discovery in our front yard in Ghachok, we joined a multi-language workshop in Kathmandu led by the world's leading tone language specialist, Dr Kenneth Pike, to help us all understand the mystery of tone languages in Nepal. And to our delight, Dr Pike confirmed the analysis we'd reached using the rhyming lists tip brought to us by Dr Pittman. But there was great variety across the seven languages taking part in the Pike workshop – unwelcome surprises to all. The papers we and our colleagues wrote, under the stimulus of Ken and Evelyn Pike, were published the following year (Hale and Pike 1970) and cemented our relationship with Tribhuvan University.

Even more bewildering than hearing and speaking the tones was how we could represent these slight differences in writing the language. Gurung had never been written before. One day, early in our village stays, one of the young Gurung men asked us, "Why are you learning our language?"

We answered, "Because we want to learn how to write Gurung so that books that will benefit you can be written."

"Oh, Gurung can't be written," he responded emphatically. "How are you going to find letters for.........?" and he described some of the challenges we were now all too well aware of. We knew they would be very difficult to represent in the beautiful Devanagari script that is used for Nepali, Hindi and most other languages of Nepal and northern India.

But as we discussed the problems and practical issues with our friends in Ghachok, they decided they needed to distinguish only the low tone, marking it with the letter *h* because of the accompanying breathy voice quality. So, soon after they made that decision, I felt confident to take up the offer of attending a large Primer Construction workshop at Literacy House in Lucknow, north India. With a primer in print, it would be possible to hold literacy classes for women in the village. Going to Literacy House, Lucknow was a great privilege, as the workshop was to be led by one of our own SIL international literacy consultants, Dr Sarah Gudschinsky.

So, with Mark and his fold-up playpen in tow, we set off in January 1968 for Lucknow. The trip was traumatic! We flew from Kathmandu to Patna, sat for hours in a hot, steamy railway waiting room fruitlessly hoping for a train to Lucknow, then gave up in exhaustion and spent a few hours to recover in a hotel before getting on a plane to Lucknow, and eventually a cycle rickshaw to Literacy House, with Mark's playpen hanging precariously from the back.

The renowned Literacy House was established just twelve years earlier by Dr Welthy Fisher, an American educationalist. The great Indian leader Mahatma Gandhi, just before his assassination in January 1948, had encouraged her to establish a literacy centre to address the challenge of widespread illiteracy in India's villages. For the 1968 workshop, along with us and a few other expatriate colleagues, educationalists from all over India came to work with Dr Sarah to design primers for the non-literates in their respective States.

Sarah stressed the importance of easy and gradual steps in introducing the learners to new letters. In a radical move, she insisted each lesson include a portion of interesting text for the learners. Most traditional Indian primers introduced five to ten new letters in each lesson and rarely included any readable sentences or stories. So it took time for the participants to accept the revolutionary changes in their respective languages and writing systems. For me, the principles were intuitive from my teaching experience in Australia and we left the intensive six-week workshop with a draft primer of 50 lessons to cover all the letters needed for reading and writing Gurung, including those words with low tone!

We were blessed in having the most unflappable and contented young toddler with us. Mark happily settled in wherever his peripatetic parents

पाठ ११

तारा
ता
राम्

राम् बनरी मुला। तारा बनरी मुला। तारा राम् बालु मुला। बनरी मल तुला। मलरी नारी मुला। बनरी नीमु मुला। लम नीमु मल मुबरी खला।

ता	तु	ती	त
ताम्	तुम्	तीम्	तम्

A page of my trial Gurung primer

dragged him. The playpen was the unchangeable interest-filled centre of his little world, but we were very grateful for the kind help of some of our workshop participants giving time to entertain him.

It would be quite a process to print this primer. We had to check the draft with Gurung speakers, get it illustrated by artists at our SIL centre in Kathmandu, and finally photocopied in sufficient numbers for testing with a trial class. All of this process took time, so it was only two years later (winter of 1969–70) that I could get the trial class going. I asked our village sponsor to nominate women who he felt would like to join the class. In due course, 15 women gathered for their night out in the little office room, enjoying the light of the pressure lamp and the blackboard. They sat with notebooks and pens before them for their first class to begin. Warren took parent duties on those nights, putting Mark to bed with the usual bedtime rituals. I blessed him and the Lord for his very willing co-parenting attitude.

Knowing how important adult participation is in learning, I felt I needed to explore with these women what had led them to join this first women's literacy class. With shining eyes each one answered with eager anticipation, "So that we can learn English from you!" Not what I had in mind! Another unwelcome surprise. However, these women did get to appreciate the easier path to literacy of learning to read in their own mother tongue first.

What other surprises lay ahead?

17 What is sin?

Write down clearly on tablets what I reveal to you, so that it can be read at a glance. (Habakkuk 2:2 GNT)

There were three of us gathered around the translator's desk – myself as the translator, the translation consultant, and our village landlord, Ram Phal Gurung. Ram Phal had come to Kathmandu with us to help check whether the story from Luke's Gospel was clear and understandable for him, an unchurched, Buddhist villager.

We'd reached the passage (Luke 5:4–9) about a miraculous catch of fish. Simon Peter had protested when Jesus told him to put down their nets again since they had already worked hard all night with no success. But he complied, perhaps reluctantly, with Jesus' command – and to their astonishment, the nets bulged to breaking point. At that point, Peter turns in astonishment, bows before Jesus and says, "Oh, Lord, please leave me – I'm too much of a sinner to be around you."

The consultant asked our friend (through me as interpreter), "Why did Peter think he was a sinner?" I relayed the question for Ram Phal, pretty confident the passage was a clear one and the question should not present any problem for him.

He responded instantly, without any need to ponder, "Of course he was a sinful man. Just a few minutes before all those fish were alive and well in the lake. Now hundreds of them are dead in the boat. A lot of sin there!"

Was this what Luke expected his readers to understand, that Peter's sin was killing fish? After all, Peter was a professional fisherman. The message my Gurung friend got was not correct!

So now, what to do? As Bible translators, our goal is that the message of the translated passage should be clear, accurate and natural to the target speakers of the language. This Gurung passage was no longer giving an accurate message for a Buddhist person for whom the taking of life is considered sinful. Our consultant suggested adding an explanatory phrase, "because I didn't believe your word... I am a sinful man." Such amplifications do raise queries for those who insist that the Word of God be not added to in any way. However, to leave this passage without clarification would make it give a wrong message. What a dilemma!

Our next dilemma came in Luke 8:22–25, when Jesus calmed the storm on the Lake of Galilee. Luke tells us Jesus was settled down in the boat having a nap, and even as the fierce storm came up, he slept on. Finally, his disciples woke him up, shouting, "Master, Master, we're going to drown." Once again, an apparently straightforward story to translate. But which *"we"* is appropriate here? Unlike English, Greek, and most related languages, Gurung has *two* forms for the pronoun *we*, which we call inclusive and exclusive.

To illustrate, I can tell you, "We've lived in Nepal for many years." In that case, the *"we"* pronoun applies to Warren and me, but not likely to you, the reader. In Gurung we would use in this context *ngi*, the exclusive pronoun, so-called because it excludes you as the hearer. Or I could say, "We've had a really rough time with COVID–19." That includes us all and so requires in Gurung the inclusive pronoun, *ngyoh*.

Now back to the boat scene. Which *we* should we use in the disciples' statement, "we're going to drown"? Did they feel that Jesus would not drown with them, or were they all under threat of drowning? We discussed this problem with the Gurung translation team. They read the wider context of how much, or how little, the disciples understood of Jesus' power at that time, and saw that in verse 25, after Jesus calmed the wind and the waves, "The disciples were terrified and amazed. 'Who is this man?' they asked each other." So the disciples had clearly not yet understood the supernatural power of their master, and they thought that Jesus would drown with them all. They were calling him to get up and help them work the boat, and join the bailing! The Gurung team agreed that the correct pronoun to use was the inclusive, *ngyoh*.

Using the correct *"we"* pronoun became even more theologically important in translating the epistles. In Ephesians 1:12,13 (NIV), Paul contrasts "We who were the first to put our hope in Christ" with "you also [who] were included in Christ when you heard the message of truth". Again, which *we* should the Gurung translation use in verse 12? The *"we"* of verse 12 is clearly a different group of people from the *you also* of verse 13, and so requires the exclusive *"we"* pronoun. However, all of the *"we"* pronouns in verses 3–11 demand the inclusive, declaring to the Ephesian believers that they already are included in the grace and blessings of the Gospel.

The criteria of Clear, Accurate, and Natural were not easy to achieve, but always our goal.

The Gurung translation team in 1976, with Shah Bahadur front row right

Shah Bahadur in mature years,
a godly mission leader

18 The first aid trunk

Those who remain in me, and I in them, will produce much fruit. (John 15:5)

The village of Ghachok was about four hours walk above the Pokhara town, where the closest hospital was situated. It was the mission hospital Dr Graham Scott-Brown had told me about when he visited Picton parish some years before. The wards were aluminium semicircular Nissan huts. The hospital was locally known as the Shining Hospital because its tin roofs were a shining beacon for patients as they came down from the surrounding mountain villages.

We were grateful for the welcome, support, and help given by the medical team there. They upskilled my very basic first-aid knowledge from Jungle Camp days, with hints about what complaints might present to our door. (The village folk assumed all Westerners were nurses or doctors, since those whom they knew down in Pokhara were indeed so.) So the Shining Hospital team also told me the Nepali names of common conditions and the simple medicines which I could stock up in my first aid trunk to treat these conditions. One very popular medicine was an injection of Vitamin B, known locally as "strength-giving medicine". The abundance of corn in their daily diet resulted in the body being less able to assimilate Vitamin B. An injection from time to time had a dramatic energizing effect.

Back home in Ghachok, before long a man called by asking if I could give him an injection of the strength-giving medicine. He had a phial of vitamin B with him, which he'd probably purchased in Pokhara, and all he needed from me was to do the injecting. My first such patient! One skill taught in Jungle Camp was this very topic. There we practised injection, using an orange! However, I wasn't too concerned and injected my patient. But I was not expecting the gentleman to faint on the grass mat in front of me within seconds of being injected! What might happen if this man died? Would I be up for medical malpractice? Was our ministry in the Gurung village destroyed at the outset? I prayed hard, and was greatly relieved when I also remembered from that same Jungle

Camp lecture that men frequently faint on being given an injection. Even greater was the relief when, after a minute or two, said gentleman regained consciousness, stood up, said, "That's great!" and took off with new strength, much satisfaction and appreciation for my help! He went on to advertise my "clinic" in the village!

Almost every day people came along to ask for help from my first aid tin trunk. One day, a very senior gentleman came along and sat quietly on the verandah till I had distributed all the worm medicines and vitamins. Then he came across and sat on the threshold asking if I had any medicine for "bloody mucus", the local name for one kind of diarrhea. Thankful that he used a term I had learned from the Shining Hospital staff in Pokhara, I was happy to help. I gave him the packet, and he asked the name of the medicine.

Since it was a rather complex medical mouthful (Sulphaguanadine) he asked me to write it out for him and he pulled from his pocket a pamphlet for me to write on. To my amazement, it was a Gospel of John in the Nepali language. Baje Baidera ('grandfather bookkeeper', as he was respectfully called) told us he'd been given it when visiting the Shining Hospital for his wife's TB treatment. (It was shining not just by the tin roofs of its Nissan huts glinting in the sunshine, but also by the team's testimony to the One who is the light of the world.)

Warren opened the booklet and asked him to read John 14:6, "I am the Way, the Truth and the Life."

"What do you think Jesus is teaching in that verse?"

Baje explained in his gracious quiet way that Jesus was saying he was one way to heaven and that like Buddha and the other pathways, they would all meet together at the top. He hand-gestured for our benefit.

A few months later, we had a first draft of Mark's Gospel ready for checking by a consultant in Kathmandu.

Baje Baidera studying
on his verandah

The consultant required that we have one or two Gurung speakers present for the check, people who had not worked in the translation process. It is important to know how the translation draft communicates to unchurched speakers of the language. After much prayer for guidance, we went across to Baje Baidera's house and asked if he would come to Kathmandu with us for this purpose.

"Well, I know little about this work you're asking me to help with, and I don't like travel. But I've always wanted to visit Nepal (most villagers considered that only Kathmandu was "Nepal") and also, I'd like to see the king before I die, so I'll come with you."

For four weeks Baje sat listening to the story of the power of Jesus over illness, demons, nature, fear, enemies and death, which is so clearly told in St Mark's Gospel. He responded with unusually clear understanding to the questions from the consultant. Our other language helpers, who shared accommodation with him that month, often turned up for work looking haggard and tired. "The old grandfather won't turn out the lights at night. He's up throughout the night reading Mark's story," they bemoaned.

At the end of the month, the grandfather told us, "Now I know that Jesus is indeed THE way to God. We must share this good news with the whole Gurung community, like when we meet for weddings and funerals when all relatives come together." We thoroughly agreed with his mission strategy and rejoiced in this reminder of how the Word of the Lord brings light to those who are open to learn.

Baje Baidera was indeed a humble and gentle man. But his gentleness morphed into fear when, on returning to Pokhara from Kathmandu, he learned of an outbreak of harassment and persecution of the Christian community. A pastor and some baptised believers were in prison for "change of religion". So Baje decided to lie low and say nothing, except that he would tell his family of this new way he had discovered to be THE truth.

Baje's two sons, Shah and Khadga, frequently dropped by our house on their way home from school. They joined with Mark and Merryn in playing trains, or enjoyed the pictures in the bound volumes we had of *National Geographic*. They were obviously of high intelligence and had an interest and open mind to learn more of the wider world beyond their mountain village.

Shah among those playing trains with Mark and Merryn

The following winter, when we were getting Luke's gospel ready for the Kathmandu external check, Warren asked Baje to help in the preparation by listening to the draft and giving suggestions for clarity or style. Each evening Warren visited their home and Baje and his family sat around the open hearth to hear the gospel story again. Since Baje's teenage son, Shah, was learning English in High School Warren gave him a copy of Luke in the English *Good News Translation* to follow. Shah was Baje's seventh child, but his first son and so was particularly precious. Shah later testified that he put his faith in Jesus during those hearth-side studies of the scripture, both in his own language and in English.

Shah with his father Baje Baidera

Some years later, when Shah had finished high school, he came to work full time with us in Pokhara to complete the New Testament for his own people. Round about that time he asked his father's permission to be baptized. Although Baje knew the risks his precious son might face, even of imprisonment, he gave permission.

One day Shah came to the office after a visit home and told us of his aunties' reaction to the news of his baptism: "You don't know how much we prayed to the gods when you were in your mother's womb, that you might be a son; a son who would give honour and pleasure to his parents and the entire family. And now look what you've done! By joining that foreign cow-eating religion you have brought utter disgrace and shame to our family and to our name. How could you have done so!" Shah told us that when he took baptism he was mentally prepared to face persecution from outsiders and even to go to jail if need be for Jesus' sake, but this tirade from his beloved aunties had all but undone him. He didn't know how to face their ostracism, but he said how much he'd found comfort in the words of Jesus to his disciples in John 15:15,16, "I no longer call you slaves, because a master does not confide in his slaves. Now you are my friends since I have told you everything that the Father told me. *You didn't choose me, I chose you.* I appointed you to go and produce lasting fruit."

After completing the Gurung New Testament, Shah worked with other mission agencies in health and community development areas. Gaining in expertise, grace and faith, he was given more and more responsibility within Nepal and also in wider Asian arenas. Tragically, in 2011 Shah died suddenly of a heart attack at only 53 years of age. He was mourned by a huge community of family, friends, colleagues, church and mission leaders, leaving behind a widow and three young sons. He had lived to bring honour and prestige not only to his family but to the hundreds of others who had loved him as a friend, mentor and work associate. His boss in the International Nepal Fellowship and then also later in the United Mission to Nepal, Jenny Collins, sent this message to add to the hundreds in his condolence book:

Shah Bahadur Gurung:

I first met and worked with Shah in the late 1970s. He was in his early adulthood and I in my late twenties. We worked together in the INF leprosy rehabilitation programme. From those early days, until I met him this past April, what struck me most was Shah's humility and compassion – whether visiting people with leprosy on the edge of the newly created Rara National Park, opening the UMN work in a new district or inspiring church leaders to engage in holistic transformation.

Shah always had time for people, to understand them and their particular situation, always treating them with dignity and a deep desire to see their situation improve positively. He saw in people the potential for them to be and live more as God created and desired them to be. He was at home in the villages of Nepal, identifying with people and their needs, often remembering and quoting his own village upbringing.

After he attended the HIM-led course, I often saw him with his camera, photographing many contrasting subjects: beautiful flowers close up and then rubbish tips. When I questioned him about this, he told me it reminded him of the contrast of the beauty of God's creation and what we (created in God's image) have done to destroy and distort creation. Shah had a deep understanding of the heart of God for all of His creation.

Increasingly Shah had a deep desire for the church to get more fully involved in God's mission in Nepal. He believed passionately and worked tirelessly to encourage the church at all levels to understand the Biblical view of mission and for them to act in their own communities. He involved himself in this in very practical ways across Nepal and handled the establishment of Micah Network Nepal to encourage the church in these activities.

He and his wife Samjhana and their three sons made me feel very welcome and accepted in their home. I learned a great deal from Shah over many years and I give thanks to God that I was privileged to work with him in both INF and UMN, for the building of the kingdom of God in Nepal.

I pray for the continuation of his vision and for peace and comfort for his friends and family.

Jenny Collins, UMN Executive Director 2001–09

Shah had indeed produced "much fruit", which ultimately led even his once angry relatives to mourn his passing and feel proud of their loved one. His dad, Baje Baidera, never followed through in taking baptism as a seal on his belief, but local villagers knew he'd changed religious allegiances. His daughter told me of an occasion when she was going around house to house collecting money for the maintenance of the village Hindu shrine. Her father had contributed a token sum when asked but, as she left the courtyard, it shocked her to see Baidera's contribution fall off the plate that she was holding completely upright. She understood this to mean that her father's God didn't want any part in the traditional religious systems of the village.

19 Banished!

In all your ways acknowledge Him, and He will direct your paths. (Proverbs 3:6)

In late May 1976, exactly nine years after our arrival in Ghachok, we started packing up from the village for yet another workshop in Kathmandu. At our landlord's request, we packed everything away in locked trunks, "to protect them from the rats." This time, I had a strange compulsion to get rid of all extra things. I passed on all the medical supplies in my first aid trunk to a local, recently trained health worker. All the copies of the bound National Geographic magazines, which the village kids had devoured with keen interest over the years, we gave to the local school. We packed into storage just minimal equipment for our next return whenever that might be.

Soon after arrival in Kathmandu, we were called to a general meeting of our SIL group, which now numbered about 90 adults, along with another 40 children. At the meeting our group director (and long-time friend from Poona days) Dick Hugoniot announced that the local university, our sponsor, had given him notice that the government had instructed them to break their agreement with SIL. Dick had negotiated a three-month grace period to allow for staged departures of all our members. No translation teams were to go back to their village to bring closure or to collect any equipment. We were very glad to have so reduced our possessions in Ghachok before departure just a few days earlier!

The official reasons given for the expulsion were that we'd been involved in "anti-government activities". For many months we speculated what these activities might have been. Did our mother tongue literacy activities violate the "Nepali only" education policy of the country, even though every item we produced in a minority language had the Nepali translation supplied? Was it because a few local people were coming to faith in Jesus through the initial translation efforts? Two language teams were named where such conversions and baptisms had taken place but, in both cases, only one or two families were involved.

The accusation that we were involved in anti-government activities often made me feel like a criminal, and guilty as a result. We had come to *serve* the people of this land, but here we were, ten years later, expelled as unwelcome. It was at these times that I was particularly encouraged by the Scripture, "Who dares accuse us whom God has chosen for his own? No one – for God himself has given us right standing with himself" (Romans 8:33).

If the almighty God, maker of heaven and earth, is for us and contends for us, who or what could ever harm us?

The real reason for our expulsion only came to the surface some years later. The Chinese government had photographic proof that a Pilatus Porter plane had been dropping arms to Tibetan insurgents. His Majesty's Government of Nepal had to get rid of the offender as they didn't want to alienate their huge neighbour on the northern border! There were only two organizations operating Pilatus Porter planes in the country at the time, SIL and another international agency. It would have been very difficult for His Majesty's Government of Nepal to incriminate publicly that very influential agency and risk losing a lot of aid from them. It was easier to make SIL's plane the scapegoat even though the Nepali authorities knew we were innocent – after all, in accordance with Government requirements, there had been a Government or University observer on every SIL flight! The arms-dropping accusation was never mentioned to us at the time.

In September 1976 a good friend, the professor of linguistics from Warren's PhD days at Australian National University, Professor Stephen Wurm, visited Nepal and the university. We were sorry to not be able to welcome him in person, as we'd just left in August, but we met Professor Wurm in Canberra on his return and he said, from his talks at Tribhuvan University, "You know why you had to leave Nepal? It was because you were doing literacy in the minority languages!" There were no doubt several factors leading to our expulsion by the Government.

During the remaining three months we were all intensely busy in production of already translated scripture materials: translation checking, keyboarding, page layouts and typing work that went on around the clock. The preparation of photo ready text was greatly helped by Flexowriters, purchased from US Government surplus, for editing the text on ticker tape. Jim Cooper had worked with the machines in Vietnam. He arrived in Nepal in 1975, sourced the machines, got the Devanagari symbols installed on the typing levers, and coached us in their use. The Flexowriters ran day and night – Warren worked the midnight to breakfast shift. The actual printing took place in the evening and night hours when University Press was not in use for University printing. Our children also worked in the print shop on the evening shift, collating and stapling books fresh off the press. Mark has often spoken of the excitement of those days and of the sense of being tangibly part of his parents' work.

Children also joined in, collating the freshly printed pages

On 11 August, we held a service to dedicate over 50 scripture selections in 21 languages where SIL colleagues had worked. Five hundred copies of all Gurung portions (Mark's Gospel, Luke's Gospel and Acts) were printed and stored with a Christian Nepali friend. Where possible, he distributed copies to local Christians for Gurung readers.

During the three pre-departure months, the then Asia Area director, Bus Dawson, and our Nepal director, Dick, met with each team to plan redeployment. Where might the Lord lead us next? We felt a nudge to think of the Australian Aborigines and Islander Branch (AAIB) and arranged for our technical library to be posted there. At least 20 parcels in all. Thankfully, there was a team handling the mammoth packing and posting task, not just for us but for all our members. The nudge to serve with AAIB was perhaps an expression of Warren's concern for Australian indigenous issues since his days in the Aboriginal Scholarship group at Melbourne University.

Amid these decisions and the heavy translation related work, we all had to face the stress of dismantling our Kathmandu homes and selling off furniture, household effects and personal items. We held huge garage sales where it seemed half of Kathmandu, from the early hours of each morning, came bargaining and arguing about the prices, already set low by the departing owners.

Our grief was further compounded with the souring of the relationship with our long-term language assistant, DB. He felt hurt that our sever-ance gift of a block of land was inadequate in comparison with what he perceived language assistants of other teams were getting. As if this wasn't hard enough to process, in our very final week our long serving village mail carrier, Purna Sarki, turned up in Kathmandu, miraculously finding us in the big city to ask for our help in getting medical attention. Warren took him to the Christian hospital, Shanta Bhawan, but he was in terminal stages of cancer, beyond medical help. He died within three days and Warren had to arrange his cremation according to Hindu rites. Death seemed to prevail wherever we turned.

The Sunday services at the Kathmandu International Christian Church were of poignant comfort to us during these heavy weeks. The first Sunday of June, after we and another Christian organisation got the order to leave, the pastor preached on Revelation 3:8 (GNT), "I know what you have done; I know that you have a little power; you have followed my teaching and have been faithful to me. I have opened a door in front of you, which no one can close." One hymn in particular spoke to my heart, "Spirit of God, Descend Upon my Heart" by George Croly. Two of the verses are:

> Did you not bid me love you, God and king,
> Love you with all my heart and strength and mind?
> I see the cross, there teach my heart to cling,
> O let me seek you, and O let me find.
>
> Teach me to feel that you are always nigh;
> Teach me the struggles of the soul to bear,

To check the rising doubt, the rebel sigh;
Teach me the patience of unanswered prayer.

Amid these death realities, Bus Dawson, our area director, shared with us that every death in God's will is followed by the promise of a resurrection. He spoke from his own experience of recently losing his wife to cancer. In her last days, the assurance of resurrection deeply comforted him. In such death situations, we can always affirm that *God intended it all for good* (Genesis 50:20).

We were to be among the last ones to leave Nepal and the repeated trips to the airport to farewell close friends and their families became an all too regular pain-filled part of the death experience. Yet we often felt that these farewells were not final, even for our earthly journeys, and that the Lord had a resurrection experience for us, too. But where was it, and which "door" had the Lord opened for us? Was it AAIB? To India? Or return to Nepal?

Little did we imagine we would never again see our 20 boxes of professional books already sent to Darwin.

20 A new resurrection

I have opened a door for you that no one can close. (Revelation 3:8)

Before leaving Nepal for Australia in August 1976, I discovered Warren wanted to buy round-trip tickets! "I need convincing that God has really closed this door to Nepal, and there's only one way of knowing – try to come back again," my engineer husband explained.

We spent six months in Australia, partly in Canberra back in ANU housing, and partly teaching again at SPSIL, now at New College at the University of NSW. Then we set off for Nepal again in February 1977. Would we be able to get a visa to enter, or were we already black listed? In Bangkok en route, we were hugely relieved to get one-month tourist visas, which enabled us to enter Nepal with no problem. And as we sat in the departure lounge for the flight to Kathmandu and had our daily scripture reading, the Lord lovingly assured us we were on the right track – "So let's not get tired of doing what is good. At just the right time we will reap a harvest of blessing if we don't give up" (Galatians 6:9).

There was no problem either on arrival in Kathmandu or when friends from our time at the University met us on the street. They were delighted to see us again, hoping perhaps that we might continue to help them in developing their linguistics department. But we were heading for Pokhara. Would we even manage a return to our village home?

In Pokhara, the Shining Hospital team warmly welcomed us and even asked us to house-sit for a family who were away on home leave. INF's Pokhara Study Centre also welcomed Mark and Merryn into their programme, relieving me of the need to home-school them as I'd done when in Ghachok village. In this place we could also welcome our former translation helpers, who with much joy took up the unfinished work.

"I can see now why you search so carefully for words that even the villagers can understand. Compared with the Nepali Bible the meaning is patently clear in our Gurung Bible." This comment from one of our helpers was a great encouragement, and Grandfather Baidera's son Shah made a similar remark a few days later.

But a few not so welcome home truths from other Gurung believers confronted us:

> "The books you printed last year are too big. They won't fit into our pockets."

> "They are too heavy for our evangelists to carry around from village to village on their backs."

> "Can't you print small portions, and give the messages on cassette to play in the villages. They love to hear songs and messages in their own language."

> "Villagers aren't in the habit of reading big books. Why not just summarise the major matters in a smaller booklet?"

The comments were discouraging, but they helped us set our priority for whatever time the Lord would allow us to be back in Nepal.

In those three months we took the Gospel narratives already in print and wrote the "major matters" in simple dialogues, printed in nine little booklets: "The birth of Jesus", "Are you ill?", "What is sin?", "You don't need to fear", "God loves everyone", "Jesus loves even sinners", "Jesus cares for us", "Can you endure difficulty?", and "The death and resurrection of Jesus".

We took some of the translation team to Kathmandu to get these dialogues recorded on cassette in dramatized format, with some appropriate newly composed Gurung hymns interspersed in the text.

On a visa renewal trip out to Calcutta, we got these titles printed and

The "major matters" in pocket-sized booklets

collated into plastic packets which could fit into evangelists' pockets. Back in Nepal, the evangelists were happy. We had no proof of their impact but were astonished to learn that the translation team who undertook a revision 35 years later wanted to reprint those same booklets. As far as we know, they are still the most widely used scripture materials and they have also been re-recorded using modern technology in the slightly different dialect. The wisdom and advice of those early evangelists proved valid.

Back in 1977, while I kept busy with these scripture engagement projects, Warren, Shah and DB continued translating the rest of the New Testament, beyond the 33% we had printed the year before. The goal of completing the New Testament now looked like being achievable within just a few years. What made this dream possible was the discovery that we could renew the one-month tourist visas multiple times. We could renew them twice by Warren's taking our passports to Kathmandu. After two renewals, the whole family had to leave the country and get new one-month visas at a Nepalese embassy or consulate in India. Over the next two years, the visa trips became a regular pattern. It disrupted school and work patterns, but was definitely worth the effort. And we could return each time to a beautiful home we had rented in Dip, overlooking Pokhara, where the team could work in peace and the family enjoy regular routines.

Our family soon faced a very hard decision. After five months, Mark finished at the Pokhara Study Centre, because it required students to leave the term before they turned 11. For the next part of his education, he would need to attend a boarding school. None of the options were attractive. The American system Lincoln School in Kathmandu was well beyond our means and in any case there was no boarding accommodation attached. Wood-stock School, in northwest India, required two days of travel. The other option some families had chosen, Hebron School in south India, was five days' travel! The prospect of being so distant from our son was very confronting. But he was keen to be in a more competitive and challenging school environment. So, hard decisions had to be made.

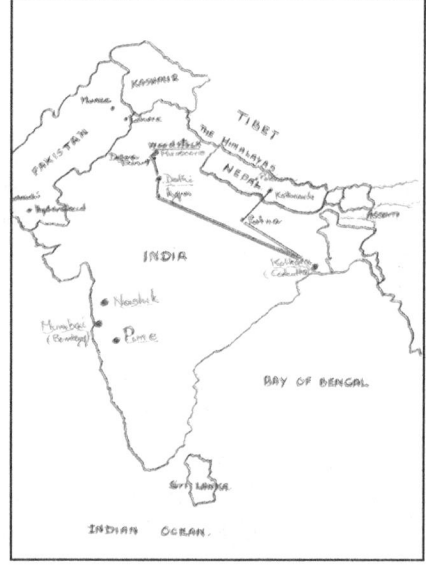

The route we took to school!

21 A short traverse of the Himalayas

Let us run with endurance the race God has set before us. (Hebrews 12:1)

We decided on Woodstock School, in Mussoorie in northwest India, for several reasons: 2½ days of travel seemed better than five days to Hebron School in south India; several other Nepal-based missionary families had their teenagers in Woodstock and spoke appreciatively of the school; and there was a growing number of students from Pokhara who already travelled together in the "Woodstock party" which could include Mark. Another amazing provision was that one of the new Shining Hospital families, Ian and Carole Meyer, were Australians and had a pre-teen son Chris. He and Mark had become friends in their term at the Pokhara Study Centre, so were pretty chuffed at the idea of going together in the Woodstock party.

The transit from Pokhara in Nepal to Mussoorie in northwest India would normally take 52 hours of bus, train and taxi travel. But in July 1977, to celebrate this important transition in Mark's life, we went as a family on an extended tour of India, including Calcutta, Agra and Delhi. Taking advantage of the greater variety of goods at some of these large cities, we could make the extensive purchases required by the school. What a kit list the school specified for a boarding student! Thus, we finished our journey to the school with several tin trunks filled with clothing, shoes, school supplies and equipment all ready for Grade 6 at Woodstock School. My memories of that first trip are indelible.

With all the school supplies securely packed in the ubiquitous tin trunks, we joined several other families from Nepal on the overnight train trip up from Delhi to the nearest railway station, Dehradun. There we asked a taxi driver how much he would charge to take us up the mountain to the school.

"Well, Sahib, as you know, it is now monsoon and the rains have caused a landslide. I cannot actually take you up to Mussoorie. But I can take you halfway up and then you can get a bus or taxi beyond the slide to continue the journey." Familiar with this system in Nepal during land-slide season, we agreed on a figure and set forth.

But barely an hour out of Dehradun, and not nearly "halfway up the hill", the taxi stopped. Immediately a horde of coolies surrounded our taxi and grabbed the tin trunks and any other portable thing in sight and set forth – not along the road towards the invisible distant landslide, but straight up the precipice of the mountain above us. We and other parents protested loudly, but with limited Hindi we understood that the prom-ised taxis and buses were awaiting us at the top of the mountain high above our heads. Nothing to do but walk *up* to find them.

So, amidst monsoon mists, we huffed and puffed uphill behind the trail of coolies, accompanied by every other traveller on the road that day. They assured us that this was indeed the only way to get to Mussoorie, so we resigned ourselves to the trek. Sadly, none of us were dressed for trekking. I was actually wearing a sari that day and open loose sandals that were totally unsuitable for hill climbing.

Some two hours later, we eventually broke out onto a plateau, where a steep sealed road was visible, and on that road was a long stream of taxis awaiting the exhausted "trekkers". We thankfully collapsed into the nearest one, along with all the tin trunks and other travel paraphernalia loaded on top or in the boot. Perhaps because of the excessive weight of the trunks and the foreign passengers, within a couple of kilometres, the taxi spluttered to a standstill. We all got out, and Warren and Mark helped **push** the taxi up and along till it could restart again.

It was at least an hour later that we reached Picture Palace, the begin-ning of the Mussoorie bazaar. We were grateful to have at last arrived. How premature! The guest house we'd booked into was another hour further up the hill, up a road where taxis couldn't go. So, back to trekking, and haggling with a new set of coolies for how much it would cost to take us, and the tin trunks, up to the guest house.

Eventually we reached a compromise and set forth once again, going up and up. Although this time we were walking along a well-sealed road, the steepness of the upward slope of the narrow road was absolutely incredible and a good reason the taxis would find it difficult to negotiate. We were used to trekking in Nepal, but the altitude of Ghachok was only 4,000 feet, while Mussoorie was closer to 7,000 feet and this higher altitude made the ascent much more challenging. How I regretted again the choice of the sari and the open sandals for a trek like this. I could feel the blisters forming between my toes!

An hour later, we gratefully entered the gate of the guest house, enjoying the first level piece of land we'd experienced since leaving Dehradun some five hours before. Appropriately called Edgehill, because from its narrow ledge of land we looked over the edge to Woodstock School 1000 feet below and further several thousand feet down to Dehradun and the Siwalik range of hills beyond. A stunning panorama almost worth the trek!

Carol Meyer, Chris's Mum, describes the Woodstock travel journey in her book *Beyond the Door* (2003:68,69)*:

> It was afternoon tea time on the day of our arrival at Edgehill when Mark and Merryn burst into the lounge looking for Chris. What a jolly reunion it was for Ian and me also, as Warren and Jessie followed hard on their heels. The next few days we spent together getting last-minute things for the boys from the bazaar, visiting the school, filling out registration forms and talking to teachers and dorm supervisors...
>
> At last the time came to settle the boys into their dormitories. They were both quite excited about it and when we left them that first evening, they seemed to be in high spirits and were already chatting with some of the other boys. The whole atmosphere of the dorm seemed very warm and friendly. The next day was to be their first day in their new school, so Jessie, Warren, Ian and I had promised to meet the boys in the playground at lunchtime to say goodbye before we headed off down the hill once again towards home. Walking up the corridor towards the Grade 6 classroom, we were all chatting about how easy it had been to settle the boys in and how grateful we all were that they had each other and seemed so happy.
>
> As we waited outside the classroom, the lunch bell went and we overheard the teacher speaking very sternly to her class. "You boys will be gentlemen! Let the girls go out first!" (This teacher had 20 boys and five girls and clearly meant to establish early on who was boss.) After the five girls emerged into the corridor, out filed the boys.

It was then that our delusions were shattered! Out came our two boys, ashen faced and in tears. Rushing over to us, they pleaded, between sobs, to come home with us. Chris promised to be so good if we would only let him do home schooling. However, Mark, who had already had enough of home schooling in their village allocation, cried. "I don't like this school. The next school I want to try is Mt Hermon in Darjeeling," They had it all figured out.

We sat with them during lunch, trying to allay their fears, reminding them that God was with them and encouraging them to think of all the fun times they were going to have. But when it came time to leave it didn't seem to make the parting any easier. As we got to the gate of the school that day, I couldn't help but think how tiny they looked. So totally different from the big courageous boys we had left at the dorm the evening before. As we hugged our boys, trying to soothe them and avert their fears once again, the ache in our hearts was like a knife jammed in and twisted.

On our return to Pokhara, the house seemed very empty and quiet. Merryn returned to the Pokhara Study Centre but life was very different for us all without Mark. Our concerns for Mark escalated on receiving his first mandatory weekly letter, which had taken *a month* to reach us, and read: "Dear Mum and Dad, hope you are well. I *hate* this school. I have decided to run away. I know how to get to Dehradun. I'll get a train from there to Delhi, Agra, and Calcutta. Can you meet me in Calcutta? Love Mark."

We immediately sent him a telegram, DON'T LEAVE SCHOOL. I'M COMING TO SEE YOU TOMORROW. LOVE DAD. And Warren set off the next day on the 52-hour bus, train, taxi journey to the school. Soon after he'd left, I got a telegram from the school, MARK IN HOSPITAL. EYE INFECTION. IMPROVING. I was doubly grateful that Warren was already on his way to visit him, and also thankful that it seemed Mark had not yet left the school as per his earlier letter!

On arrival in Mussoorie, and en route to Edgehill, Warren met some Woodstock lads on the lower road. "Oh, you've come to visit Mark, have you?"

"Yes, I'm on my way down to the dorm now."

"Oh, he's not in the dorm. He's in the hospital here."

That certainly shocked Warren, who up to that time knew nothing about the eye infection. There were no mobile phones or text messages in those days, and the school's telegram had actually taken 10 days to reach me in Pokhara anyhow!

Warren went straight down to find Mark in the hospital – his eye was protruding from its socket like a large plum, but the staff assured Warren that the swelling was less than before and was decreasing. They released Mark to spend some days with his Dad at Edgehill, enjoying the company and culinary delights of Dora Barklay's kitchen. Warren extended his time there with Mark till he was feeling better and able once again to face the martinet teacher who seemed to have it IN for the boys in her gender-imbalanced classroom. Mark's eyesight has never been strong, but his currently weaker eye is not the one which was infected in his first weeks at Woodstock.

That first semester proved for Mark to be the hardest of his Woodstock experience, and for us in getting used not only to having our son in boarding school but also to the inordinate time it took for letters and even telegrams to reach us. Phone calls were not possible since the Shining Hospital in Pokhara didn't even have a phone. Praying for his safety and emotional adjustment was our only weapon against discouragement and doubt. We held onto the assurance that since the Lord had so clearly called us to this ministry, that call and covenant blessing was not just for us as parents but also embraced our whole family. We had to hold on in faith till we saw those promises fulfilled

Woodstock School campus amongst the deodar pine trees

PART 5 Give me this mountain

22 Bags and stuff

Don't take any money with you, nor a traveller's bag, nor an extra pair of sandals. (Luke 10:4)

During our many years of travel as Jesus' followers, we rarely got down to the minimum of stuff which he instructed his disciples for their outreach journeys. Our first weeks in Ghachok with just one enamel plate, mug, bowl and cutlery pack each were perhaps the closest, but for the rest of our sojourning history we would have to confess to carrying around a plethora of stuff.

In 1979 we as a family had a respite from boarding school separation while living together for five months in our beautiful Federal Capital, Canberra. Warren was a Visiting Fellow in the Department of Linguistics at the Australian National University and the children had a spell in local schools experiencing the Australian educational system. Mark didn't like it. "I want to go back to *my* school in India." Much to his disappointment, we had to extend our stay by an extra five months.

On our return journey to South Asia, this time we had not only the pile of bags and stuff our family inevitably travelled with, but also 21 additional large boxes of unaccompanied baggage! Our Indian colleagues had asked us to bring them for a linguistic training programme soon to begin. Not a happy look when entering India as "tourists", that is, not in regular employment with an Indian firm – as Commonwealth citizens we did not in 1980 need visas to enter India. Some of our boxes contained electronic equipment such as overhead projectors, others had teaching manuals, or stationery supplies not easily available in India. Might the Lord work it that customs officials wouldn't even notice these unusual extras? Some of us thus prayed.

At 9.30 am on 23 February 1980 we gratefully arrived in Calcutta and not only retrieved all our personal baggage but also discovered in the customs shed all 21 additional boxes of equipment waiting for us. "How come you've got all these boxes if you're only coming to India to be tourists?" And the official demanded we open the boxes so he could inspect the contents. We tried to explain that all of this baggage was not personal stuff but was for an educational institute in India. We showed him letters to prove this institute existed, but it was too hard. He went away to get a supervisor to handle this unusual request. That was the beginning of a long wait. We all were deeply aware of our dependence on God to help us over this seemingly insurmountable hurdle.

Merryn and I took a taxi to the city to pick up from a travel agent the train tickets prebooked on the Doon Express leaving that evening. We looked forward to the 36-hour journey as a restful break after the stress of packing and departure, and it would bring us closer to the now much-loved Woodstock school. Tickets in hand, we went on to the railway station where we found a cool ladies' waiting room to await the arrival of Warren, Mark and all the baggage, hopefully in time to catch the train. We also faced a long wait.

Back in the Customs shed, progress was not happening. The man who'd gone off to get his supervisor just never returned. Warren and Mark were hungry, hot, and frustrated. Warren sent Mark off to find something to eat. When he returned, Warren also went to get a quick snack, leaving Mark to guard the boxes. Coming back barely half an hour later, he was alarmed to find Mark missing and then stunned to see a rather official jeep speeding across towards the custom shed with Mark sitting beside the driver.

"We have been waiting for over five hours, and need to catch the evening train to Dehradun," Mark had protested to the official. He was only 13 years old but, given an early growth spurt which included a beard, at six feet tall he looked quite adult. His new safari suit added to his businesslike appearance. So, when he had demanded to see a superior officer and that someone come immediately to process the bags still waiting to be cleared, he got a response. The superior officer – perhaps in embarrassment, perhaps in sympathy for this Australian family – lost no time in coming to the shed and, with nary a question, query, or demand for inspection, chalked the clearance mark on every item and had taxis summoned forthwith. A good partnership between prayer and action!

At Mussoorie, the time had come for us to rent a house on the hillside year-round so that Mark and Merryn could be day scholars instead of boarders – in the times we could be there. So, in late February 1980, we had the joy of moving into "Lower Bethany". It was a bungalow built during the British Raj for families escaping the heat of the plains to the coolness of the hill stations. From this home the children had only a 10-minute scamper down to the school in the mornings but a 30-minute climb back home at the end of the day. But they had been well schooled in this kind of mountaineering when they lived in hostels further down the hillside from the school campus. From higher up, we enjoyed gorgeous views of the scattered community around the hills and to the vast Gangetic plains sweeping out across the far horizon to the south. The climate was pleasantly cool and the fellowship with school staff and other folk living on the hillside was very stimulating and encouraging.

However, the house had little furnishings and all our own household belongings were still back in Pokhara, stored there when we'd left some 18 months before. So Warren and I returned to Pokhara and spent most of March sorting out and repacking what we needed for our new life in Lower Bethany. Late March I took a friend visiting us in Pokhara from Australia on a north India tour by air and train, to Agra, the Taj Mahal, and Delhi. Meanwhile, Warren began the slow, convoluted trip back to Mussoorie, with 22 boxes of haberdashery, kitchen equipment and books for our new home! The trip involved a bus to the Indian border at Sonauli, another bus three hours to Gorakhpur, two trains (to Lucknow and then Dehradun), a taxi up to Mussoorie and more coolies to get back up to Lower Bethany.

We actually joined forces again on the Dehradun railway station as the Doon Express from Lucknow pulled in. I saw Warren immediately as he

was waiting for the railway coolies to help with not only the 22 boxes of our stuff but also a rolled up large coir mat that he'd bravely added to the luggage. Lower Bethany soon became our comfortable home, a haven not only for us but for many who came for meals and visits over the next three years.

Just three months later, we had to make another long journey with boxes. We needed to deliver to the training venue at Nasik, in central India, the 21 boxes of educational equipment we had brought from Australia. The trip would involve more taxis, trains, and rickshaws until we could get all the cargo to Nasik, ready for the first training course for Indian Bible translators and literacy workers

23 India challenge

So give me the hill country that the LORD promised me. (Joshua 14:12)

I draw from Warren's book *Making a difference: training Bible translators in India* (2002:10,11,22):

> During our last weeks in Kathmandu [before we had to leave in August 1976] a new turn in the road opened up. The SIL director in charge of assisting the Bible translation work in India passed on to me a request from leaders of Indian missions to help set up a training course for their field staff. "Our missionaries are having great difficulty in learning the languages of the communities where they are working. Could you send SIL teachers to help us in preparing them for the challenges of learning unwritten languages?"

> Jessie and I agreed I would immediately help with teaching a preliminary course in Danishpet, in south India, while she took Mark and Merryn to Australia. There we would seek the Lord's direction for the future after the seeming closure of our project with the Gurung.

"Give me this mountain"

In September 1976, I was waiting for a plane to rejoin my family who had gone ahead to Australia. I was back in Calcutta after four challenging and stimulating weeks in south India with 21 young Indian Christians. God spoke to me there in Calcutta through the story of Caleb, as recorded in Numbers 13 and Joshua 14. The Bible records how Caleb asked Joshua for a tough assignment, "Give me this mountain". (Joshua 14:12 KJV) He recalled their earlier reconnaissance into the promised land, when they saw that "their cities were large and fortified" (Joshua 14:12 NIV) but Caleb put his faith in the LORD's help to win the inheritance promised to him.

That was a reassurance for me as I reflected on India. As I reflected on my own "career path" within SIL, I could see that Jessie and I, with our Gurung translation team, could complete the Gurung New Testament fairly soon. What then? The default assumption in SIL was that after finishing a New Testament in one language, the translator should move on to tackle a second language. But I saw what seemed a far more rewarding and strategic possibility. Instead of simply *adding* another project, we could *multiply* our experience and training by investing in the lives and work of Indian brothers and sisters such as the ones I had just been sharing fellowship and study with in Danishpet. What a "mountain" to claim, by the Lord's enabling!

That night in Calcutta in September 1976 following the Danishpet course, I received new insight through the Caleb story: India has enormous challenges ("mountains"), but it also has birthed a missionary church – faithful servants of the Lord who, like Caleb, trust in the Lord's help to tackle mountains. I wanted to be part of facilitating their vision.

Through the next two and a half years, while being based mostly in Pokhara, Nepal, and while still giving primary focus to the completion of the Gurung New Testament, we worked on the practicalities of beginning a formal linguistic training course, similar to the SIL courses which had helped us in Australia. This one was to be called The Indian Institute of Cross-Cultural Communication (IICCC).

I quote from a letter we sent to our prayer team from the beginning of the first course in June 1980, using the IICCC acronym:

With two of our IICCC students

*I*nevitably, one or two came late! But eventually by the second week we had the full complement of 16 students in residence for the first linguistic course in India for potential Bible translators. All are committed to ministry among India's 40 million tribal people, and some will almost certainly be moving into Bible translation in the years ahead.

Thank you, Lord, for the privilege of helping train these dedicated young folk.

*I*nexplicably, none of the ordered textbooks had arrived in time for the commencement of the course. So we six staff were all running like scalded cats, trying to get lesson notes and language problems typed up and duplicated in time for classes. Just imagine our relief when the first shipment of books arrived last Thursday, near the end of the second week. So the typing pressure is greatly relieved.

Thank you, Lord, for such willing staff colleagues.

*C*oncurrently with the IICCC, another course started this week for Indian missionaries who will not likely work in Bible translation but will have to learn another language in their field of service. We are providing staff to teach language learning, phonetics, and semantics for this group. It is another great opportunity – but it means that some of our staff are adding to their teaching load, and we are all feeling close to exhaustion already. Can we keep up this pace for 10 more weeks? And several of our expected staff have not arrived yet, which leaves us feeling rather panicky. We especially hope that our Australian SIL/WBT mates Ray and Elisabeth Christmas will join us soon, but there's no word from them yet. Some of you have heard that Warren was sick in April at Mussoorie – bedridden for weeks with an enlarged spleen (cause unknown). He recovered full strength just the week before we left for Nasik.

Thank you, Lord, that you don't try us beyond our endurance.

*C*hurch involvement in the distribution of the Gurung scripture portions encouraged us very much during our March–April visit to Nepal. Both congregations of the Pokhara township held dedication services for the newly printed Mark's

Gospel and book of Hebrews. There is even a recently opened Christian bookshop right in the heart of the Gurung section of Pokhara. They are happy to stock whatever portions we can supply them with.

Lord, use the distribution of your Word in Gurung to transform lives.

*C*an you imagine the culture shock we're going to experience come late August when we leave IICCC one Thursday and, God willing, start classes ourselves the next Monday in Dallas (Texas, USA) to upgrade our consultant work in Literacy and Translation? Warren will also work with the Printing Arts Department at the WBT centre there in preparing the Gurung New Testament photo-ready manuscript. I think the greatest shock, and one that won't be easy to overcome, will be the separation by half the globe from our children. Since the courses we are taking are for only one semester, it seemed unwise to uproot the children once again from Woodstock school. While we've been here at Nasik, Merryn's letters from school have been rather sad. What happens if they get sick and I'm right across the other side of the world?

Lord, supply all that is needed for this Dallas trip, especially confident trust and peace of mind for us and the children.

Just one week before our August departure for Dallas, the weekly letter from Merryn brought a request which nearly tore my heart apart, and one which I could neither fulfil nor ever forget

24 A hundredfold

Will receive now in return a hundred times as many houses. (Mark 10:29,30)

For most of our Bible translation journey in Nepal and in India, our lives had been full. Stretching in energy, energising spiritually, but often faith challenging. Friends often marvelled at our faith or sacrifice, but we'd hardly seen it as sacrifice at all – until we had to grapple with the family separation involved in boarding school. But with Merryn's letter in August 1980 pleading that I not go to America, the sense of sacrifice and impossible dilemmas sank in.

I sat on the outside steps of the antiquated Bible Fellowship Centre in Nasik, on the private side of the building where others wouldn't see me, and I cried out to the Lord as I'd not cried out before, "Lord, what would you have me do? My daughter needs me sorely, and my husband also needs me to go with him to Dallas. I don't know where my priorities lie. I know Merryn will be cared for at Woodstock, but what about her emotional needs? If not met, these may impact upon her for the rest of her life."

It was a HUGE relief to get a second letter within a few days, and fortunately before I cancelled my ticket to the US. "Mummy and Daddy, please don't worry about that letter I wrote last week. I'm now feeling fine and I'm really OK about you going off to the States. I'll give you a list of the things I want you to bring back for me."

Soon after reaching Dallas, we received another letter: "Mummy and Daddy, these days I am feeling that Jesus is very close to me and that He loves me very much." I wondered if my returning to Mussoorie when she originally asked might have robbed her of that genuine experience of the Lord Jesus in her young life. We are not to know, but we bowed in awe and thanks to the Lord for His grace and love toward her in that very vulnerable time of her life, and of ours!

A similar challenging question had come a year earlier. We were in a small University flat in Canberra while Warren worked on the massive pre-publication editing and checking of the Gurung New Testament. Jim and Marjorie Houston had long been among our generous financial and prayer supporters. They lived in Canberra, and we were glad to take up their invitations for a visit. Like most Canberrans at the time, they lived in a new house in a newly developed suburb. They welcomed us with great generosity and love.

As we drove away after one visit with them, 10-year-old Merryn asked me, "Mummy, why don't we have a nice house like the Houstons'?"

Another question that stabbed at my heart! Was she to feel that, because of her parents' life choices to live and serve among the world's disadvantaged, she would suffer deprivation?

I knew at that moment what telegram prayers are: "Lord, please show me how to respond to this one." And in an instant the promise of Jesus to His followers in Mark 10:29,30 came to mind, "And I assure you that everyone who has given up house or brothers or sisters or mother or father or children or property, for my sake and for the Good News, will receive now in return a hundred times as many houses, brothers..."

I turned to Merryn and said, "I can't tell you why we don't have as nice a house as the Houstons right now, but I can tell you something absolutely amazing about the houses we've lived in." I quoted the verse from Mark's Gospel and we made a game together of counting how many houses we'd already lived in. In her lifetime, we'd only enjoyed about 25 up to that point. She seemed excited at the prospect of how many more the Lord might have for us. No matter in her young mind that we had not actually owned any of them!

When Warren and I went over the full 57 years so far of our marriage we counted over 60 houses where we've stayed—not yet up to the "hundredfold"! Some of the more significant ones in Merryn's counting were:

1.   A nice ground-floor **apartment** in central Kathmandu, where Merryn joined the family 12 April 1969.

2.   The **converted barn** above a cattle shed of our Gurung landlord (October–December 1969, February–June 1970, February–July 1971). Mark celebrated his second and third birthdays, and Merryn her second birthday, in this barn.

3. **University flat** supplied by the Australian National University, Canberra (five months from October 1970).

4. Another **ANU flat** in Canberra (April–November 1972, February–November 1973)

5. A **new barn** (custom-built for Warren's height) in Ghachok (April 1974 to May 1976).

6. A **house** in Kathmandu (July 1974 to July 1975), while still maintaining the Ghachok house.

7. A fairly new **SIL house** on Tribhuvan University campus (August 1975 to August 1976)

8. A **house sit** in Bag Bazaar, Pokhara, for an INF family on home leave

9. A **Thakali 2 storied house** in Dip, Pokhara (November 77 to August 78, with interruptions)

10. Another **ANU flat** in Canberra (February–November 1979) **our longest uninterrupted stretch in any one house** to that point since marriage (10 months!).

The little fun activity with Merryn helped to remind us of the Father's never-failing care and provision which certainly has blessed us all the way. A family devotional activity around that time included designing a family flag with our motto on it. I forget what we wrote, but I have never forgotten the motto Merryn wrote on her flag, "God's happy nomads."

25 Stirring up the nest!

Like an eagle that rouses her chicks. (Deuteronomy 32:11)

Let me quote once again from Warren's book *Making a Difference* (2002:40).

> It was obvious from many angles that we must work for the development of Indian leadership. Expatriates faced uncertainty as to how long they could live and serve in India. There was increased scrutiny from Indian police authorities and restriction on travel to areas where tribal communities lived. Positively, the Indian church and missions were ready to assume responsibility for fulfilling the Great Commission, including the specialised work of translation and literacy within India...[So] we adopted a faith goal, "an Indian Principal within five years." By 1985, the sixth year of operation of IICCC, there should be an Indian national serving as Principal.

We expected to serve in IICCC leadership for those five years, and looked forward to developing a strong training school under Indian leadership and an empowered translation movement, but there was a surprise coming! During our second year in the job (1981) our regional director, Don Gregson, came to Nasik on his annual visit. Don came directly from visiting a new advance in Pakistan and told us of the need for new leadership there.

The situation Don described deeply concerned us. As Warren and I prayed together, we felt we should offer to help. Back to Don, we asked, "What qualifications are you looking for?"

"God moves in mysterious ways! We were planning to ask you to consider the move. We need someone with Commonwealth citizenship to minimize visa issues, someone who had actually worked in a translation project themselves, and someone who's had experience in training nationals. A bonus would be if they were Anglicans, since we're working with the Church of Pakistan, a member of the Anglican worldwide communion."

We felt awed. Obviously, we had all those qualifications. Warren was ready to decide right away. He felt God was stirring up our (comfortable?) nest in India! But I wanted time to think and pray more, and work out the implications of our moving across the western border. Further, we needed to find someone who would carry on the leadership of IICCC for the rest of the initial five years.

Our two teenage offspring had to be included in the decision, as it might be difficult for them to border-cross to Pakistan for school holidays. It was certainly not as friendly a border as to Nepal! They would join us for their Christmas vacation later that year and that would be our chance to discuss it with them. So we agreed with Don to pray about it, and promised to let him know our answer by the end of the year 1981.

We were teaching at the Australian SIL school again that summer, at New College on the UNSW campus in Sydney. Mark (now 15) and Merryn (12) were to fly home from India, unaccompanied this time. Woodstock school staff would put them on the plane at Delhi and THAI ground staff would coach them through the Bangkok transit. But a heavy snowfall that winter delayed all flights out of London and the THAI plane was late arriving in Delhi. Hence, Mark and Merryn missed their connecting flight from Bangkok to Sydney. The airline put them in a hotel to await the next flight, 24 hours later, and Mark and Merryn enjoyed their luxurious layover. An SIL friend there, Dot Thomas, very kindly escorted them around tourist spots during the day of waiting! After many phone calls and delays they eventually got to Sydney, and we went out to Mascot airport to welcome them back to Oz. How should we open the discussion regarding Pakistan? Don was pressing us for a decision, and we had promised to let him know by 31 December. Lord, open the way.

One day, as I was ironing, I commented to Mark, "I wish it were a simple matter to know the Lord's will in changing situations."

"We've been talking about that in Bible club this last semester," said Mark.

"What did they say?"

"Well, you pray for God to guide you, you look at the situation and see what you believe is the right thing to do in the light of scriptural principles, and then you do it. Why, what are the factors involved in your situation?"

Our teenaged counsellors

I thought, "Here's a switch, being counselled by my teenage son!"

I explained to Mark, "There's a lot of tribal people in the Sind desert in Pakistan very responsive to the Gospel, but they speak different languages. Neither the national language (Urdu) nor the provincial language (Sindhi) is adequate for teaching the converts the truth about their new life in Christ. Also, very few of these people (perhaps only 1%) can read. So the Church of Pakistan has asked Wycliffe to send people to help in Bible translation and literacy. But there is nobody to lead the Wycliffe team. Don has asked Dad and me to do it, and we are praying about whether we should go."

"It's obvious. You've finished the New Testament in Gurung. The tribes in Pakistan need the Bible too. If you and Dad can help in that, that's where you ought to go," concluded our counsellor.

"But it might affect your own holiday plans. You might even have to change school to Pakistan. You and Merryn are important factors in our decision making." (By this time, both of them were happily and fully involved in life at Woodstock School.)

Mark and Merryn quickly said they certainly wouldn't leave Woodstock, but they would go with the flow regarding border crossings for holiday travel. They seemed almost excited at the prospect of living in yet another Asian country.

So, we faced a change of assignment come December 1982 to a country, people and spiritual environment very different from anything we'd so far encountered in South Asia. The promise for the descendants of Jacob whom the Lord led in the wilderness seemed especially relevant:

> Like an eagle that rouses her chicks and hovers over her young, so he spread his wings to take them up and carried them safely on his pinions. The LORD alone guided them. (Deuteronomy 32:11,12)

PART 6 **Heading West**

26 Life in Pakistan

I have learned the secret of living in every situation…with plenty or little. (Philippians 4:12)

The third session of IICCC concluded in November 1982, and we returned to Lower Bethany, our lovely cottage in Mussoorie. We packed up for the move across the border. The move was just one instance of an aspect of our pilgrim lives that Merryn expressed so lovingly in her poem written for my 60th birthday, part of which I quoted in chapter 13:

> My mother's hands are big
> from holding, carrying,
> packing, heaving
> bags and children on and off
> buses, trains, motorbikes,
> planes, horse drawn wagons,
> bicycles, buffaloes, boats.
>
> Dry with the dust of deserts,
> the cold of mountains,
> the wastelands she made home.

Mark and Merryn came out of boarding at the end of the semester to join us for their long winter holiday. Together we travelled down to Delhi and flew to Karachi on 8 December 1982. Warren came down with a tummy bug, and couldn't face three hours on a bus going east to the large city of Hyderabad. We explored going by train. Warren loves train travel anyway and we found the Pakistan trains cleaner and less jam-packed than the Indian ones. We quite enjoyed the three-hour trip.

At Hyderabad we got all our bags onto two horse-drawn tongas (open carriages) which took us to a spacious, ancient bungalow at 53B Liaqat Rd. The house had been the verger's home for the former garrison church in British Raj days. Its box-like architecture reflected its antiquity. The walls were all about ½ metre thick and stored heat from the midday sun. Two redeeming features were the flat roof for sleeping and the lovely long verandah which shaded the front of the building. Even in its shade, the thermometer on the verandah often showed 32 degrees. At the verger's house we met Sami and Miriam, the gardener and the cook, a married couple who lived on site and eagerly welcomed us. They became an indispensable duo in helping us get settled and cope with life in this new city.

53B Liaqat Road, Hyderabad

We were delighted to find that the national language, Urdu, was grammatically identical to Hindi, of which we all had a good smattering. But once away from the most basic bazaar contexts, the vocab was completely different. Many words derive from Persian rather than from Sanskrit. Mark did many odd jobs necessary to get our large old house livable. He ended up knowing the Hyderabad bazaar better than we did, since he often dashed off on a pushbike to get more screws, wood, nuts, curtain rods, or brackets. His knowledge of Hindi was a great help in this. (He was functionally fluent, even though he had objected to the method of teaching Hindi at Woodstock and had resolved, in protest, to get the lowest possible passing grade. He achieved his goal, thus minimizing his chance to make the highly coveted Honour Roll in the semesters in which his Hindi grade was low.)

It was Merryn's second long vacation as a child carer, since she had been on the SPSIL child care staff the summer before in Sydney. She now took on the three preschoolers of our two new British Wycliffe teams as her special project, and thus allowed the parents to concentrate on learning Urdu. Warren and I also needed to learn it!

For ourselves, we found that there was a big difference from being Principal of a linguistic school in Australia or in India to leading a new field team. We felt nervous at being responsible for these folk whom the Lord had led to join us here in Pakistan – for their families' welfare and for their translation goals. But God reminded us that we are all His children and in fact the work is His. "He who calls you is faithful, and he will do it" (1 Thessalonians 5:24 RSV).

Although Urdu is very similar to Hindi (or Hindustani), Pakistan differed greatly from India and Nepal. There appeared to be more affluence and a

Suitably clad, Merryn and I try a camel ride on a Karachi beach holiday

larger middle class. Lots of people had telephones in their homes – this was before the days of mobiles! But the Christian community in the cities was a poor, marginalised minority living in cramped ghettos. Those in rural areas were even more oppressed, being largely bonded labourers of Muslim landlords.

Women were not free to leave their homes unaccompanied, but we were relieved to find many women out and about in the clothing bazaars. If we wore the Pakistani dress (shalwar kamiz) and kept our heads covered we could go shopping in Karachi and Hyderabad, though not without some ogling, whistles, comments, brushing against and sometimes outright groping.

Regional places were worse, such as Quetta, the capital of Baluchistan province. Our beautiful 15-year-old Merryn went with me on a pastoral visit to one of our new teams there, and we went down to the bazaar for a look-see. Merryn quickly attracted a following of male eyes, and physical harassment by one man. So we jumped into the first available autorickshaw to retreat to the house. Horrors! The man got into a rickshaw himself and followed us all the way home! We scurried into the safety of the courtyard and found our colleague having her language lesson with a quite sophisticated lady Urdu teacher. We told the teacher of the unpleasant incident and asked her what we should have done.

Without any hesitation she said, "You just go straight up to such men, grab them by their shirt collar, and scream out in a loud voice so everyone can hear, and say, 'Stop harassing my daughter! You should be ashamed of yourself!' That's the only way to shame such men. Once you shame him in that way, all the other men will pile out of the shops and kill him on the spot."

I couldn't imagine myself taking such aggressive action, so decided that neither Merryn nor I would venture out again for any more shopping expeditions in Quetta. We were glad to return to the relative safety of Hyderabad.

Of course we all needed to get fitted for the beautifully cool national dress – shalwar kamiz. I found out rather embarrassingly that clothing issues were a sensitive matter for the Christian community. I had assumed that the styles of the women's shalwar kamiz outfits were consistent year on year, but it was soon made clear to me that there were slight changes from year to year which meant that folk were immediately aware as to whether you were wearing last year's shalwar or the currently more fashionable one! When we first settled into the Liaqat Rd house, I noticed in a cupboard a selection of carefully folded shalwar sets left by the previous Wycliffe occupant, labelled "Old shalwar sets, for house use only." When I unfolded them, I couldn't believe how such gorgeously embroidered colourful outfits could be "for house use only". Nevertheless, I obediently went to the tailors to have some suitably fashionable shalwar kamiz outfits made for me.

When a Canadian family arrived in 1986, I passed on to Angela some of the older outfits with the same caution, "For household use only." But, like me, she could not believe that such pretty clothes would not be good enough to wear to church on her first Sunday in Pakistan. (She hadn't had time to go to the tailor to get any others made.) As we left the service that morning, one of the church elders came up to me. "Elder Sister," he began cautiously, "Please don't let Angela wear such old clothes to church. You see, we Christians do not have many ways to hold up our heads in the face of ridicule and ostracism from Muslim neighbours, but we DO take care to dress our women in the nicest and most modern of shalwar suits. For any of you Western women to come out in ancient styles doesn't help us in this matter." I was very embarrassed and apologised that I had not realised how important clothing was to our Christian family.

Another challenge was learning to read and write Urdu, a language written in the Nastaliq, Arabic-based script. It goes from right to left on the page and largely marks only consonants, with just a few vowel markings. Further, the consonants take on up to four different shapes according to where they occur in the word. We were well and truly back to kindergarten again. I wondered how it might ever be possible to help village people, with whom our teams would work, to learn such a complex writing system. It didn't take long for the new Wycliffe teams to come up with creative ways to display and teach the varied shapes of the script. Indeed, for most of the communities in Sindh, the script challenge was greater since the provincial language Sindhi had an even larger inventory of consonants than Urdu and used even more dot clusters to distinguish them.

Physically challenging was the climate – nearly 40 degrees most days of the year, with only slightly lower temperatures in the winter months of January/February. But it was a dry heat, so it did not always feel so oppressive. Like most locals, we enjoyed sleeping out on the verandah or up on the flat roof to enjoy the cooling night breezes coming in from the desert to the east. We made sure that we tucked our mosquito nets in well under the mattress lest the strong breezes become gales during the night and blow our sheets off the beds, and even off the rooftop!

We enjoyed very much the monthly retreat days held at Ratanabad, a Church of Pakistan centre further to the east. A wonderful chance to escape the dusty city and to catch up with fellow missionaries and Pakistani church leaders. Together we could pray, sing and hear God's Word in English, a special treat.

Many of these folk had long served in the tribal contexts where our Wycliffe teams were just beginning. We had much to learn. Many of these pioneering heroes shared of God's miracle workings amongst the Hindu-background landless tribal peoples of the desert areas. It thrilled us to learn how the tribal folk, whose culture was rich in dance and drama, had used song and dance to share the Gospel story once they themselves had come into a trust relationship with the Lord. These were the people most receptive to the Gospel in the Church of Pakistan's mission outreach, and the ones in focus when Bishop Jiwan invited Wycliffe to come to Pakistan some five years before.

In Nepal and India, the rainy season, the monsoon, lasts typically three months, but in Hyderabad it was only about five days, usually the only rain of the entire year. But when it came, it absolutely deluged! Dust, plastic and city refuse had already clogged whatever drainage system existed and the flood waters had nowhere to go except across the city thoroughfares. One year, the deluge happened on the very day Mark and Merryn were returning to school and needed to catch a train up to Lahore for the border crossing back to India at Wagah, near Amritsar. How were we to get them to the railway station? The city was already awash with knee deep floods. Dear Salvation Army sisters, who had a high floored jeep, offered to get the travellers down to the Hyderabad railway station. Just getting from the house to the waiting jeep outside the door left the kids and their packs absolutely soaked. Then the challenge of driving through the flooded city to the station. Thankfully, the jeep made it without stalling and unloaded the passengers and luggage under the porch of the railway station. Apparently, the train took off without too much delay. We never heard how our kids coped with the drenched packs and clothes en route or on arrival at Woodstock.

Monsoon dramas were to become even more memorable in our Pakistan journey.

It was July 1984. Mark had just graduated from Year 12 at Woodstock School, and we were heading down to Karachi en route on a round the world excursion furlough trip – partly to celebrate Mark's graduation by visiting school friends literally around the world, and partly for Warren and me to take part

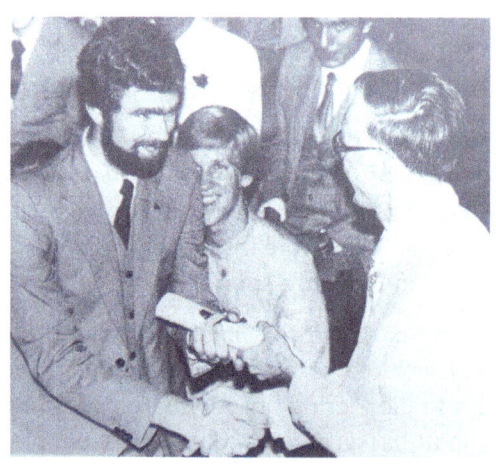

Mark receiving his Woodstock diploma

in a linguistic conference in Europe. The children had spent the summer vacation with us in Hyderabad, helping with the inevitable sorting and throwing out involved in preparing for home leave. We'd also had fun doing lots of shopping in the bazaar, carefully choosing suitable gifts for the many host families who had offered us hospitality in the various countries on our travel route. To make the gift-giving easier, I bought up lots of colourful Pakistani wrapping paper and had all the gifts pre-wrapped and labelled. I felt quite proud of my level of organisation at this point.

Up to our departure time, the rains had not begun. We took our customary pile of large and small suitcases down to the bus depot in Hyderabad where we were to begin the first leg of the journey – by bus down to Karachi. We were to fly out late that night to Germany. As was the practice, the bus staff threw all our well packed cases up onto the roof, and quickly took off. Problem! I was not yet on the bus when it took off, and I mistakenly thought it was just going to a nearby petrol station to get fuel for the trip and would return for the remaining passengers. When I realised that this wasn't the case, I jumped onto the next bus, due to leave in four minutes. But now I had to explain to the bus driver that I needed him to speed up in order to catch the previous bus and my husband and daughter Merryn. (Mark was already in Karachi, working in the engineering office of Mr Bavington, a good friend.) I knew Warren would be frantic, wondering where his wife had got to this time! Thankfully, within a couple of kilometres, we caught up to the first bus, easily identifiable amongst the throng of vehicles because Warren was hanging off the ladder at the back of the bus, looking frantically back along the road for me! With great relief we were reunited on Bus #1, and with some sense of the ridiculous about all of this drama we sank with relief into our seats. If only we knew it, the excitement had only just begun.

Half way down the four-hour trip to Karachi, the buses always stopped at a roadside café for tea and comfort stops. While Warren went into the café to fetch us tea, Merryn and I looked across to the east and saw the most ominous black cloud rolling in from the horizon. It looked like a tremendous dust storm, or the piled-up waters of the Red Sea in the film *The Ten Commandments*! The annual monsoon was about to deluge upon us! And unlike buses in Nepal, there was no tarpaulin to protect the luggage on top of the bus! The driver called for all the passengers to reboard quickly, as he wanted to beat the storm to Karachi.

To no avail! Within seconds the heavens opened with the loudest and heaviest monsoon rains I can ever remember. By the time we got to Karachi the streets were awash with water about 50 cm deep. The storm water drains, blocked with 11 months' accumulation of dust, dirt, plastic and other unmentionables, couldn't possibly handle this torrent of water. It flooded the city within minutes. As we gingerly waded off the bus like drowned rats, we looked hopefully for rickshaws to get us to our Karachi friend's home. Amazingly we found three and piled ourselves and our baggage in, and set off for the Bavingtons' house. Since the roads were still awash with water, there was no way the drivers could see any open drains, potholes, or obstacles still on the streets. Whizzing around a street corner, the wheel of my rickshaw went down an open drain, leaving the vehicle dangerously leaning on its side. Merryn and I found ourselves almost out the door into the watery muck, with two large suitcases falling on top of us. Fortunately, men from the nearby tea shop rushed to the rescue, and a group lifted the rickshaw back onto the road. Once again, Warren looked on with horror from the following rickshaw, wondering, "What next can happen to Jessie?"

At the Bavingtons', we showered, changed our soggy clothes, took a most welcome evening meal and then went to the airport. Because of security concerns, each passenger had to identify their suitcases out on the tarmac before the ground staff would load them into the plane. So, once again in pouring rain, we revisited the bedraggled suitcases, now having their second dousing of the day.

We landed first in Frankfurt with all the bedraggled suitcases. Warren went off to get a luggage trolley and was alarmed to find that trolley staff did not understand English, and even more alarmed to find that trolleys did not function well on airport escalators. The entire load came tumbling down on top of us. Somebody must have pressed the emergency stop button, because the escalator stopped and we were extricated from the mess. It was only after arrival at our next destination in Holzhausen, central Germany, that we opened the suitcases. With horror I looked at the gifts, carefully prepacked in colourful Pakistani paper, none of it colour-fast. Few of the gifts were dry or ever presentable again!

Each of us left South Asia after a very stressful and heavy schedule of work, study, and travel. Thankfully, the next six weeks proved less drama -filled. The cleanliness, orderliness and beauty of Europe, Britain and the US was a balm for our weary souls, minds and bodies.

Our Indian travel agent had secured us a special deal with KLM – business class tickets from Karachi to Los Angeles via Europe. We flew to Frankfurt, then travelled by train to a station near Holzhausen where the Wycliffe Germany director met us. He had served with us in Nepal! A wonderfully relaxing time at Holzhausen and touring Germany and Switzerland, including seeing the amazing passion play in Oberammergau! Warren and I attended the conference on applied linguistics in Belgium, and it was a special delight then to visit many friends in England and Scotland.

The next leg of our round-the-world journey was with KLM again, to Los Angeles. We flew from England to Amsterdam to connect with it, and KLM gave us an overnight stay before the intercontinental flight. What an overnight stay! We were in absolute five-star luxury in the hotel's honeymoon penthouse apartment. The kids ran from room to room to test every switch, tap and appliance, in wonder and amazement.

Next morning, we fronted up to the airline desk to be greeted with, "We're terribly sorry, but business class is full. We'll have to put you in Royal Class." In that luxury, throughout a day lengthened across several time zones, we flew through a cloudless sky over the top of the world. In the front seats of the top deck of the Jumbo Jet we had superb views on either side of the icebergs floating off Greenland far below and of the North American coastline as we flew on! And of course, we enjoyed the superb food as well. We were learning, like Paul, both "how to be abased, and... *how to abound*" (Philippians 4:12 RSV, my italics) and enjoying every minute of it all.

We had a great time visiting with my sister Gwen and her family in California. Highlights included the Huntington Museum and of course Disneyland. Then we flew on (not with KLM) across the Pacific back to Melbourne. In Australia for six months, we gave priority to seeing Mark settled into tertiary education. Most significant was the Lord's provision for him of very supportive accommodation at the Kew Baptist student hostel. This well-managed facility, set up primarily for the benefit of country students studying in Melbourne, proved a strong emotional support for Mark, somewhat akin to his well-loved Woodstock hostel, his home for much of the previous seven years. Merryn continued her studies by correspondence in Australia until February 1985 when she could return to Woodstock for Year 10, and we to Pakistan .

27 Shadowlands

Even when I walk through the darkest valley, I will not be afraid, for you are close beside me. (Psalm 23:4)

One of the most challenging aspects of our distanced locations in South Asia was that we could not attend important family functions back in Australia. Funerals and weddings particularly. These days (apart from during COVID-19 years) international air travel is much more economical and available. In earlier days, the expense was prohibitive and the timing difficult when news of a death sometimes didn't reach us till long after the event.

My Mum

January 1984. It was early morning in Hyderabad, and Warren leapt out of bed to answer the phone ringing in the office. (What a novelty! In India or Nepal, you had to go down to the Central Telegraph Office to make a phone call. That our Liaqat Rd house had a **telephone** was one bonus of our move to Pakistan.) But the news was sombre. My sister Norma was phoning from Sydney to say that Mum had fallen and broken a hip. She was in hospital and, at 88 years of age, was not in a good way. Dad was thus alone in the house at Wilton, now needing much support. Warren said to me, in his usual direct and matter-of-fact way, "You need to go home. This is the eventuality we have known may come."

Mark and Merryn were nearing the end of another winter vacation with us. We had bookings on the train to Lahore and would go by train and bus through India for our annual visit to Nepal, before they returned to Woodstock, and we to Pakistan. What to do now? How to pay for my flights to Australia? In the next day or two we received our gift income statement from Wycliffe and were humbled at several significant unexpected gifts we had received that month. So we could book my tickets. Thank you, Lord! But we decided I would still go with the family up to Lahore and fly back from there (to Karachi, then on to Bangkok and Sydney) in a few days' time.

We travelled 18 hours by train to Lahore (over 1000 kilometres) and had a day or two at a mission guesthouse. I recall we saw together the film *Chariots of fire*. Eric Liddell's courageous witness for Christ in refusing to run on a Sunday moved us greatly.

What was also moving was a typical Glover rendezvous foul up. Shopping in the bazaar to get things for the kids to take back to school, we boarded two autorickshaws to return to the guesthouse. Warren and Mark got into one, which roared off immediately, leaving Merryn and me in the other. Properly segregated, but also separated! Warren worried that neither Merryn nor I might know the way back to the guesthouse, so he had their rickshaw driver circle round and round the market looking for us. In Pakistan it's rather hard to identify passengers in a discreetly curtained rickshaw as they are totally shielded from view! We did eventually all meet up at the guesthouse, but I don't remember how.

I took the plane to Karachi and had ten hours to wait in the airport there before the THAI flight to Bangkok arrived from London, due about 4 am. After an evening snack in the terminal restaurant, I settled down in the departure lounge for the long wait. The loudspeaker announcements in the departure lounge were all in Urdu and the reception inaudible with static. After a couple of naps, come 2.30 am, I became more alert to listen for the THAI flight arrival from London and for our boarding call. I was watchful of my fellow THAI passengers, who all had pink boarding cards peeping out from the pockets of their jackets.

I made a quick trip to the toilet and returned to find all of my pink boarding card holders missing. Or rather, that those still wearing pink boarding cards told me they were in fact heading for Budapest! I raced frantically to the exit gate. "When is the THAI flight to Bangkok leaving?"

"Oh Madam, that left an hour ago. Where were you?"

Obviously, I had been unable to understand the confused departure call. My plight now was serious: having come through the immigration counter, I had legally already left Pakistan. Would they let me back in? And even if they did, where would I stay? How to get the next flight to Bangkok? Would I still be able to connect with my Sydney flight? After several hours of panic and confusion, all of the questions were resolved. The later flight did actually get to Bangkok in time to connect with my original flight down to Sydney. What a demonstration of how good God is for those who call upon Him in trouble – and for those who only depend on the colour of fellow passengers' boarding cards in departure lounges!

Back in Sydney I met sister Norma and her husband Roy and we drove directly out to Camden's rural hospital. I hardly recognised the emaciated, wrinkled Mum lying there. She soon woke up and with joy at seeing me by her side, whispered her earlier tribute, "Jessie, you didn't grow under my heart, my love, but into it." One of the most poignant moments during Mum's hospitalization happened when our beloved "brother" Allan came to visit. We two prayed at her bedside and as Allan and I sang one of Mum's favourite hymns, "Praise my Soul the King of Heaven", she weakly tried to join in with us.

After weeks in hospital, Mum contracted a staph infection and the nursing staff told me it would be better if we could care for her at home. But because she would need 24/7 maximum nursing, the family agreed it was simply not possible. She died 7 March. My *Daily Light* reading that day was, "To all who mourn He will give: beauty for ashes; joy instead of mourning; praise instead of heaviness" (Isaiah 61:2, Living Bible). Dad stayed on alone in the house at Wilton. After two months away from Warren, I needed to leave Dad, still grieving the loss of his long friend of 60 years. A difficult wrench.

At Dad's 100th birthday in Wilton - Front row: me, Shirley, Dad, Norma
Back row: Merryn, Warren, Mark, Bruce, baby Nathan, Robyn, Roy, Susan

My Dad

Dad turned 100 on 29 October 1987 and, since we were in Australia, we could join the family celebration in his beloved Wilton home. Soon afterwards, with failing eyesight, he accepted that living alone was no longer viable. Unpredictable TIAs were also getting more frequent. So he moved into the Queen Victoria veterans' retirement home in Thirlmere, not too far away from Wilton.

Two years later, Warren and I were teaching at Asia SIL in Singapore in August 1990 when a phone call came, once again from sister Norma, that Dad had died. And again, Warren insisted I go home – not as difficult a journey as the 1984 trip from Pakistan! I flew to Sydney to join my family for Dad's funeral. Mark and Merryn drove up from Melbourne and at the funeral they sang together *Abide with me*, one of Dad's favourite hymns. The timing of this connection with Merryn proved to be very important in helping her negotiate an extremely difficult and distressing decision she was facing. Another touch of our Father's loving care in her time of need.

My brother-in-law, Roy Wark

In February 1992 Warren and I were working in the UMN Gorkha project. On a supervisory trip to the women's literacy classes, we were trekking between two villages when we saw a man coming up the hill waving to us. He was bringing a faxed message from Mark to say that my brother-in-law Roy had died suddenly of pancreatic cancer. There was no way I could get back to Sydney in time for the funeral, as it took days to get to Kathmandu, and then more days to Sydney via Bangkok or Singapore. All I could do was suspend the supervision trip and trek six hours to Gorkha bazaar, the district centre, where I could phone Norma to grieve with her. Only when we returned to Australia on leave months later could we mourn with Norma and her family in person. The tyranny of distance.

Warren's mother

"Mother" (as Warren always called her) had serious health conditions for several years in her 80s. In April 1997, the day after Warren and I arrived from Nepal to Horsleys Green, UK, we opened our email to find a message from Warren's sister Alice with news of Mother Glover having suffered cardiac failure. If it were possible, it would be good for Warren to visit her. He got a flight back to Australia the next day and spent a week there until Mother's condition stabilised a little. Mother was then on a roller-coaster path of one day being able to function well, and the next in intense discomfort with increasing difficulty in breathing, needing oxygen. (Some years earlier, Warren had had to make a similar dash from the UK to Melbourne.) We felt far removed from the daily drama of her fragile health, and we struggled with divided loyalties, recognising the burden on Warren's two sisters and wishing to be more supportive, but unable to just remove ourselves from responsibilities in South Asia.

Mother celebrated her 90th birthday 4 April 1998, at Warren's sister Alice's house in Thornbury. We had plenty of notice of this event (!) and had planned a trip back from Nepal to join the occasion, and also to attend the wedding of his youngest brother Philip. Later that year we had another trip to Melbourne following Warren's heart attack in Nepal in August. That unscheduled visit was also, of course, an opportunity to spend quality time with Mother, who was very content in the aged care centre she had chosen to enter five years earlier.

The following year, just 9 days after her 91st birthday, Mother died of heart failure, while actually in hospital for a different matter. Word reached us in Kathmandu and the question was, "What to do?" Having seen Mother on two visits the previous year, and being now in the middle of a very pressured project with the Royal Nepal Academy, Warren decided we could have a family memorial in Kathmandu, kindly hosted by Mark and Jenika at Sanepa. He left the Melbourne service to his siblings. Mother had already specified that the service should be the same as for Warren's Dad in 1988, so that was already planned. Alice did a superb job in organising the arrangements and giving the eulogy.

It was not only funerals that we missed. We could not attend the weddings of Warren's sister Margaret or of my Sydney nieces, and we were sad to miss such events. All part of the shadows that inevitably clouded an otherwise well-lit journey

28 Farewell to Pakistan

I appointed you to go and produce lasting fruit. (John 15.16)

Civil unrest and curfews were becoming frequent in Hyderabad in 1985. Often there were only a few hours of the day when people could go out to get food or medical supplies.

Visas became a bureaucratic challenge. Up to 1984, as Commonwealth citizens, we had the privilege of visa-free access to both India and Pakistan, and this was great for the travel back and forth between Hyderabad and Woodstock. But in early June 1984 Indira Gandhi sent the Indian Army into the Golden Temple in Amritsar to put down a Sikh insurgency. Then she imposed visa requirements on citizens of most Commonwealth countries to control the flood of Sikhs returning to India to join the protest. So the first visa for India Warren had to get was at the Indian Embassy in Karachi. It was mid-June 1984, to attend Mark's graduation from Woodstock School. Then we all needed exit visas to leave India after the graduation.

In August 1986, Pakistan also began requiring Commonwealth citizens to get visas. More bureaucratic hassle!

Around this time the landlord of the old verger's house ended our lease, saying he wanted to pull down the old and build a bigger and better place. We needed to find suitable accommodation for our office and for the growing Wycliffe team. Merryn was home at the time of our search and joined in the fun of resettling in a much more modern, open plan house in Latifabad, a suburb of Hyderabad. Hours of disruption to our work as we transported furniture and got the new place functional for office, library and accommodation!

In March 1986, the Thomson family arrived. Their family of eight needed the abundance of rooms in the new house where we had been living, so Warren and I negotiated with our new landlord to renovate a rooftop room into a penthouse apartment for our use. Once again Merryn was around during this fun interior decorating process. We soon transformed the room into an excellent kitchen/lounge/en suite unit. But, with no room for a bed, we did what most Pakistanis did, sleep outdoors on the rooftop.

Soon after settling in, we welcomed several missionary friends for a house dedication. Noting there was no bedroom, one asked, "Jessie, where are you going to sleep?" and I drew her attention to the outside bed set up around the side of the room.

"But Jessie, what are you going to do when it rains?"

"Lilli, when did it last rain in Hyderabad?"

This convinced Lilli that we needed no indoor sleeping arrangements – at least not till the July five day monsoon downpours. But that night, almost our first one on the new rooftop, it rained!

Holiday travels for Merryn now involved the six-hour trip from Woodstock to Delhi, a flight across to Karachi, and then a bus (usually the next day) up to Hyderabad. She was increasingly feeling a great deal of pressure from school expectations. Merryn is very much an all-rounder and had a finger in lots of extracurricular activities, as well as facing increasing academic demands. She continued to star in dramatic productions. In addition, through unforeseen and unhappy events, she became, as an 11th grader, President of the Student Council, which brought more responsibilities and time pressures.

She returned home for holidays needing complete rest and recuperation. Days spent down at an Interserve-run guest house on a beach outside Karachi were life-savers. On that beach on moonlit nights we got up to witness the miracle of mother turtles laying large batches of eggs in deep holes they had laboriously gouged out with their back flippers. They themselves had hatched at these very beaches years before and as mature adults returned year by year to drop their eggs. Sometimes our beach trips coincided with the hatching of the baby turtles from their sandy nests. They faced a long waddle down to the ocean. We delighted in chasing off the dogs and birds to help the baby turtles make a safe journey. We knew how important that long waddle was in strengthening their legs for the big swim they faced on reaching the ocean. So we resisted the temptation to just pick them up and transfer them down to the sea.

In May 1987, the time had now come for us to leave Pakistan and help

Merryn prepare for her transition back to Australia. We wrote to our prayer supporters:

> Can it really be four and a half years since we first rode up in two horse-drawn tongas (open carriages) to that old British Raj bungalow in Hyderabad? So much has happened, so many deep friendships made, so much to praise God for!
>
> Providing translators to work in six language groups, representing five to six million people.
>
> Helping us develop writers and artists in those communities.
>
> Blessing the early efforts in translation. Teams in four languages prepared New Reader Selections from Genesis in the recent April translation workshop.
>
> Providing English colleagues, Geoff and Jacki Tonkin, to take over hosting the group guest house, a fulltime job.

Our colleague Mike Payne sharing a display of booklets in Dhati , one of the desert languages of Sindh

> Leading us in the development of a Pakistani Bible Translation movement by calling one of our teams to work full time in liaison with the Pakistani church in this endeavour.
>
> Encouraging several of our teams to share the administrative and technical jobs needing to be done.
>
> Challenging us (in 1985) to rent larger office facilities when we couldn't see how the rent could be covered. The premises have been fully used over the past two years, and the rent paid!
>
> Surprising us with the provision of A$6,000 to buy a photocopier

for preparing literacy and translation materials in the office.

Overwhelming us with a US$1,000 gift from SIL colleagues in Peru which helped us air-condition our office library this summer.

Postscript: In March 2009 we revisited Pakistan, 22 years after our May 1987 departure. We had been asked to evaluate a long-term translation and literacy project (in six languages) among the Hindu-background tribal communities of Sindh province. A tremendous joy to revisit many of the places which had been home to us for those five years, and to meet many whom we had known as young men in the '80s and were now in positions of significant leadership. Even more joyful to see the fruit of the translation and literacy training these young people have received – they are now almost independently running community development, translation and literacy projects for their own communities.

We were glad that we had followed Mark's advice back in 1981, "That's where you ought to go."

29 Farewell to Woodstock

For the Lord is good... His faithfulness continues to each generation. (Psalm 100:5)

After Mark's Woodstock graduation in June 1984, we vacated Lower Bethany cottage in Landour, with regret! So our regular trips between Hyderabad and Woodstock now required not only international flights and visas for both India and Pakistan, but also finding each year new accommodation for the eight to ten weeks, mid-April to late June, that I spent on the Mussoorie hillside. For Merryn's three remaining years at Woodstock, then, we rented three different cottages to support her during the pressure-packed last weeks of each school year. Not only final exams for the year but also a wealth of cultural and community events.

In celebrating our 40th wedding anniversary (28 November 2004), good friends Yvonne and Cy Satow brilliantly described well one of the school's end-of-year activities:

> Memories of you two are mostly associated with our days at Woodstock School. Merryn and our Steve were classmates and during one particular summer, we served together on the June Sale Committee. I was chairperson, an awesome responsibility!
>
> In case you have forgotten, June Sale was not just a fundraiser for the school. It was THE summer event with a long and illustrious history. Who hadn't heard tales of Mrs A cranking gallons of homemade ice cream from before dawn? Of parent S, whose creative games and booths attracted shoppers from miles around, and of Mr D who brought such high-quality goods from Bombay that even the Delhiites were impressed?
>
> So there we were. Not trying to compete exactly. We knew that these were different times, with fewer parents to help. But we did want to make some money for the school and we did want everyone to have a GREAT day.
>
> Jess and Warren were on the Sale Committee, and I remember [we were all] working hard to make ours a Sale to remember. And

it was! I think we made a sizable profit and everyone had a good time. We exhausted Committee members staggered off (up or down the hill or both) to a long overdue early night. And, since the next day was Sunday, perhaps a wee lie-in in the morning.

But I didn't reckon with our Sale Treasurer extraordinaire, Warren. At around 7.30 am there was a loud knocking on the door. We staggered out to find Warren, freshly shaved and very awake. Going through the books the night before, he'd found that we were Rs 3.75 short. He was concerned. So was I!! I thought he had lost his mind. I would have gladly given him not just Rs 3.75 but Rs 3,333.75 if I'd had it.

On this bright Sunday morning, I didn't want to think or hear another thing about the Sale. But Warren wasn't going to let it go until the money was traced. Every paisa.

Apart from these fun events at the school we could witness some end-of-year activities which involved our children – concerts (we'll never forget Mark's perseverance and steady beat on the kettle drum during Ravel's Bolero); plays (Mark figured in *The Company of Wayward Saints* and Merryn performed a one-woman play, *The Dreaming Child*, about Isak Dinesen, of *Out of Africa* renown); and sporting events. But the ultimate parent interest was always in the graduation events, including the Baccalaureate church service. The school not only farewelled the fresh graduates after their years of Woodstock experience but also encouraged them to make an impact in the wider world where they were beginning their journey – and indeed many of the graduates have! We came to understand why Americans call the graduation ceremony "commencement". The young adults shed many tears, feeling they might never again see their Woodstock family. But in fact, our two have had several reunions over the years in different countries, to which many Woodstock colleagues have travelled from all over the world.

June 1987 saw Merryn graduate from Woodstock, a very encouraging culmination of her nearly 10 years at the school. Brother Mark had deferred his engineering studies at Melbourne Uni for a year and worked in Nepal six months to get practical engineering experience. Then he fitted in a visit back to Woodstock to help in the staging of Merryn's one-woman play and also be present for her graduation. Both Mark and Merryn had served, in their respective years, as President of the student body.

We very proud parents and our adult offspring were now returning to Australia for an extended time. Warren and I might "call Australia home" but our children had limited preparation for it or cultural knowledge of it.

Merryn graduating

PART 7 Heights to conquer

30 Home?

I will sing of the LORD's unfailing love forever! Young and old will hear of your faithfulness. (Psalm 89:1)

Equity in a house?

We arrived back in Australia in late August 1987, and Wycliffe provided us an apartment at its national centre. A beautiful rural location 30 kilometres from Melbourne, where we could live for a few months – a great transition in a supportive community. True to its name, Kangaroo Ground is frequently visited by mobs of kangaroos from a creek nearby. The rural setting surrounded by undulating hills and eucalyptus trees was a very welcome environment for us as a travel weary family. Warren and I worked once again in the SIL training school. Mark and Merryn each managed to get work to earn some money toward their growing independence.

It is an idyllic location, and Warren went to our Australian Wycliffe director, Darryl Kernick, to explore the possibility of a more permanent stay at Kangaroo Ground. But Darryl said, "Warren, that's not possible. You need to get some equity in a house at this stage to give your kids stability and support during this important transition, and of course to make provision for the future."

We looked at one another in despair. "Get some equity in a house!" What with? We might have about A$1,000 in our bank. How could we purchase a house? We had been married for close to 23 years, and here we were just about to embark on our first home purchase.

"You'll need to look at a hundred houses before deciding," warned Jenny Williams, our Wycliffe Australia member care facilitator. With the promise of some financial help through bridging loans from Wycliffe, and some generous loans from family and friends, we began searching. Our limited budget meant our options were at the lower end of the market.

We looked at a couple of places north of the Yarra, somewhat close to Kangaroo Ground, but nothing excited us and everything was well beyond our financial range.

Then a friend said, "Go look south of the river. You'll find similar places for about $10,000 less than around here." So we found an agent in North Ringwood, and told her our price range. The very first house she took us to was a lovely weatherboard cottage which had all that was necessary for our family of four adults.

Our "first home" - 31 Oban Road, Ringwood

But Jenny had said we needed to "look at a hundred houses", so the agent showed us other places. We quickly decided that this home in Ringwood was God's place for us. Not exactly in the same class as the Houstons' Canberra home, but attractive. A local builder friend, a heavy man, checked it by jumping up and down. "It's well built!" he affirmed.

A house, but what about furniture? Tom Hibberd, a dear friend of many years and "Mr Wycliffe" for NSW, came to our aid. A friend disposing of a houseful of furniture in Sydney when her parents died had contacted Tom. Warren and I were going to Wilton to celebrate Dad's 100th birthday, 29 October 1987. So Tom invited me to look at his friend's house and choose what we would need in our Ringwood home. Every-thing we needed for the house – double bed, single beds, dining suite, dressing table, kitchen equipment – arrived on the truck from Sydney at just the right time when we moved in! We are still comfortably enjoying the Sydney double bed – probably 50 years old by now!

On 27 November 1987, just one day before our 23rd wedding anniver-sary, we moved in and soon after had a thanksgiving service. Friends from Wycliffe and our local church joined us in thanking the Lord for His provision through friends, family, Wycliffe and the Australian govern-ment's First Home Owners Assistance scheme. We were probably their oldest "first home owners"!

A wonderful joy was to be reunited as a family after the years of many separations while the children were in boarding school. Mark, still working on his engineering degree at Melbourne University, rejoined the family with some ambivalence, as life in our small nuclear family was not nearly as engaging as his life at Kew Baptist Hostel over the previous two years. But maybe Mum's cooking had some attraction?

Not just a house

During the next two and a half years we made a home in a country none of us knew well. When asked about this transition in an interview for a mission magazine, Merryn said, "We'd been in Australia several times, so it wasn't a great shock. Our main problem is on the personal relationship side – coming back this time to live as a family in Melbourne, we found that we have no roots; nobody our own age that we'd known for a long time; no good friends. At the boarding school, we could just walk down the hallway to see our friends, but here we actually had to learn to use the telephone. It was very uncomfortable at first, and making friends here took us a long time. Not that people were unfriendly, it's just that developing friendships took a lot more time."

Mark had a slightly more pragmatic reflection: "One disadvantage of our missionary life is that I don't think I will ever be able to settle down in suburbia with an ordinary job for 40 years, doing the same thing day in day out." (Which proved to be another of Mark's prophetic statements!)

We gave our new house an Urdu name *Dil Araam* (Heart Peace). It was our prayer that many people who entered our house might experience heart peace, whatever their current situation.

Merryn and Mark did soon make many friends. Mark already had some close friends from the Kew Baptist hostel and associated church, while Merryn also made friends from the local church she had joined. These friends were soon some of the heart-peace seeking visitors at Dil Araam.

1988 was a year of high stress and less heart-peace as the family dived into study and work. Mark resumed his engineering course at Melbourne University, after his deferral in 1987 to get some practical experience with the United Mission to Nepal.

Merryn began a Bachelor of Education degree at Rusden College, part of Deakin University. She was very stretched in doing a triple major of English, Drama and Dance.

Early after returning to Australia, I felt I should work towards a BEd at La Trobe University. The reasons for this were not clear except that the SIL training schools expected continuing professional development for all teaching staff. So, after much prayer and consultation with the family and SIL staff, I also became a tertiary student (mature age!).

Warren was teaching, and acting Principal for some months, at SPSIL, the training school at Kangaroo Ground, and I was also teaching there.

Four adults, four different tertiary institutions! At the end of the year we wrote to our prayer team about 1988 as a time of learning:

What have we learned?

Jessie:

That study is *hard* – maybe my age and academic limitations are showing!

What a great support my family are to me.

That God's grace and love are sustaining even when we feel weak and pressured.

That computers can be friends, especially when writing essays.

That life goes on even when ironing and house cleaning don't get done.

Lots of interesting things in anthropology – on other cultures and our own Oz values – and in my other BEd subjects, insights into language, second language learning, reading and writing, and the teaching of them.

Warren:

To stretch lots academically in teaching new courses, such as language program planning and survey of grammatical theories.

The joy of meeting friends, old and new, in our link parishes.

How to be a normal member of a local church here in Oz, and leading group Bible studies.

The adjustments needed after the first death in my immediate family (my Dad). We have felt this loss, but also experienced the comfort of God and of friends.

Mark:

That there are many more interesting things to do than study.

That I am impatient to get into *practical* engineering. The formal education system here strikes me as inappropriate in its emphasis.

That many (most?) Christians in Australia are obsessed with the exclusive "rightness" of their denomination and I see this belief as in conflict with the prayer of Jesus in John 17.

Merryn: Immanuel is: With us; Within us; And without us: crucified, again and again, and again.

I think she must have written this reflection around Good Friday? Her faith walk, energised by many folk she met at her new church, included an outreach to a women's remand centre nearby.

31 Teaching others also

Teach these truths to other trustworthy people who will be able to pass them on to others. (2 Timothy 2:2)

Warren and I both believed strongly that our commitment to mission should always be to train and empower others to share the Gospel. In training other cross-cultural workers, we would multiply our efforts. This we had certainly seen happening in the Indian training program. We were mindful of Paul's injunction to the young man Timothy, leader of the church in Ephesus: "entrust [the teachings] to reliable people, who will be able to teach others also" (2 Timothy 2:2 GNT) and this verse featured on our prayer card for many years.

We had counted it a privilege to work in setting up the Indian training programs from 1976 to 1982, similar ventures in Pakistan in the mid-1980s and in Singapore in the early 1990s, and to serve regularly on staff at the SPSIL training schools whenever we were in Australia. During 1988 we were both on staff once again at SPSIL, now moved to a year-round home at the Wycliffe national centre at Kangaroo Ground. A poem by Elizabeth Givens seemed to capture something of the vision and purpose of these courses:

Ants in the Sugar bowl

So send I you:

To ants in the sugar bowl,
To things that fly, creep, and crawl into the house,
To uncertain water, sporadic electricity.
To long hours, sweltering heat, exhausting days,
To uncomfortable vehicles, crowded jeeps, smelly buses,
To noisy, early, EARLY mornings.
To rice, rice, and more rice,
To poverty you didn't believe existed,
To masses of people like you have never seen,
To know and work with people who have never known comfort,
So send I you, and expect you to adjust.

So send I you:

To people who will give to you from their poverty,
To friends that will embarrass you with their generosity,
To pastors that will entertain you from their lack, with bounty,
To hungry, receptive, questioning people who want to know God.
To study, to teach, to learn from your study and teaching,
To probe your own motives, values, and beliefs,
To learn about yourself and the culture that has reared you,
To know God and to understand more deeply dependence on Him.

So send I you.

Are you going? I'll go with you all the way.

Four couples in the SPSIL community that training year exemplified the truths of Elizabeth Givens' poem. I wrote about them to our praying friends.

Stephen and Wendy Moody

Drawing on my years of being first aid orderly in the Gurung village, as well as my research on the belief system of the Gurungs, I was really excited to work with Stephen in his preparation for an essay on the Himalayan peoples' attitudes to physical illness and Western medicine. Stephen hopes to serve as a doctor in another Himalayan country. To add a touch of excitement to life at SIL, Stephen decided that Wendy Humphreys, one of our childcare staff, would make just the right resident nurse to have with him in the country of his calling.

In the virtually roadless land they will be going to, Stephen and Wendy won't need to worry about the "uncomfortable vehicles, crowded jeeps, and smelly buses". It'll be Shank's pony most of the way.

P.S. Stephen and Wendy lived in that Himalayan country for over 10 years helping to establish a hospital in a very remote part of the country where thousands of people received the story of the God who loved them. Over 20 years later, God has opened the door for them, as almost "empty nesters", to serve again in the same Himalayan country.

John and Sally Padgett, with their two small children, Alison and Luke, are off to Bangladesh as medical missionaries. They will work in community health at a hospital in the northwest of the country. We were particularly encouraged by the cultural sensitivity and language skills John and Sally showed.

We hope we can visit them one day, and we know they'll one day absolutely *love* "rice, rice, and more rice"!

P.S. In fact, John and Sally ended up working in Nepal and we had the joy of working alongside them during our three years in the Gorkha project where I worked in women's literacy. By then, little Becky had also joined their family. In 2019, after finding themselves empty-nested back in Australia they returned to Nepal where they continue serving, coping perhaps with "ants in the sugar bowl" and certainly with the tremendous challenges of a rural hospital in the COVID-19 pandemic. The actual number of infected people is hard to identify since testing sites are few.

Daniel and Wei Lei Jesudason

We are especially delighted to have Daniel and Wei Lei here as Asian missionaries. Theirs is a cross-cultural marriage – Daniel is of Indian ancestry and Wei Lei is Chinese. They took their theological and initial linguistic courses in their native Singapore, and are completing their training in Australia to prepare for literacy work with SIL in Papua New Guinea.

As they go from bustling, prosperous, clean Singapore, we pray they will make a good adjustment to "ants in the sugar bowl and things that fly, creep and crawl into the house."

P.S. Daniel and Wei Lei plus son Jonathan served for many years in PNG where they not only saw many people come to Christ through reading the scriptures but also witnessed an amazing revival among the people as they came out of the deception of cults endemic in the area.

Mark and Anne Osborne

Mark grew up in Papua New Guinea and, with a fellow student from there, often called in to our place in Canberra for a meal in 1979. Perhaps we contributed to Mark's awareness of needs in the Indian subcontinent. Certainly this was a challenge Mark already had through Navigators in University. Now Mark and Anne, with little Timothy, are heading for South Asia with Wycliffe. They are seriously praying about serving in Pakistan, where the

5 am calls to prayer from the mosque will guarantee them "noisy, early, EARLY mornings"!

P.S. In fact Mark and Anne went to another part of Asia where they have continued significant involvement in Bible translation in a very sensitive country. As we had done for Mark and Merryn, they also spent some time back in Australia to help their three sons transition back to OZ as young adults, and then returned to their project and to train others. Mark also served several years in mission administration.

Just recently we had news of another former student, also Singaporean. With her German husband, she has facilitated translation and literacy for a people group in Asia, and is now leading a new team in yet another sensitive Asian country.

These vignettes represent just a fragment of stories about the many folk we've had the privilege of equipping for the service the Lord was calling them to. All of them "reliable people...able to teach others also" (2 Timothy 2:2 GNT).

32 Guilt-free Language Learning

O Lord, I am not very good with words…I get tongue-tied, and my words get tangled. (Exodus 4:10)

Saturday 17 February 1996

Dear Warren and Jessie,

Last night as I lay in the courtyard of my host B. family, looking up into the stark Saharan sky and thanking the Lord for the cool air that brings relief after the onslaught of the relentless sun, I thought of you. And I smiled. My ears ringing with the music of strange vowels, flapped 'r's and backed 'k's, the bleating of goats, and the scolding of children, I thought you'd be proud of me.

You see, in the almost dark (except for the flickering coals heating the eternal sweet, green tea) I was a silent listener, drinking in the exotic sounds and letting my head rise and fall with the words as they spilled out and filled the air. I was a silent, non-participating listener, and thoroughly enjoying it.

Thanks (at least in part) to your enthusiastic presentation of this language learning approach, I wasn't feeling in the least guilty about not even wanting or trying to open my mouth. But I found my lips involuntarily, from time to time, dancing with the melody, forming shapes that one day will serve to communicate. But not yet. I'm a listener. An active, enthusiastic listener-learner.

The first word I heard was "aba". I heard it in a pleading tone, an accusing tone, a submissive tone, and noticed the father's response. I heard it dozens of times and now it can never be just a word on paper, but a word that belongs to children, that communicates. It is a real people word, not a paper word. I heard dozens of other phrases, repeated in similar contexts which probably mean, "Stop it!", or "Come here!", or "How are you?" or "Do you want more?" etc.

Someday I'll know what they really mean. Today I don't even really try to guess. I listen and feel that I am being absorbed into this lovely language. I can't repeat these phrases, but when I hear them again, I will recognise them!

Just thought you'd like to know.

Andrew S.

Andrew wrote his beautiful letter as an entry in his diary but didn't actually mail it to us. However, just last year, some years after Andrew's untimely and sudden death, his widow Hélene found it in his papers and sent it to me. My mind travelled down memory lane to the years I had taught the Language Learning class as part of Andrew's prefield training program at SIL Australia.

The thrust of that approach contrasted with the traditional approach to learning a second language. In years past many of us spent hours upon hours in memorizing grammatical structures, learning long lists of vocabulary, and trying to repeat model sentences and words until both pronunciation and grammar were adequate for communication. In contrast, the research of Stephen Krashen, a Canadian linguist, showed that a second language was more successfully *acquired* (as distinct from *learned*) in similar ways to how we master our first language, that is, by good exposure to simple chat that includes repeated utterances. This input in time gives the child confidence to practise responses which they've heard often. Krashen's research has led to several language learning schools adopting the natural approach language learning method.

I had seen the principles applied when a new Wycliffe family joined our team in Pakistan in 1986. As the language learning coach for our group, I sat down with them soon after their arrival to discuss how the family might tackle learning Urdu. Early in the conversation, Greg interrupted my spiel on the options possible, with a new thought: "Jessie, would you be open to us using a somewhat radical approach to learning Urdu, in that we won't be following any textbook but will learn by listening and living in situations where we can hear the language?" He went on to describe the theoretical background to this experiment.

I responded something like, "I'll be glad to give you three to four months to try it and then we can evaluate if it's been successful."

His wife Angela quickly interjected, "Jessie, don't just evaluate the method according to how Greg succeeds. He'll learn a language whatever method he uses. Just evaluate this approach by checking how I can speak Urdu in three months' time. I'm coming to this country with a history of failure in language learning behind me. We arrive here with five children, one of whom is still a baby. If I succeed, then Greg's method is definitely worth looking at."

The family, including Angela, did indeed succeed by following the *listen* approach. I was very impressed, and so the natural method became our method of choice for all new members. Their success also prompted me to do further research on it in my postgraduate study in education at La Trobe University just a few years later, and to teach this method in our prefield language learning module at the Australian SIL training school. And that method is what Andrew's diary entry referred to in his early days of language exposure in the Sahara.

Going back to our early days in Ghachok village, I didn't have any theoretical basis for language learning then, but after the initial trauma of over-exposure in the open tea shop, we experienced the benefit of the natural method in the next house we lived in.

The tea shop where we lived our first months had overwhelmed us with language exposure. From dawn till dusk the onslaught of questions fired at us by the never-ending stream of visitors coming by on the various paths converging at our house was not only unintelligible but frustrating and exhausting.

After only eight weeks in the tea shop, we unexpectedly had to go back to Kathmandu for an administrative role. Nine months later we returned to Ghachok. Because of our physical problems in the tea shop, we planned to ask if there might be some other house which was a bit higher. But before Warren could even raise the matter, our sponsor Ser Bahadur jumped up to greet him and to apologise that the tea shop was no longer available. He would find us something else! What a gift from our loving Father. "Before they call, I will answer." (Isaiah 65:24)

Ser Bahadur introduced us to his younger brother, Ram Phal, who showed us his barn, above the buffalo shed and facing the family home across the courtyard. It was high enough for us to stand upright, just about everywhere! We were overjoyed.

It was not long before we realised how ideal this setup was for our language learning. Just like Andrew that evening in Africa, we could hear the family conversations going on without our being expected to take part or respond. We heard the greetings and the responses of the various neighbours and of visitors who came and went with such regularity. The first greeting exchange was inevitably *kaen tsai wa?* (Have you eaten rice?) to which the response was a single word, either *tsai* (I've eaten), or *aatsaingyu* (I haven't eaten).

We had fewer visitors up the steps to our barn than to the exposed tea shop – and when they came, it was usually for a purpose that we could understand and respond to, such as to sell us eggs, or to beg some medicine. We learned the kinship terms as people began addressing us, either as *surjemae aama* (mother of Surje – the name they'd given Mark), or *surjemae aaba* (father of Surje) for Warren.

For Mark, it was also a great natural language learning environment, demonstrating the success of the natural method. On his second birthday, he amused the gathering of friends and neighbours who celebrated with him by going around to each one with a question. None of us knew exactly what he was asking, but we all knew it was a question because each utterance ended with the question particle *wa* and rising intonation.

When his younger sister Merryn was a toddler, she would join with three-year-old Mark down in the courtyard or on the verandah of the main house playing with the landlord's children. On one occasion I called out to Mark from the barn window opposite, "Look out for Merryn that she doesn't fall down to the courtyard."

Mark's playmate asked him, *"aamadi to bi?"* (What did your Mum say?)

He responded in perfect Gurung, *"nani aakxurige ro."* (She said, don't let your sister fall).

The grammatically complex response flowed off his tongue with ease. The natural approach was working for him, too.

Natural language learners!

146

33 Go to Galilee

With your unfailing love you lead the people you have redeemed. (Exodus 15.13)

In early 1990, Mark and Merryn moved to inner city Melbourne to involve more in their church's outreach there. SIL leaders had spoken of us being based in Australia for perhaps two to five years to help our children transition back to their home culture. After two and a half years in Ringwood they decided to move out, and so we felt free to return to South Asia. I still felt concerned about removing ourselves so soon from the support that Merryn particularly might need for a few more years, but we felt a strong nudge to be ready for the next door the Lord might open for us back in Asia. But when, Lord? Surely not yet? "The Galilee Song" by Frank Andersen MSC well expressed our challenges at the time:

Deep within my heart I hear
Voices whispering to me
Words that I can't understand
Meanings I must clearly hear,
Calling me to follow close
Lest I leave my self behind,
Calling me to walk into
Evening shadows one more time.

> So I leave my boats behind
> Leave them on familiar shore
> Set my heart upon the deep
> Follow you again my Lord.

In my memories I know
How you send familiar rains
Falling gently on my days
Dancing patterns on my panes.
And I need to learn once more
In the fortress of my mind
To believe in falling rain
As I travel deserts dry.

> So I leave my boats behind...

As I gaze into the night
Down the future of my years
I'm not sure I want to walk
Past horizons that I know.
But I feel my spirit call
Like a stirring deep within
Restless till I leave again
Beyond the fears that close me in.

> So I leave my boats behind...

But where, Lord? Back to the dry deserts of Pakistan? Resume working with IICCC in hot, humid Nasik? Help with the Asia SIL training school in always humid Singapore? Or return to our first love amongst the Gurung people, in the cool hills of Nepal?

So, on an exploratory visit in April 1990, we entered a Nepal very different from the autocratic, monoethnic state we'd left in 1976. The people's revolution demanding ethnic, religious and political rights had climaxed just four days before our arrival in Kathmandu on Good Friday. On Easter Sunday we were in high spirits as we went to the international church on the outskirts of the valley. On the church bus I was delighted to meet with Margaret McCombe, a friend who was working in literacy with the United Mission to Nepal (UMN).

"Oh Jessie, I'm so pleased to see you. Next week I am running a training for literacy facilitators out in Pokhara. Please, come out to Pokhara with us tomorrow." I really wasn't ready to leave Kathmandu so soon, having just arrived only two days before. But that morning, the director of UMN based his sermon on Matthew 28:9: "Don't be afraid. Go tell my brothers to leave for Galilee, and they will see me there." Wow! If we were to hear what the risen Jesus wanted to say to us, we'd better go out to our Galilee – Pokhara.

During that workshop I met the Minister of Education who spoke of the government's new policy of "Education for All", and wanted to address particularly the issues of access. I mentioned to him the challenge of access for peoples whose first language is not Nepali, and he assured me that multilingual education would also be part of the government's new focus. What a contrast with the 1976 "Nepali only" policy! The Lord was clearly directing us to pursue returning to Gurung work to contribute to the Government's new multilingual education emphasis.

In its Gorkha Project, UMN had a hospital in Amp Pipal. Many years before, when we'd been printing Western Gurung scripture portions, Dr Cynthia Hale at that hospital had told us that, although many of the patients at that hospital were Gurung, "The Gurungs here say they can't understand what you've done there in Pokhara. *Mildai mildaina!* (It doesn't match at all!) You need to come over here and do a translation in their dialect."

In 1975, Warren had worked with a good friend John Landon on a survey of Gurung dialects, and had certainly confirmed Cynthia's observations.

John Landon and Warren with our Ghachok landlord, on dialect survey

Was this now, in 1990, the door the Lord was opening to us, fifteen years later? Here we were in 1990 exploring the possibility of taking up a translation project for that eastern (Gorkha) dialect of Gurung. We had published the Western Gurung NT in 1982. To enable Warren to adapt it to Eastern Gurung, I might get a post to do women's literacy outreach with the Gorkha Project's Community Health Department – and hence get visas for us to live at Amp Pipal.

But negotiating the administrative details of this secondment would not be a simple process. We needed to check first if the UMN Gorkha Project needed a Non-Formal Education (NFE) consultant, and then to explore whether UMN would accept me for the post, despite the history of SIL's banishment from Nepal in 1976. How quickly that all happened!

When we made initial enquiries with the UMN HQ office in Kathmandu, David McConkey, UMN's Education Director, advised us, "You'll need to go out and talk directly with the Gorkha Project director."

As we left David's office, we wondered just how were we to get out to the Gorkha Project. At that moment, we met Mariane, a German member of the Gorkha Project team, standing by the mailboxes in the corridor just outside his office. She said she was leaving the very next day to return to her post, and that we could travel with her. She offered to show us the way up to Amp Pipal, though admittedly going a circuitous route via Gankhu, a more north-easterly village where she worked. "And," she said, "it's a Gurung village." Wow!

We took up her offer, packed quickly, and found ourselves next day huffing and puffing up the very steep trail to Gankhu, after a long bus trip and a further two-hour trek along the river valley below. We were lagging far behind the lean and energetic Mariane, finding ourselves to be very out of condition. Five years in essentially flat southern Pakistan and 2½ years in suburban Australia had not been good preparation for

Nepal's hills once again! Plus, Warren was just recovering from an attack of bacillary dysentery the week before, an unwelcome 50th birthday present! As dark came on we collapsed on the verandah of a Nepali house two-thirds of the way from the river valley up to Gankhu. There we received a hospitable welcome, a meal and a bed – wonderful Nepali hospitality to strangers! We reached Gankhu next morning.

We planned to go on to the project office in Amp Pipal in a few days' time, going via Thalajung, another Gurung village, much higher up the mountain. A Christian Gurung couple lived there, and it was where Margaret McCombe herself had worked. However, the plans had to be aborted when, on day two, Warren severely damaged his right knee. Backing out of a bush latrine sited on the edge of a terraced field, he fell three metres to the terrace below (the slope of the hill is steep!). He landed on his feet, but his knees took the worst impact. He could barely walk, let alone make a lengthy detour to Thalajung. How were we now going to make the six-hour trek across the ridges to the office and hospital at Amp Pipal?

Next day we felt we must move on. With the help of some willing porters who carried all our backpacks, we gingerly wended our way around the hills and across landslides until at about 5 pm we eventually staggered into the little Amp Pipal bazaar on the saddle of a high hill. Only one hour's walk down to the project office on the other side of the hill!

"I can't walk another step forward," moaned Warren. "Let's just spend tonight at their guest house here, and go down to the office tomorrow morning to meet the project director."

So, within two minutes, he collapsed thankfully into a bed at the nearby mission guest house – and we found that the hostess, Sally Smith, was actually a nurse who applied poultices to the injured knees. Even more amazing was that her husband, Ian, was the very Gorkha Project director we wanted to meet – and that he had just arrived back from an administrative visit that day and was leaving on another trek the next morning! So that very night, and in that very place, was the only time we could have possibly met with him. That wouldn't have happened if we'd gone directly down to the hospital, or if we'd detoured to Thalajung!

Ian came over that evening to explore our assignment. WHO statistics have shown that wherever women are literate, mother and child mortality rates are significantly lower. Hence Ian saw the assignment of an NFE consultant as strategic in the community health outreach: it could make a life and death difference to the women and their families in the surrounding villages. When he learned of my literacy experience and the recently acquired BEd degree, he assured me there was a post for me!

Warren could do the translation work in his own time, and in his own space, as "unassigned spouse" in the UMN system! We rejoiced in this confirmation of the Lord's hand in the assignment, and in His directing our steps to meet Ian. The visit to "Galilee" had certainly been an amazing meeting with the Lord, showing us that His next step for us was not back to either India, Pakistan, or Singapore, but a return to the Gurungs of central Nepal, and to serve many other communities as well in Gorkha district.

During my three short years in the Gorkha NFE project, Warren worked with a Gurung speaker to learn the eastern dialect, and used a newly developed computer program for adapting the Western Gurung translation into the Gorkha dialect. We could print Dr Luke's two volumes (the Gospel and Acts) and two epistles before we left the project in 1994. The Amp Pipal hospital hosted a dedication which was attended by patients and staff, and we held another event up in Thala-jung, the home village of Pastor Padam Gurung. He had helped with checking the translation for accuracy, clarity, and naturalness.

One of our dear Gurung friends from Ghachok, Khadga, came to Thalajung for that dedication. Before starting his speech, he said, "I know that my dialect might be difficult for you all here. Would you prefer if I spoke in Nepali?"

"NO!" they all replied. "This is a Gurung occasion. We'll follow what you're saying!" And they did.

*Acts of the Apostles
in Gorkha Gurung*

34 If you give them a literacy class

The needy will not be ignored forever: the hopes of the poor will not always be crushed. (Psalm 9:18)

I dreaded the early morning arrival at my new NFE office in Amp Pipal of a little, almost mouse-like lady, Thaili Didi. *Didi* is a respectful term meaning elder sister, and the Thaili part identified her as a tailoress who makes the little cloth draw-string purses (thailis) worn by most Nepali women in their cummerbund to keep any precious money safe. Thaili Didi, probably in her late 40s, although mouse-like in her stature, was strong and lively in her spirit. She wore a simple cotton sari with the classic bright blue cummerbund around the waist, causing her old faded velveteen blouse to crimp up above her waist. As typical of her poor community, she wore little jewellery.

After the mandatory polite greetings asking about each other's wellbeing, she would inevitably return to her advocacy on behalf of her poor village of tailors, Harmi Kot. The wider Nepali community does not hold tailors in respect or high regard, although everybody needs their skills. Mostly illiterate, they had little option for other employment. "If the mission (UMN) were to give a literacy class to our village I know that the entire village would turn to Jesus and put their trust in him," Thaili Didi reiterated on each daily visit.

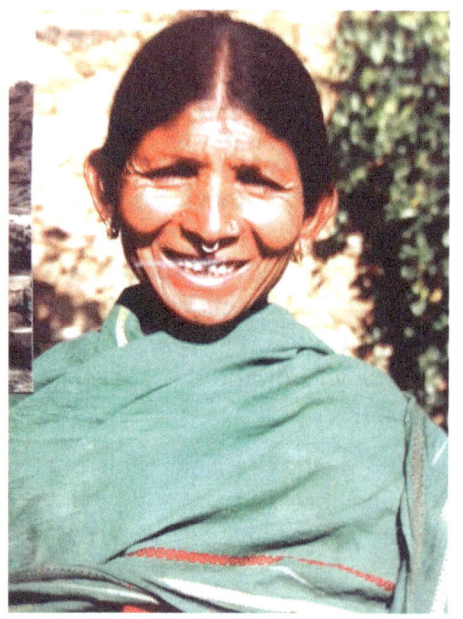

Thaili Didi

While I regarded her confidence with a grain of salt (my lack of faith?), I did assure her that her village, Harmi Kot, definitely had priority for a class by our project criteria, but I couldn't make any promises at that stage. These were early days for the addition of adult literacy classes to the services offered by the Community Health Project of the Amp Pipal hospital.

Day by day, Thaili Didi darkened my office door, trying to ensure that I'd not forgotten her request. In frustration, one day I decided to give her half an hour each day to take her through the government's adult literacy primer that we would use in the classes. This would give me a chance to evaluate if the primer was pedagogically sound, and help me in training locally appointed facilitators in how best to teach from it.

After about a month of these daily tutorials with Thaili Didi, I concluded sadly that either the primer was not designed well, or that Thaili Didi was just not able to learn, or perhaps both.

As she and I had hoped, Harmi Kot was among the villages chosen for a class. As self-appointed chair of the village education committee, she worked on motivating her people to sign up as learners and facilitators for the new class, and then to attend regularly.

About eighteen months later, when the classes were developing reading fluency, I found myself one cold night visiting to see how the Harmi Kot class was doing. Like so many village classes, this one was held on the verandah of the facilitator's house. The participants sat around on woven grass mats, huddled up in their shawls against the winter cold. Their only light was from a kerosene lantern or two spread along the verandah. I was glad to see that the class had not diminished in numbers during their second year of operation. A testimony to Thaili Didi's shepherding! In fact, other semi-literates had come along to enjoy the library club, which operated out of a tin trunk two nights per week. As I sat on the verandah with the rest of the learners, someone behind me was reading from a simple Bible story reader the local church had donated to the class library. I turned around to see who it was. Imagine my amazement in discovering none other than Thaili Didi! I couldn't stifle my amazement. "Thaili Didi. You can read!"

"Yes," she replied with a broad smile. "When the class started I asked the Lord to help me learn to read so that I can one day read the Bible in church."

The Lord also rewarded Thaili Didi's faith in that a large proportion of her village did indeed come to faith in Jesus, and the class facilitator subsequently trained to become a church leader. He is now an ordained pastor in their local church and Thaili Didi is a regular Bible reader in the church services. What joy!

Her daughter Sun Maya was also a learner in another village. I didn't get to visit her village very often, so wasn't aware of her progress. Recently, we visited Sun Maya, now living in Kathmandu, and she excitedly brought out a plastic bag of a powder which she assured me was efficacious in improving ladies' skin blemishes. The shine on her own middle-aged face was a good advertisement for her product. Excitedly, she told me she was earning income by selling this product to the many beauty salons dotted around her neighbourhood.

"Where did you get the recipe from?"

"From that book called *Where there is no Doctor*. At the back of the book there is a part about good recipes." And then she hastily added. "And Didi, I can read that book because you taught me how to read in our village literacy class so many years ago." Actually, I'd never taught her class, but in her mind, I'd made the classes possible, and I shared her joy at the result.

She insisted that I also take a packet of the powder. "Didi, I'm sure that this will also do wonders for your wrinkles."

The three years in Amp Pipal, from March 1991 to January 1994, working on behalf of illiterate women, were my most busy and productive assignments in Nepal. Over that period, the NFE team of the UMN Gorkha Community Health Project served about 60 villages and at least 1000 women became literate and more confident carers of their family's health needs. Because of those three years of trekking over the middle hills of the project target area for facilitator trainings and class supervisions, I recovered my marriage weight and felt healthier than I could remember for some years. What a nice unexpected personal benefit from the women's literacy assignment! Though I'm still waiting for the wrinkles to go, despite Sun Maya's powder.

But there was one other trek for which I wondered if I'd aimed too high.

35 Higher than ever before

How beautiful on the mountains are the feet of the messenger who brings good news. (Isaiah 52:7)

Issue one of the 1992 TEAR magazine, pp. 6,7, reported on their proposed project among the Tamang people in the village of Jharlang, partnering with Nepal Christian Fellowship (NCF), an umbrella organisation for believers in Nepal.

> Few of our global neighbours are as remote from us as the Tamang people in the Jharlang area of northern Nepal, and few would be as poor. The region is 12–15,000 feet above sea level, and five days hard trekking from the nearest road.
>
> In early October 1991, four of the NCF staff made a long trek to Jharlang and spent 10 days with local leaders and assessed the needs of the population. They noted that approximately 80% of the 5,500 people in the 9 separate villages of the region were Christians. Seven of the villages had constructed church buildings. Most of them consisted of two stone walls and a thatched roof attached to the pastor's house. It was obvious to the NCF team that the needs of these people are very great, and little, if any, government assistance has been forthcoming because of their isolation...
>
> Illiteracy is a major problem. At the present time (1992) there is only one school with one untrained teacher serving the whole region. Not surprisingly, only 1% of the population are literate.

In September 1993, the UMN project in Gorkha received a request for help. For some months, the NCF staff had been working amongst the Tamang of Jharlang trying to teach literacy skills, using Nepali as the medium of instruction. They had little success, as most people in this remote area spoke only their own Tamang language. So, recognising the success of the Gorkha project's classes in using Gurung experimentally, the Non-Formal Education office in Kathmandu asked, "Could Jessie help

NCF use the Tamang language primers which the SIL team had prepared some years before?" Hence my visit to the Himalayan heights, higher than I'd ever trekked before:

We woke to a very wet morning in Amp Pipal 22 September. The monsoon was still hanging around. It had poured rain all night, and this was the day I had to set off at 6 am, with a Nepali companion, for a two-week training course for literacy teachers in the north of Dhading, the district immediately to the east of our Gorkha district. Although perhaps only 25 kilometres directly east of us, the route we had to take was very circuitous!

We picked our way carefully for four hours down the wet, rocky and slippery (red mud) trail to the road at Turture. The rain had damaged the road sufficiently to block all motor traffic and so we had no choice but to walk on another four hours south to the main east–west highway at Dumre. A bus there took us the three-hour trip east to a small bazaar called Malekhu, where we crossed the swollen Trisuli River by a swaying footbridge. There buses would line up to take passengers up the unsealed road to the District capital, Dhading Besi. But no buses were running when we arrived at 7 pm, so a reckless driver (drunk or un-skilled?) took us on a two-hour wild jeep ride to the town. Quite a journey! We settled for the night into a little hotel, thankful for safe arrival. But that was only day one!

Next morning a Tamang pastor met us. He had come down to escort us back up to Jharlang, where the training was to be held. (We were not holding the training in the principal town because there was considera-ble hostility there toward Christians.) We did the trek in two long days. The continuing rain provided welcome cover from the tropical sun but made the rocky stepped paths treacherously slippery, particularly when going down. I prayed much for the Lord's protection on these stretches; a false step would have landed me down the steep ravine with nothing to halt the fall or to prevent serious injury. At this point I was really feeling I had now achieved the missionary credentials that many folk imagined was a normal part of our lives! Our path brought us higher and higher into the Tamang area and it thrilled me to see small crosses atop many houses. I learned these were actually marking the village church – the ones made of just two stone walls referred to in the TEAR article above. Finally, as the sun sank in the west, we were told that we'd now reached Jharlang. I was exhausted, relieved, and very thankful to get there safely and to meet the Nepali staff NCF had assigned to the project. (This literacy and community development project was the one supported by TEAR Australia.)

The rigours of the trip faded somewhat with the joy of seeing 300 folk flock into their newly constructed village church on our first Sunday there. (Building this larger, tin-roofed structure had clearly required financial help – probably from TEAR.) I noticed many women had brought little bottles along to have them refilled and consecrated by the pastor and I learned they used the oil through the ensuing week for any healings needed, either for family members or for household animals! Lacking even the most basic health services, the new believers in these remote areas depended totally on the Lord their God for all aspects of health care. God graciously heard the prayers of this infant church as they brought Him their needs, and He worked nothing short of New Testament miracles to show them His presence and power.

I experienced firsthand one of these miracles when our elderly landlady came upstairs one morning to the loft where we were all staying. "You've to come down and pray for our cow. She calved two days ago and her milk has not come down."

We all joined Grannie and the sick cow down in front of the barn, singing some praise songs and praying for the Lord's healing of the cow. Grannie handed me the little bottle of oil with which to anoint the sick cow. But where was I to apply it? The udder? The head? Or where? My delay and fumbling frustrated Grannie, so she finally snatched the oil out of my hand, dug her finger deep into the bottle, and firmly smeared the oil over Daisy's horns. When I asked next morning how the cow was, Grannie replied, "Fine, fine. The calf is now drinking contentedly." Why should I even need to ask!

The simple faith of these first-generation Christians made me wonder why we Western Christians give so little heed to James, Jesus' brother: "Are any of you sick? You should call for the elders of the church to come and pray over you, anointing you with oil in the name of the Lord. Such a prayer, offered in faith will heal the sick and the Lord will make you well." (James 5:7) Only in rare cases do our churches in Western countries follow this practice and that often only when all else fails.

During the training of the literacy facilitators, my goal was to help the ladies in their classes become confident readers. so that they could read from their New Testament. It had been translated into the Tamang language by one of our Australian Wycliffe colleagues, Doreen Taylor, and published in 1990.

Sitting in the tin-roofed church, I heard the local church leaders using only Nepali language for scripture reading, songs, prayers and teaching. I noticed that most of the women (probably 75% of the congregation) sat in their places totally uncomprehending and not taking part in the worship. I became convinced of the urgency of using mother tongue instruction in literacy skills, especially for these women.

In the two weeks of training, I helped the local teachers write hymns and songs in Tamang and print sufficient copies on silk screen that each facilitator could have one to use in their classes. It thrilled me to see them begin immediately to teach these new hymns in the village church, and to see the now animated participation of the women. That response, along with the example of the simple faith of these mountain people, made the entire trip worthwhile.

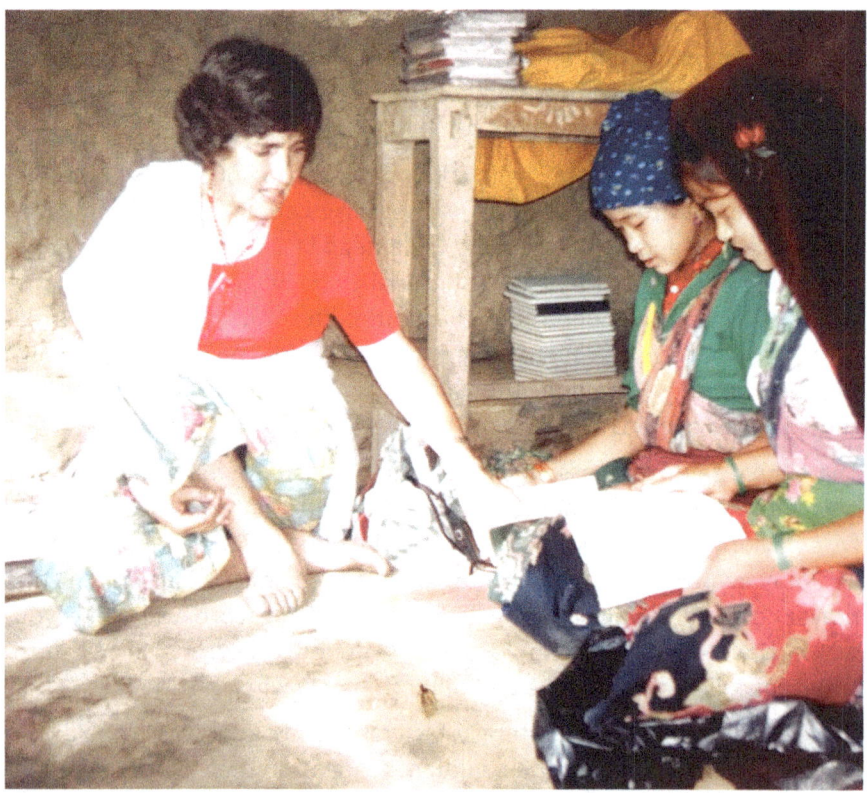

Helping Tamang women in Dhading read their own language

36 A full day

Today's trouble is enough for today. (Matthew 6:34)

Was it this morning, or was it yesterday, that a knock at the door woke me at 6.30 am? Putali, one of our class participants from nearby Harmi Kot, wanted a loan to pay off her dad's hospital bill so he could be discharged. She'll repay me next week when I collect the cloth purses (thailis) she has made to sell in tourist shops in Kathmandu. How I wish that all the requests for money that come my way were as easy to resolve as Putali's.

I gulp down a bowl of porridge and then head up the hill to our Non-Formal Education office. We are in a ten-day training program for 44 trainee facilitators for 22 new classes beginning next month after the busy rice planting season is over.

Ram Chandra is at the office when I arrive. He is the local church worker and has been running a voluntary devotional half hour before each day's training. This morning I'm thrilled to note that 12 of the 44 trainees, and all three of my Nepali NFE staff colleagues, are present. Ram Chandra sets us all thinking with some challenging questions about the Prodigal Son, a good non-formal approach to Bible study.

Today I have to take one of the training sessions. It is always a challenge to convince the staff that they do not need to be "teachers" standing up in front of a class, but that adult learners can discuss and teach one another in small groups. It really means treating people as adults who have lots of life experience and knowledge to share with one another.

After my session (hopefully, I demonstrated the participatory model) I make a few makeshift toys for the eight toddlers we have at the training this year. It's great that the mothers can teach in their villages, but a real challenge is to cope with the crying, crawling, grabbing wrigglers they bring with them to the training sessions! Mental note to self: "Next year we'll have to insist they bring their own babysitters."

Then down to the kitchen to help our kitchen helper to make 100 *chapatis* (flat bread) for lunch. We're making these with a "super flour" to show the Mums the benefits of this multi-mix flour of different grains. After lunch we also show the women how to make porridge for their babies and toddlers from this same mix. It is a great sales pitch to see how eagerly the eight toddlers take to the sample porridge – the first time they have been quiet and happy all day.

Sessions end at 4 pm and we can have a staff meeting, sharing a cuppa after that. I'm just so thankful for the terrific NFE team God has brought together this year – Hal* with skills in forestry and fodder grasses, Giri* in animal husbandry, and the new supervisor, Ivan*, who has had 27 years' experience as an agricultural science teacher. All three men will pass on their skills to the follow-up groups of newly literate adults, to help them practically and in income generation.

My NFE colleagues, Ivan, Giri and Hal, after a staff meeting

From 7 pm I walk 45 minutes to the relatively nearby village of Patlepani to see the new trainees in their practice teaching sessions. For two hours I watch in disappointment as the new trainees stand awkwardly in front of the local ladies, totally unsure of how to discuss the topical introductions that we'd practised in the afternoon. One seems to be unaware of what to do with the key reading word for the lesson, with no idea of how to discuss the word in their cultural life or of how to explain its visual representation in print. It seems our training strategies haven't impacted these ladies at all. What to do?

But then the host class of Patlepani takes over! They share how the literacy classes have helped them over the year that they've already been functioning. One lady tells how she feels she's come out of darkness into light. Several others express their appreciation for the classes held in their village. Another quoted from a well-known proverb – originally, she likewise couldn't distinguish a letter on the page from a black buffalo, but now she can read those marks on paper! Rudra, the director of the Community Health Project under which our classes function, is currently back home in Patlepani from Leeds University and he tells the class how thrilled he was to receive in England the first letter his wife had ever written. I am at last beginning to feel encouraged again!

As I climb back up the hill to home round midnight, Padam, a new trainee facilitator and a keen Christian from Thalajung, walks with me. He tells me he thanks God for giving him the opportunity to serve his community as a teacher, and thus to provide a bridge of trust and love that he has not previously had in his village.

I fall into bed, exhausted but encouraged!

37 Writing Gurung – again!

But, my child, let me give you some further advice: be careful, for writing books is endless and much study wears you out. (Ecclesiastes 12:12)

In the late 1960s we developed a writing system for Gurung, with lots of input from Gurung literates who had already learned to read in Nepali. The 1982 Western Gurung New Testament made some slight changes in the writing system, and it proved easy for Western speakers to read.

Some 24 years after my trial literacy class with Gurung ladies in Ghachok, I could include six Gurung-medium classes in the Gorkha Non-Formal Education (NFE) Project. 1 January 1992 marked a bright spot for us personally – the beginning of a teacher training seminar for 12 folk representing six Gurung villages. This venture marked a historic moment in non-formal education (NFE) in Nepal. The first time, to our knowledge, that a tribal vernacular language was the medium of instruction in a formal literacy program.

Since there were no previously written teaching materials, it was a case of do-it-yourself (DIY), with the participants writing their own stories and teaching materials. Like most Nepalis, Gurungs love folk singing and dancing, so we used that as the core teaching component. Learning to read by reading songs is an application of the "learning to read by reading" approach that many educationalists support.

The two weeks were incredibly busy. We needed to type and print assignments for the following day's teaching session. We found too that the weak winter sunlight was not really adequate to keep the solar-powered equipment functioning, so often the computer and/or printer malfunctioned. However, even these dark moments of stress could not dim the excitement we felt in seeing 12 eager folk turn up each morning for the voluntary devotional slot when we taught them some simple Gurung choruses and introduced them to the story of the birth of Christ from Dr Luke's report. Warren was particularly encouraged by the 95% acceptance of the draft he'd adapted by a computer program (CARLA) from the Western Gurung base text of 10 years earlier. There were still a

A trainee teacher, Cini Maya's Dad, and a chart of a song he wrote

few vocabulary items to be changed before he could feel confident to run off the whole Gospel.

In those two weeks, the participants wrote about 20 short first-person local incident stories and from these we developed simple readers. They had prepared enough material to begin classes back home. About two weeks later, the classes held their official opening programs, and Warren and I could trek around to their villages for the events. Imagine my amazement to find that in one particular village, they had chosen one of the Christian choruses as their class song!!

Come, come, brothers and sisters of the world!
Jesus is calling for you.
Your dwelling place is not really in this world.
Your purpose in life is not in this world.
To give you a kingdom Jesus is calling you.

As we had lived in a Gurung village ourselves without electricity or running water, the very basic nature of these village "classrooms" did not surprise us. Frequently, they were barns cleaned out for the classes to use each night. The barns were open-sided, and cold in midwinter in the Nepali hills with breezes finding easy access. But the events had warmth and vitality with 20 or so participants plus all the hangers-on keen to watch this new village entertainment. The brightly lit village Petromax kerosene pressure lamp made it easier for the learners to see their bazaar-bought blackboard.

A month later, we called the teachers together again. This time we met in one of the Gurung villages. One of the trainee teachers, Cini Maya, absolutely amazed me when she turned up with her week-old baby

New teacher, Cini Maya, with her dad (a teacher in another village), her baby and a girl for babysitting!

Printing materials by silk screen

Silk screened primer covers

daughter. Culturally, a newly delivered mother should remain cloistered in her home for four weeks to ensure her cleansing from the perceived spiritual defilements of childbirth. However, for Cini Maya this new experience had been so life changing that she didn't want to miss out. So, with her husband's and parents' approval, she ventured forth for the second training. Her dad, a teacher for another village, was also present, and she brought another girl to babysit if necessary.

During that training they wrote more stories and added more lessons into their resource folders. They also learned to use a silk screen for duplicating their work. They silk-screened the new lessons and designed a colourful cover for their books entitled "The Way for Opening our Eyes".

Twelve facilitators received certificates as trained teachers and returned home with enough resources to complete a four to five month basic literacy course for their fellow villagers. Amongst these happy trekkers was Cini Maya, carrying her baby on her back wrapped up in a shawl and her new teacher's manual tucked into her shoulder bag.

Another eight years later, in late 2000, Tamu Bauddha Sewa Samiti (TBSS), a Kathmandu-based Gurung ethnic society, approached Warren. Two Gurung scholars had collected data, representing their own dialects, and asked TBSS to publish their dictionaries. Warren's job was to edit the two manuscripts into one publication. He worked with a skilled Gurung co-editor, using the same writing system as before. They added the roughly 3,000 words from our Ghachok dictionary (Glover, Glover, and Gurung, 1977) – a western Gurung dialect – plus data from our time in Amp Pipal (an eastern dialect). TBSS published the resultant Gurung-Nepali-English Dictionary in 2003 and distributed it mostly among Gurungs resident in Kathmandu.

But more changes were to come! A disadvantage of our Gurung writing system from a linguistic point of view was that it used unnecessary symbols for each of the two high vowels (/i/ and /u/). The traditional long and short written forms for each vowel do not represent any sound contrast in either Nepali or Gurung, but most literate Gurungs prefer to use both forms of the two vowels since Nepali uses both symbols, and so to them it looks right aesthetically.

50 years after our start in Ghachok, in 2017 two Nepali NGOs (MTCN and HIS Nepal) worked together with Nepali linguists and Gurung scholars and community leaders to devise and promote an orthography for the Gurung language – again! After a final consultation in September 2019, MTCN published a spelling guide for the Gurung language. The resultant orthography was, thankfully, consistent with that used in previous publications, except that they insisted on using only one form for each of the two high vowels. It is ideal to have only one symbol for one sound, and so the decision to avoid over-representation is linguistically good.

The Gurung community leaders accepted the MTCN spelling guide, and so we had to revise the spelling in the Gurung mini-Bible to be published in February 2020. The translation team leader accepted the decision, but it was not welcome to the main translator, nor to Warren as the editor. At the last minute, he had to make massive regular changes throughout the Gurung Bible, with many exceptional cases to be protected from change, before submitting it to the printer! But will that really be the last word on writing the Gurung language? We now know that there are several quite different and competing writing systems for Gurung being promoted, some of them in different parts of the country, and in different countries. More endless study for the writing of Gurung?

PART 8 The family joins the journey

38 The visiting Scottish doctor

The Lord always keeps his promises. He is gracious in all he does. (Psalm 145.13b)

It was November 1991. Our daughter Merryn was flying into Kathmandu, en route back to Woodstock. The school had invited her to join the English department for a semester to fill in for a teacher who was on home leave. The semester didn't begin till February and she came early in order to spend some months with us at in the Gorkha project en route to India. Her November flight also avoided the Christmas spike in fares.

We needed to go to Kathmandu to meet her and bring her back to Amp Pipal. "While you're there, could you meet up with a Dr Alistair Appleby and welcome him? He's coming just for six months," asked our Gorkha project director as we left. "Just give him some idea of how to get out to the project, and assure him that if he wants to do his intensive Nepali study there in Kathmandu, or out here in the project, either is OK by us."

So, after the joyful, and tearful, reunion with Merryn (after typical Glover confusion over where we would actually meet her!), we settled into the mission guest house at Pulchowk while Warren went down to meet Dr Appleby at the Thapathali guest house. We both had the impression that this Scottish doctor was a dour, pipe-smoking, grey-haired retiree willing to fill a short-term need in Nepal. He was not at the expected place (another rendezvous foul up!), so Warren left a note, inviting him to join us for dinner at Pulchowk that evening and alerting him that we were returning to Gorkha next morning.

Nobody turned up at dinnertime, so we went ahead with the meal with other mission friends. We were just finishing a lovely dinner when there was a knock at the door. Imagine our surprise on seeing the young, athletic, handsome Dr Appleby on the doorstep! We warmly invited him to take the vacant chair awaiting him at the table as the group shared some of their hopes for the coming year. In Dr Appleby's turn, he said something about expecting that 1992 would be a memorable year for him. Looking at Merryn across the crowded room, did he have an inkling of just how memorable 1992 might be?

He quickly decided to do his Nepali intensive study out in Amp Pipal and arranged to join the team in time for the pre-Christmas potluck dinner. For that occasion, Merryn was putting out the place cards for the meal, and I noticed that hers and Alistair's were at the same table – strange!

There was a New Year's picnic up at the guest house where we'd first met Dr Ian Smith and been invited to join the Gorkha team. The winter snows of the central Himalayas were clearly visible from the lawn in front of the guest house, resplendent in the warm sunshine, and seeming to tower over the middle hills. (At Amp Pipal we were at about 1000 metres in altitude and looked up to the Manasulu Himal which reached 8163 metres!)

We decided we could all learn some Scottish reels after the meal. Merryn had already learned some during her dance and drama course at Rusden College. So she and Alistair, along with another two UK staff members, taught us all how to prance around with some level of fun if not of competence. The chemistry between Merryn and Alastair was obvious to all.

At the completion of Alastair's six-month locum in our Gorkha project hospital I farewelled him with the following affirmation, "Alastair, I feel God has gifted you with an incredible ability to mimic people's speech and to learn languages. You are what we call a language soak. Keep that in mind when thinking about what and where God may want you to serve him in the future." It was probably obvious to Alistair that I hoped he would move towards cross-cultural mission in the years ahead.

In June 1992 Merryn completed her semester of teaching at Woodstock, including directing a marvellous outdoor performance of *Midsummer Night's Dream*, and Alistair finished his six months in the Gorkha project. They arranged to meet again in the UK, and there they worked through the complications of a cross-continental life journey. They married 26 March 1994 at Kangaroo Ground. At the wedding reception on the lawns there, once again they led the guests in a few Scottish folk dances.

We had little expectation then of seeing them back in Nepal again, but of course we rather hoped so.

Al & Merryn's wedding at Kangaroo Ground, 26 March 1994

39 Mark and Jenika journey together

Your children will be like vigorous young olive trees as they sit around your table. (Psalm 128.3)

When Mark visited us in Amp Pipal in 1992 I took the risk of asking, "Any special ladies in your life yet?" He responded in the negative. So imagine our surprise and pleasure when, soon after his return to Australia, he emailed us, "When you get home I'm looking forward to introducing you to a special lady who I hope to spend the rest of my life with."

We were delighted to meet Jenika and enjoy a meal at her home when we were on leave in Australia later that year. Mark wanted to bring her back to India and Nepal to show her his roots and the places where he had spent most of his life. Jenika says it was just as well they were already engaged when this trip took place in October 1993, as their encounters along that journey left much to be desired, but much to be remembered for the rest of her life:

- The long overnight flight into hot, oppressive Delhi at midnight
- The crazy horn-blowing taxi driver that careered through the streets taking them to the Old Delhi railway station
- The hot steamy railway waiting room where Mark insisted they needed to rest ALL DAY until the 10.30 pm train departure for Dehra Dun. She still wonders why they couldn't have used the time to do some interesting touristy things around Delhi, including finding some A/C restaurants or shopping malls. Mark's only plea is that they were totally exhausted from the plane trip and needed to just rest! He hadn't discovered yet that he was engaged to a travel-phile who delights in sightseeing and exploring in any unfamiliar country. Sitting around doing nothing in such situations is anathema to Jen.
- While they were visiting the Woodstock School campus, they came across an accident scene on the hillside. A student had just fallen down the roadside cliff to his death. A very sobering and sad experience, which reinforced for her the risks involved in living in a developing country.

- On their arrival at our Gorkha project in Nepal, my staff wanted to celebrate their engagement with a huge party and invited all the staff and their friends. (Of course, neither Jenika nor Mark knew any of them.) They flooded the enormous platters of rice with a mutton curry that included not just the meat, cooked in a huge vat of oil, but the attendant furry skin, bits of bone and hoof, and dear knows what else. After trying to stomach this meal, Mark and Jen had to join in the dancing – inevitably a part of any Nepali celebration. I'd lent Jenika a sari, the blouse of which was far too big for her, and the outfit unsuitable for trying Nepali dances she'd never seen before.

Mark was very fortunate that she still said, "Yes", to their life together, probably in Nepal.

One bonus of the trip was an invitation to join us in a missionary retreat for CMS Australia folk serving in Nepal. David Claydon, one of my old friends from Sydney League of Youth days and now Federal Secretary of CMS Australia, was the main facilitator of the weekend, and he was quick to assure Mark and Jen that if they wished to work in Nepal, they would be very welcome to serve under the CMS umbrella.

They married 26 February 1994 at Community Church of St Mark, Clifton Hill, and applied to CMS for service in Nepal. With Jenika's experience as a nurse, and Mark's as a civil engineer, CMS accepted them for service with the United Mission to Nepal (UMN), as we had been four years earlier. Their first child Rebekah (Bekka) was born during their CMS orientation at St Andrew's Hall in 1995. They arrived in Nepal in January 1996. During their nearly 12 years of service with UMN, they served in their respective professional roles.

For Mark that included building Nepali engineering expertise, including in the construction of dams for hydroelectricity projects and irrigation. This development was an obvious need, since power outages of increasing length were part and parcel of life in Nepal. We all had to ensure that computer batteries got charged during the ON hours and to juggle other work during the OFF hours. The makers of candles and various kinds of kerosene lamps were thriving! Thankfully, a weekly load shedding schedule of ON/OFF hours was available in the local newspapers. The huge potential for hydro projects in the multitudinous gorges and fast running rivers augured well for the end of such power outages. Government and people valued UMN's commitment to the country, and to training a growing cadre of national engineers. Sadly, lack of political will and bureaucratic integrity meant few projects came to successful implementation.

Mark also served in UMN administration and drew on his experience there and with Nepali engineering companies for case studies and research for his Masters of Business Administration.

Although Jenika was the "unassigned spouse" in the UMN system, she was very active not only as the primary caregiver for their four children but also in women's empowerment activities, working with the leader of the Nepal YMCA. She supported the first Nepal hospice, trained the Nepal palliative care team in providing home-based care, and also worked in a vaccination clinic.

In the early days of firming up their CMS assignment none of us had any inkling that for much of Mark and Jen's Nepal experience, the three branches of the Glover family tree would be all living in Kathmandu, within easy walking distance of one another. What a contrast with the family separations of previous decades when Mark and Merryn were in boarding school, thousands of miles away from us!

40 A fresh challenge!

Be strong and courageous! Do not be afraid or discouraged. For the LORD your God is with you wherever you go. (Joshua 1.9)

It was February 1995. Warren and I were teaching once again at the SPSIL summer training course at Kangaroo Ground.

We were enjoying a cool evening out on the shaded patio of our Ringwood home after a hot, busy day. That morning I had noticed a letter in our mailbox from our field Executive Committee chair, Clare O'Leary, offering nomination for election as the next director of our SIL work in South Asia. I took this quiet moment to discuss the matter.

"How do you feel, Warren, about Clare's request for you to consider nomination as field director?"

"That letter wasn't addressed to me. It's you they're asking," came his instant response.

The peace of the cool summer evening shattered. "Me! Why me? I've never served in any administrative positions on the field, nor been a delegate at an area or international conference." (Those are all valuable preparatory experiences for potential directors.) Maybe they just need an extra name on the ballot, I thought.

Warren and I had both been looking forward to returning to our consulting and teaching roles back in South Asia. But director? It was a completely new and confronting idea. The ensuing weeks found us both doing a lot of soul searching. Was this God's next challenge for us? Or not? I have never seen myself as an up-front leader, but as one who facilitates others in doing their work. However, Warren (a "female chauvinist" from way back) was enthusiastic and encouraging as ever. (I only found out much later that he had actually dobbed me in. He had suggested my name when Clare asked his advice on nominations!) And I had to acknowledge there were positive indicators:

- The field committee's confidence in making the request.

- My varied and extensive experience in South Asia with heavy administrative responsibility in UMN's Community Health Programme in Gorkha district.

- My freedom from family commitments to our children's education. They were now married to wonderful people and pursuing their own walks of discipleship.

- I still had a reasonable reserve of energy and health.

After prayer and much thought, I wrote to Clare accepting nomination given that:

- I saw the role of director as being a servant to all members, helping each one fulfil God's purpose and plan for them in South Asia.

- I saw no scriptural prohibition of women from fulfilling that kind of servant leadership.

- Warren and I work as a team. I would only consider taking on the responsibility with the full cooperation, support and partnership of my husband, though we would have separate and distinct job descriptions.

- I would seek to be resident in South Asia to carry out my duties there. (Previous directors of the group had been resident offshore, visiting South Asia regularly, but some members found the lack of on-site leadership affecting their morale.)

In December 1995, the South Asia Group (SAG) conference elected me director and I took office in October 1996. I believe my intention to live in South Asia was a significant factor in the members' decision.

My job as SAG director was not only a 100% time commitment while in Nepal but also called for regular visits to the other parts of South Asia where our members worked and also back to the SAG head office in England. For security reasons, and the difficulty of getting visas for South Asia, previous directors had established the SAG office in England, and that office still had several staff and important administrative functions, including recruitment from the students at the British SIL training school.

But how was I to get a visa for residence in Nepal or India? SIL's presence in Nepal was no longer official after the 1976 banishment. All our members had to find individual visa routes for residence in the country. Several had research visas through our still friendly university; others got visas through getting jobs with NGOs who served in rural areas. But in each case fulfilling their employer's work expectations consumed much of their time and so left only limited opportunity to work on their language and translation goals. Often, though, the spouse of a visa-holder could get a spouse visa and take primary responsibility for the translation work.

Warren's support became vital. If he could get a visa, then I could tag along as his spouse, with no commitment to the employer. (Similarly, I had held the visa post in our time in the UMN Gorkha project, leaving Warren free on a spouse visa to work on the Eastern Gurung translation.) Thankfully, a friend knew of an opening for a linguist with the Royal Nepal Academy (RNA) and took Warren to meet the director of a large dictionary project, funded through the Indian Embassy in Kathmandu. RNA secured a residential visa for him to work as a computer consultant on the project and thus got a spouse visa for me. My getting a visa through Warren's work with RNA was a confirmation of the Lord's green light for this fresh challenge. A poem by Eddie Askew, former General Director of The Leprosy Mission, struck me as very relevant.

> Lord, turn my mind around,
> Help me to realise that what I see
> As never-ending quest, a constant learning,
> Is not a threat, but an adventure, lived with you.
> Help me to understand that the infinity that beckons me
> Is an infinity of love.
>
> And as I take the road afresh, each day,
> I'm not sure where it leads, or where I'm going,
> But I'm going there with you. And that's enough.
>
> *No Strange Land* (Eddie Askew 1987:71).

41 "An infinity of love"

See how very much our Father loves us, for he calls us his children, and that is what we are! (1 John 3:1)

Kathmandu, Nepal, November 1998. I babysat the children to allow Mark and Jen to attend the funeral of a dear friend. During one of our play activities, 3½ year old Rebekah asked, "Did you know, Nana, that today is a very sad day?"

"Why is that, Rebekah?"

"Well, Richard's funeral is today. Mummy and Daddy are very sad."

"Yes, that's right. But you know this is also a happy day too," I ventured, thinking this might be a wonderful moment to share the truths of Richard's ongoing life with Jesus even after his death.

Rebekah sat pensive for a while, obviously racking her brain for some happy thought to brighten her day. Then her face lit up. "Oh yes, our pussy cat has just had kittens and they are in our store shed!" I gave up on the theology lesson for that day.

This little family interlude was just one of the many loving exchanges we could enjoy by choosing to base in Kathmandu while I was director of the South Asia Group of SIL (SAG). Painting interludes and sleepovers with the grandchildren were particularly memorable. For most of my five years in that position (from October 1996), we were blessed to have both of our children, with their spouses and children, living close to us – "an infinity of love" as Eddie Askew had written.

Mark and Jen arrived in Kathmandu, with ten-month-old Rebekah, in January 1996, to serve under UMN. During their time in Nepal they added three more children to their family – Joshua (December 1996), Sarah (March 2000), and Rachel (August 2005). Their formative years in Nepal shaped the concerns of all four children about the inequalities of life in the developing world and awareness of how significantly NGO advocacy and support could help facilitate change.

Like Mark and Jen, our daughter Merryn and her husband Alistair came to serve in Nepal – for a longer period of service than the six-month fill-in which brought Alistair to Amp Pipal in 1992 for their original meeting. They arrived in Kathmandu as a couple in January 1997 for a two-year assignment, Alistair as a GP in UMN's Patan Hospital in Kathmandu, and Merryn as an English teacher in an international school there. After extending their service for a further two years, they returned to Scotland in July 2001.

And so it was that even though we were separated by thousands of miles from our kids during their high school years in India, the Lord had kindly and lovingly led us all back to Nepal – to serve Him and the peoples of Nepal in the "spirit and name of Christ" (one of the key phrases in the UMN mission statement). Mark and Jen and family lived just 900 metres from our house in Bakhundol, Merryn and Al lived even closer. It seemed our lives had come full circle.

Alistair served in the Accident and Emergency department of Patan hospital, in Kathmandu. In that role, he set up and trained the staff in triage regimes to handle emergency cases.

Just a few weeks later, in August 1998, during our daily swim in a nearby hotel, Warren cut short the swim and sat breathless by the pool. When I climbed out, I realised he was grey and clammy to the touch! Heart attack? Help! Where was I going to find a taxi to get him to the hospital? It was quite a search, till I found one 500 metres away at another hotel. Arriving at the hospital, Warren proved how well the staff had absorbed Alistair's training! They responded quickly and even sent their head of Pharmacy out around the Kathmandu chemist shops to find the clot-smashing drug streptokinase. For maximum effectiveness, it needed to be administered within three hours of the attack, and there was none in the hospital's pharmacy store. The timely supply of the drug was a significant factor in Warren's full recovery.

Only weeks before, Merryn was claiming the prize of needing family coddling when she came down with hepatitis. Her Dad's heart attack seemed to eclipse the sympathy focus she'd been enjoying. Thankfully, she also recovered and was back to her English classes after ten weeks of rest and recovery.

Our proximity in Kathmandu meant that Merryn and Al felt the time was right to address some negative consequences of the boarding school experience. The minister of the Kathmandu international church, Neil Hall, and his wife Rosalie proved sensitive moderators of the family discussions. We came to understand some of the long-term painful effects of separations and geographical distance in those boarding school years. Rather a painful process, but ultimately a healing one for which we are very thankful.

Another of Eddie Askew's poems seemed to resonate with us during these years:

Lord, you are the still centre of every storm.
In you is calm, whatever the wind outside.
In you is reassurance, however high the waves.
In you is strength, however contrary the tide.
Many voices, one voice (Eddie Askew 1985:29).

Several years later, as Warren and I approached our 40th wedding anniversary, 28 November 2004, we brought forward a celebration to early October. Jenika and Mark were still living and working in Kathmandu. They offered their lovely garden as the venue for an afternoon tea with our friends, mission colleagues and our wedding attendants from 40 years before – Pam Rendell, my lifelong friend from Wagga Teachers' College days, and Warren's mate from Wollongong (and Wycliffe India), Ray Christmas. The Appleby family came from Scotland for this special event, bringing with them a cake beautifully iced for the occasion and two albums of greetings and cards that Merryn had secretly elicited from our wide circle of family and friends.

At the end of September, the annual monsoon was still hanging around the valley. Daily downpours had no intention of stopping imminently. Should we order a large marquee for the occasion? What was the forecast? Fine days were predicted, so we took the risk and went ahead, wet soggy lawns notwithstanding.

Eight-year-old Rebekah marshalled her siblings and the Scottish cousins to sing a little ditty she'd written to the tune of "Jesus loves me".

NANA LOVES GRANDPA AND HE LOVES HER, THEY'VE BEEN MARRIED FOR FOURTY YEARS, FIRST CAME MARK THEN MERRYN TOO, AND NOW YOUR GRANDKIDS SING TO YOU.

Yes, indeed, an "infinity of love"! But what about the "never-ending quest" and the "constant learning" that Eddie Askew's poem also alluded to?

42 The "never-ending quest"

Come to me, all of you who are weary and carry heavy burdens, and I will give you rest. **(Matthew 11:28)**

My role as director of SAG often felt like the "never-ending Quest" of Eddie Askew's poem:

Happily passing over some of the burden to Linda Proudlove, my rescuer!

The *quest* to keep my email IN box down to just what I could see on the screen, with nothing below. I RARELY achieved that. Often there were 300 mails a week. Two or three folk stepped in from time to time as my personal assistant, which eased the stress. I was VERY thankful for their skill and support – and especially for Linda Proudlove. She came to Nepal with husband Barry on a long-term assignment to be my PA and took over the management of the email deluge – helping to prioritize how we should handle the various messages. Many emails came from the 18 Wycliffe home offices of our multinational team.

The *quest* to keep these home offices worldwide assured of the safety and security of their members in South Asia. The region is frequently blighted with civil wars, earthquakes and other natural disasters, train crashes and populist revolutions, so communication to reassure home offices was a top priority. We RARELY achieved that quest either. (These days we appoint a Field Security Officer to handle that job full time – and during the current COVID-19 pandemic it must be of particular pressure.)

The *quest* for a work-life balance when I had minimal office support. Warren was very overloaded in his efforts to support me. He was working at the Royal Nepal Academy to get my spouse visa and also as finance manager – not only for the entire group but also for me person-ally in fulfilment of his promise years before, "I'll be your treasurer." No doubt the accumulating pressure contributed to his 1998 heart attack. In addition, we had our two children and, by mid-2000, four grandchildren in Kathmandu, with whom we wanted to spend time regularly. It was challenging because all of us were busy with full-time work or parenting, or both. I'm still not sure how successful we were in the quest for work-life balance. Two things were very important to help us in the search – a daily devotional with our soul friend and housemate Mary Morgan, and taking regular "Sabbath weekends". Every seventh week we got away from the office (which was the front room of our Bakhundol apartment!) and went to a mission guest house well outside the city for R and R. Over the years we have continued to prioritize Sabbath weekends into our otherwise tight schedules, though now only three or four a year, COVID permitting!

The *quest* to plan and book a workable itinerary. I needed to visit each of the three major countries where our SAG members worked. My dear husband's skill, attention to detail, and tenacity achieved that goal. Remember that he is a train-phile, and he maximised my use of trains in India, to tot up my kilometres of train travel for the Guinness Book of Records! Not to mention the dozens of hours spent on aeroplanes and waiting in airports. Another excerpt from Merryn's poem, "My Mother's Hands", reflected on life as an administrator at this time:

My mother's hands are quick now,
on computer keyboards,
briefcase buckles,
telephone buttons,
and appointment diaries.

She handles the business of today as deftly
As she fed clothes through her
own mother's mangle,
and threw fistfuls of seed
to the backyard chooks.

The most challenging *quest* was to build trust and cooperation amongst our many national partner agencies. We worked together toward the goal set at the June 1999 SIL International conference: "We embrace the vision that by the year 2025, a Bible translation project will be in progress for every people group that needs it."

The vision statement elaborated, "Our desire is to build capacity for sustainable Bible translation programs and scripture-use activities. Therefore, we urge each entity within the family of organisations to give priority to strengthening present partnerships, forming additional strategic partnerships, and working together to develop creative approaches appropriate to each context."

At the conference, Warren commented to the Wycliffe Australia director, Kirk Franklin, that we in SAG had been operating in India that way for over two decades. In 1980 we'd helped birth the national Bible translation movement (IICCC) which had already trained scores of translators and literacy personnel. Kirk immediately asked him to write up the history to help in recruitment of new Australian members. They would need to embrace this vision of partnership when joining Wycliffe. Warren spent our next home leave writing *Making a difference: training Bible translators in India* (Wycliffe Bible Translators Australia, 2002). I've quoted from this book in several chapters already.

In all South Asian contexts, we wanted to work with other missions and Bible agencies, who shared a vision to bring the Gospel to previously unreached people groups. Warren's book lists some of these partners:

- *Indian Institute for Cross Cultural Communication* (now Wycliffe India), in training translators and literacy specialists.
- *Indian Evangelical Mission* (IEM) and *Friends Missionary Prayer Band* (FMPB), as major Indian missions working in church planting and holistic mission including Bible translation.
- *New Life Computer Institute* (NLCI), in technical support and innovation (especially in computing and linguistic survey) as well as translation.
- *Serampore College*, a premium theological training college in India, with whom we sought to develop a Masters degree in Bible Translation, and basic training for mother tongue translators.
- *The Association for Theological Education by Extension* (TAFTEE), in enabling senior translators to get postgraduate degrees through the University of Wales.

In May 2001 I wrote to our prayer team about working with partners, "Along with the excitement comes the sobering realisation of the hard work involved in good communication – time spent together, not just in meetings, but also in getting to know one another and sensitively understanding the different cultural backgrounds from which we operate." On this topic Peter F Drucker wrote: "The most important thing in communication is to hear what *isn't* being said."

In Nepal, we were particularly happy to see people who themselves had worked on translating Scripture for their own language group found and lead groups for outreach to other languages. Such partners included the Nepal National Language Preservation Institute (NNLPI), the Mother Tongue Centre Nepal (MTCN), the Mother Tongue Translation Society, and the Himalayan Indigenous Society (HIS Nepal).

Our original partner in Nepal (1966–76) had been of course Tribhuvan University, and out of that partnership had developed the Central Department of Linguistics of Tribhuvan University (CDL). Long after the formal agreement of cooperation ended in 1976 CDL continued as an important partner, sponsoring the research visas of a number of our members and facilitating events such as the annual meetings of the Nepal Linguistic Society.

Over the years, despite increased complexity of relationships and cultural needs, these partnerships are still growing and bearing fruit. The number of people groups in South Asia still lacking language development and a Bible translation project is now greatly reduced. Many language communities have received the New Testament, and work toward completion of the whole Bible is progressing in some of them .

With a population around forty times that of Nepal, hundreds of different languages, and huge geographical and cultural diversity, India is a complex challenge for the Bible translation movement. I needed to appoint an India Training coordinator to make a priority of building trust relationships with Indian leaders in order to forward the training of Bible translators, literacy personnel, and linguistic surveyors. They were working in communities all across north and south India. But North East India is very different, and the linguistic and cultural diversity in those states (the "Seven Sisters") required a separate SAG coordinator to build partnerships there.

Working with a different set of partners to address the complex language development needs in North East India would consume much of my energy and attention over the following fifteen years of my South Asia journey (2003–17), beyond my term as field director.

PART 9 Retirement triathlon

43 Re-entry

Now that I am old and grey, do not abandon me, O God. (Psalm 71:18)

"You mean I need to pay $8 fee for cashing my travellers' cheques and US dollars?"

"Why did you send our VISA cards to the Collins St branch in Melbourne when we'd phoned three times from UK and India requesting you send them to the Sydney address we gave you? Now I have no easy way to access money while here in Sydney."

"Jenika, I can't get this borrowed car to work. I think the battery has gone flat. I need to get out to the airport right away to meet Warren. What should I do?"

These were just a few of the challenges I faced in my first weeks back in Australia in October 2005. Later dramas related more to the restoration of a very neglected house and garden at #31 Oban Road, and dealing with the takeover of fences and trees by climbing ivy and wandering jew. I don't know how we could have coped without the help of Mark and Jen, particularly in that first week, and several Wycliffe angels who visited weekly to help with garden and house restoration. Thanks, Roy and Janet!

Re-entry apprehensions might have delayed our decision to retire. But in 2005 we both qualified for the Australian Age pension and Warren had increased pain and discomfort from ill functioning knees. His knees had first experienced serious stress in 1967. He and another young Wycliffe colleague walked five days in eastern Nepal seeking a place for them to live and work among the Sherpa people. On their return journey they ran down Himalayan mountains in hopes of reuniting with their Kathmandu based wives perhaps a day earlier than planned. A very unwise decision. Subsequent treks for language surveys and visits to Ghachok and throughout Gurung territory exacerbated his problem. The time had now come for surgical intervention.

Roy and Janet Gwyther-Jones attacking the Ringwood wilderness!

We had visited Australia in 2003 to consult a top knee surgeon. We'd barely walked three paces into his office and Mr Bartlett said, "Those knees will last another four to five years, but you'll need to do something about that right hip within a couple of years." What! Warren had no idea he had a hip problem. "I don't do hips," he said, "and I'll recommend another surgeon for you. Meanwhile, if you use a walking stick in your left hand it will take at least 20% of the load off the right hip."

The hip operation two years later was successful. As also one on the left knee some time later. We were very grateful for their expertise and the steady work of post op rehabilitation teams. Then, because of ongoing requests for consultant help we negotiated a retirement plan with our Wycliffe home staff and our South Asia administration to include three months a year back in South Asia.

Colleen Humphreys' little ditty, penned at the time of our 40th wedding anniversary in October 2004, foreshadowed our likely retirement scenarios.

Our Darling Gypsy Friends

Where in the world are the Glovers?
What's happened to Warren and Jess?
Just stick a pin in the atlas
And the answer is right, more or less.

They travel the world with 'No worries!'
They pack travelling bags with such flare.
Their passports are stamped full of countries.
Mention a town – they've been there.

They now and then mention the R word,
They talk about settling down.
But children in Asia and Scotland
Will draw them to more flying around.

I don't think we'll see them in Ringwood,
These gypsies will be on the roam.
The travelling is now such a habit,
The airport's their natural home.

FF points must be quite record breaking.
They've earned them, they sure have the knack.
To use them they'll celebrate 50
By flying to Venus and back."

Our August 2007 letter to our faithful prayer team read:

Retired? Retreaded? Reduced Assignment? Repaired?

No doubt you have heard people in retirement say, "I don't know how I had time to go to work." We have rather struggled with the dreaded R word and wondered what label is appropriate for us at this point of our pilgrimage. Semi-retired? Or maybe Retreaded? A number of R words are filling our diaries and calendars so we leave you to draw your own conclusions.

Retooling

Right now, in Kangaroo Ground, I (WG) am in the middle of a two-week workshop on training trainers of translators – to use a fairly new textbook *Introductory Course in Communication and Translation*. A stimulating time of thinking, reading and discussion about recent developments in communication theory (under the title Relevance Theory, if you are familiar with the field). Training and mentoring younger colleagues continues to be an important part of my life.

Retreat Facilitation

Following on the training in leading *days of reflection and prayer* that we attended in Bangkok in February Jess has led a Half day of Prayer at Wycliffe Australian national centre in April and has been asked to lead another in early September. We will be helping to facilitate a similar workshop in Chiang Mai, Thailand, in late November.

Relieving Administrators

Our friend Erik Andvik, coordinator for North East India (NEI), requested a year's leave from administration in order to concentrate on the translation project he's been part of for many years. Since Jess knows the significant partners in NEI and has led workshops in Multi Lingual Education (MLE) she volunteered to relieve for part of his job. She will thus have the responsibility for *MLE and for Government and university liaison* for a year from 1 October. This will involve her in a few trips to NE India. Hopefully the sum total will not exceed our original reduced assignment intention of three months in South Asia per year. (But what about the email load?)

My NEI assignment in fact went on for much longer than the one-year relief requested by Erik.

44 The "constant learning"

Learn to use good judgement. (Proverbs 9:6)

In 2002, Erik Andvik, SAG's coordinator in North East India (NEI), had asked me to go with him to Guwahati, in Assam state, to meet with some key potential partners. With them we hoped to address the complex language situation there. Hundreds of minority language communities, all pleading for development of their own language or dialect, both for Bible translation and also for language development in schools and media.

Many people said these small minority languages would soon die out. "The next generation must develop fluency in the respective state, national, and international languages – Assamese, Hindi, and English." But would the languages of NEI really die? They'd been around for centuries already. Australian Baptists and Welsh Presbyterians had evangelised some of these groups in the early 20th century. For some of the larger languages, they had also translated some scripture and hymns. Strong indigenous churches had sprung up and thrived in these communities. More recent linguistic surveys had identified hundreds of languages in NEI, still unreached, or undocumented. These groups were knocking on the doors of Bible Society and educational institutions., pleading, "Come and help us."

Language loss and death is a burning issue around the world. There is a widespread trend for children of minority communities to give up using their parents' language in favour of whatever language the schools and the wider community use, the Language of Wider Communication (LWC). Not only do they give up using it, but they also come to disparage their mother tongue as tribal or inferior. But often the children do not have a full command of the LWC and so fail in school and become dropouts, under-qualified for any employment.

We have seen generations of children caught between these two worlds, neither valuing their own culture nor succeeding in the outsiders' language and culture. Experience in the world of Wycliffe, and increasingly in secular educational contexts, shows that children who learn to read and write initially in their mother tongue can more easily use the LWC as medium of instruction once they have experienced successful learning in their own languages. Hence the advantage of bilingual education. Governments that have adopted bilingual education policies include Australia for indigenous languages in the 1970s, PNG nationally in the 1990s, Mexico in the 1950s, Soviet Union in the 1930s and more recently the Philippines and India. Once the transition to the LWC as medium of instruction has taken place, the mother tongue component in the curriculum ideally continues up through sixth grade to continue language enrichment and use throughout the child's primary education.

In considering the call to NEI I was already pretty impassioned about the importance and value of multilingual education (MLE). I became increasingly convinced that a commitment to this work was a very important aspect of bringing justice to the oppressed and marginalised, a high calling for the people of God.

Building on my work in Nepal for women's literacy, I was glad to visit NEI in 2002 to meet with partners concerned about the disadvantages hundreds of minority group children faced in mainstream schooling. In Guwahati, Erik and I met Dr Barkataki, director of the **State Resource Centre**, and Dr Jyoti Tamuli, Head of the **Linguistic Department at Guwahati University**, and his wife Dr Anita Tamuli. They were keen to work in partnership with SIL. They knew us as a well-respected INGO committed to minority language documentation and development.

I wondered how the Tamulis had heard about SIL. "Oh," replied Jyoti with a broad smile, "when I was a PhD student at Deccan College in Poona in the 1970s, I got to attend a linguistic workshop led by Dr Kenneth Pike at the Central Institute of Indian Languages in Mysore. He recognised me as a struggling PhD student and daily took me for a walk in the relative cool of the evenings. He helped me process my linguistic thoughts and theories and to articulate and then write them down coherently. I will never forget his love and commitment to me. That is why I am keen to work alongside SIL personnel again."

Erik and I felt the smile of God, and thanked Him for His humble servant, Ken Pike. Ken was a world-renowned expert in tone languages and had helped us enormously in unravelling the pitch problems in languages of Nepal in 1969, eleven years before the workshops at CIIL which had so impacted Dr Tamuli.

Workshop on how to make a good alphabet with Gauhati University Department of Linguistics

Over the next 12 years, 2003–14, I gave much of my time to working with the State Resource Centre and the Linguistics Department of Gauhati University, and also a range of other partners who had similar commitments:

- *Don Bosco Communications Centre*: A Catholic publications department already publishing small primers and Christian catechisms for the communities they worked with. They had community networks of writers and leaders who came in goodly numbers to the first workshops we ran.

- *PAJHRA*: a social justice wing, birthed by Catholic activists, working primarily to uplift the oppressed tea plantation workers of Assam. They were already active amongst four communities and wanted to start a school for the largest group, Adivasiya (Sadri). Pajhra had the

With one of my protégés, Luke, who has now completed his PhD program

support of one of Dr Jyoti's linguistic students, Luke Horo, himself a Sadri speaker.

- *Singpho, Sema, Tangsa, Tai Phakey, Tai Khamyang, Tai Turung, Tai Khamti* and *Tai Aiton Development Council* communities amalgamated to facilitate language revival and development. The chairman of the council hosted workshops in his newly opened eco-lodge in Margaretta, upper Assam. In this idyllic lodge, modelled on tribal longhouses, I met with community representatives to help them plan their mother tongue program, write materials, and train teachers to use them in the schools. The program was further strengthened by the commitment of another of Dr Jyoti's linguistic students, Palash Nath, during his fieldwork.
- *Rabha Students Union (Dudhnoi)* facilitated a large writers' workshop to increase the number of titles available for children to read in the schools. Fifteen new titles in three days! Dr Jyoti had assigned yet another of his students, Subhash Rabha, to work with his own Rabha community.

Dr Tamuli routinely seconded his fourth-year linguistics students to work with me in the workshops and seminars that were needed to forward the multilingual education projects. They helped develop writing systems for unwritten languages, train writers, develop primers and motivate local communities to form village school management committees. The committees, comprising local leaders, were responsible to oversee and monitor the program at the local level. Dr Tamuli's students faithfully worked in these activities over many of the fifteen years I was privileged to be involved. And after graduation some were full time employed as staff by some of the NGOs listed above.

As encouraging as these non-formal developments were, Erik and I recognised that for change to be sustainable, we needed the Government educationalists also to commit to the MLE model. At a national level, the curriculum framework prescribed basic education in the mother tongue of the learner as foundational. It seemed a good basis for SIL to begin a dialogue with the Assamese state Dept of Education, and Erik and I regularly visited the leaders in the State Centre for Educational Research and Training (SCERT) and the Education Department of Assam.

Erik got an agreement from the person in charge of the Education Department to start a trial program among the Sadri, one of the larger linguistic communities who worked as bonded labourers on the tea plantations. The Department of Languages at Tezpur University would facilitate the program. I arranged a team of six international literacy consultants for a two-week workshop to produce materials and a curriculum for a kindergarten phase.

Just as I was about to leave Kathmandu for the workshop, Erik emailed me that the state government had pulled the plug on funding the workshop! It was "not included in their budget for that year"! Erik insisted we go ahead anyway – SIL would try to fit it into our budget to cover the Assamese Government's withdrawal. We consultants and over 20 teachers attended and worked nonstop for the two weeks. The teachers were excited to see their Sadri language honoured, respected and put in writing for the benefit of their children. Tribal dances by colourfully dressed women blessed the closing program, reminding us of the vibrant culture of the community.

That experience showed me how difficult it is to get partners to work together. Over the years, Erik and I continued to facilitate seminars to help different partners learn together the complexities of their situations, to hear how the mother tongue based multilingual education (MTB -MLE) model was being used in other countries such as the Philippines, and to recognise what they needed to make it work in their contexts too. We also funded several participants from the larger partner agencies to

Visiting discouraged Amri MLE teachers and supervisors

attend international conferences and seminars on MTB-MLE. They appreciated the stimulus and cross-fertilization of ideas gained at these events, but in most cases, they found it difficult to work together back on their home turf to implement the programs.

"It's easy to get good partners. Getting 'em to play together, that's the hard part." (Casey Stengel)

By the time of the last workshop for the newly established non-formal schools in July 2014, I could see that interest in these local informal programs was waning. Parents increasingly felt that there was no future for their children in using their mother tongue in school. "They need to become proficient in Assamese, Hindi and English to improve their status in the wider world." We couldn't argue with that, but tried to show them that the children would gain fluency in these languages of wider use better if they learnt first in the language they understood best. By 2014, our funding had ended, and I felt this would be my last visit. I packed my bags, stored all the archive copies of materials from 15 different language communities into a tin trunk, and left Guwahati wondering what my twice-yearly visits to the North East had actually achieved.

But there was yet more for me to learn in this mother tongue saga. Could the church once again have a role in promoting and using the mother tongue amongst these smaller communities? Western missionaries were now largely long gone from India. But the indigenous missionaries, many trained by the IICCC programs, had a strong conviction of how important the language of the heart was for the peoples they ministered to.

By 2016, SIL was increasingly working to encourage collaboration among all missions to achieve shared goals. The missions were now convinced of two realities. First, the Gospel message must be lived out in good works which would glorify our Father God's love and compassion for the people; and second, to achieve widespread impact in multilingual India, they needed to work together with other partners in the communities. Thus, one of our long-loved mission agencies Indian Evangelical Mission (IEM) agreed to be the chief facilitating agency for missions working with the churches of NEI. "Would SIL literacy consultants help train the local church leaders in these communities in preparing materials and teaching from them?" they asked. So SIL staff worked tirelessly to help form and strengthen collaborative outreach in mother tongue literacy.

In January–February 2017 I felt privileged to be part of the very first materials production workshop for about eight languages from Assam and a further eight from the neighbouring state of Tripura. What a contrast with the earlier work in NEI seeking to get several secular partners to work together! In our work with secular agencies, we needed to form local school management committees, and they did not function well. But now there was already in place an infrastructure, the local church, to facilitate the classes, and an IEM staff member to monitor and support the program. Sustainability built in right from the start.

It further encouraged me to see that one trainee from the Rabha team was Karuna, who had been one of the chief coordinators in the secular program just a year or two earlier. The smile on his face showed his confidence that *this* program would last. It did not surprise me, on a closer look, to see that the materials the Rabha team were developing in this workshop used English orthography, not the Assamese script we had used in the earlier program. Did this reflect the aspirations of the community? Maybe so, since the parents had told us before that they wanted an education that would open the gate to English competence for their children. (Memories from my very first literacy class in the Gurung village of Ghachok, some 50 years before, came flooding back.) And the use of English orthography was in harmony with the script used in the Catholic publications already in print. So the wider Christian community, whether Catholic or Protestant, would welcome them. I saw it as another smile from the Lord. Sustainability possible here too!

With Palash Nath and his wife at my NE India farewell

Recent reports from my University friends in the North East speak of some mother tongue medium schools continuing to function. Some of Dr Jyoti's students are currently working to document the growth and impact of the schools and one, Prafulla Basumatary, is writing up his PhD research on that topic. Encouraging glimpses of grace for these oft-neglected minority peoples of NEI.

But for myself, in 2017 I realised I needed to get back to Nepal to give my undivided attention to the burgeoning work amongst the Gurung people, to whom we had lost our hearts some 50 years before.

45 Some 50 years before!

It is the same with my Word; I send it out and it always produces fruit. It will accomplish all I want it to, and it will prosper everywhere I send it. (Isaiah 55:11)

We had first gone to live in a Gurung village in May 1967. The Western Gurung New Testament was published in 1982 after 15 years of slog: nine years living in the village of Ghachok where we learned the language and culture, followed by two more years, based in the city of Pokhara to bring the translation to completion. This process included all the village and consultant checks, a lot of work in editing in corrections on punched paper tape on a Flexowriter machine in Kathmandu, and

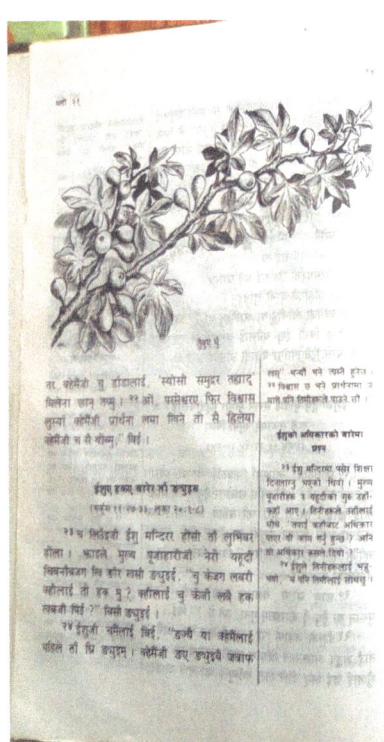

checking the consistency of spelling, parallel passages between the Gospels, and the use of key theological terms. Then Warren got a position as Visiting Scholar back in the Department of Linguistics at ANU for the year of 1979 and worked night shifts in the computer centre on more editing – rather a technological upgrade from the Flexowriter in Kathmandu!

*Matthew 21:21-24
in Gurung-Nepali diglot*

But if you're counting, that only makes 12 years! There was much more to come. Remember, "writing books is endless" (Ecclesiastes 12:12). We had to print the New Testament in the Devanagari script. Linguistically and aesthetically beautiful, but a tremendous challenge for SIL's Printing Arts Department in Dallas. The Gurung New Testament was #173 produced by Wycliffe, but the first in non-Roman script. The technical team there had to design fonts for each of the 56 letters in Devanagari needed for writing Gurung, and the many combinations of consonants that get written together. Finally, after two four-month stints in Dallas (August 1980 to June 1981) for Warren to work with the Printing Arts team, he carried the precious typeset document back to Ambassador Press, a Christian printer in New Delhi.

1982 Gurung-Nepali New Testament

They printed 1000 copies which were brought into Nepal on the Operation Mobilization (OM) trucks. OM frequently brought "helpful" books across the border for their ministry outreach. We dedicated the Gurung NT in Pokhara in July 1982, in the only two small churches then existing in the town.

As far as we knew, few of those present were Gurung. Only 36 copies were bought on the day – quite a few by expatriate missionaries to distribute to their Gurung friends. Not very encouraging!

Over the years we made regular visits back to Nepal, from India and from Pakistan. We sought to promote the use of the Gurung scriptures, and particularly to encourage the Gurung believers to meet for worship, hymn singing and scripture reading in their own language, even though they were members of different churches in Pokhara.

In September 1987 we wrote to our prayer team:

> Doesn't everyone need the Bible in their own language? But many Gurungs themselves and Christian workers generally answer the question negatively.
>
> > "The Gurungs don't need the Bible in their own language. They can all speak Nepali."
> >
> > "Gurung books are too difficult to read. It is easier to read Nepali ones."
> >
> > "You shouldn't be encouraging Gurung Bible studies. That could be divisive in a church struggling to overcome caste and tribal barriers."

These comments were typical of the reaction to the Gurung New Testament (published in 1982), and any other Christian literature which we produced. Not a very encouraging response to 20 years of hard slog, painstaking research and sustained prayer!

The Gurungs are one of several large ethnic minorities in the hills of Nepal. Their language is quite different from Nepali; it is related more to Tibetan. About 80,000 speakers of Gurung live in mountain villages in three districts around Pokhara. Another 80,000 speak a slightly different dialect and live further east. From our experience of living and working in a Gurung village we know that they cannot *all* speak Nepali. But they do need to use Nepali for shopping and business purposes in the market towns. Hence the town folks' perception that they "can all speak Nepali".

Most Gurungs who have become Christians have been persecuted by family and neighbours and have eventually moved down to live in Pokhara or other towns. Here they have benefitted from the warmth of Christian fellowship and teaching of the Nepali churches in town. Therefore, they have come to feel that the only language appropriate for Christian worship must be Nepali. Further, in the teaching of the multi ethnic town churches they have been taught that caste and tribal distinctions are to be broken down in Christ. We are "all one in Christ Jesus" (Galatians 3:28). This truth they have accepted and sought to live by, many even entering into cross cultural marriages. However, since the vast majority of Gurungs still live in the villages, the question remains as to how best to reach them. Surely by using the language they love and understand best.

In this decade [the 1980s], leaders of several churches in the Pokhara valley, and Gurung believers in particular, have realized that for the purposes of evangelism and outreach to village folk particularly, it is obviously better to use the language of the heart. In July 1986 a small monthly home fellowship began in Pokhara, attended by Gurungs from several of the Pokhara churches. The fellowship has needed strengthening and leadership, together with a clearer understanding of their purpose in meetings. This seemed to be an encouraging beginning for outreach to their home communities.

Much later than when I wrote that in 1987, Campus Crusade similarly encouraged Gurung believers to form a committee *with membership from different churches* to pray for the *Jesus* film in Gurung. They wanted a diversity of Gurung believers to work together for the ongoing use and distribution of the film. However, the Gurung Prayer Committee did not last long after the release of the film in October 2003 and we saw little evidence over the years of Gurung believers from different churches in Pokhara cooperating together for Gurung village outreach.

The 1986 Gurung fellowship, representing different churches in Pokhara, with Tirtha Kumari the song writer and Ras Kumari, my Ghachok close friend, in the front row.

46 Back to the Gurungs

I am about to do something new. (Isaiah 43:19)

In August 2008 , we were surprised (and delighted) to receive an email written in Gurung: "My name is Bhim Gurung. I know that you once helped write a Bible for us Gurung people. But it was for the Gurungs of Syangja and Kaski districts. There are no more copies left and the one or two we have are difficult to read because we speak differently. We are now a group of 20 people who meet weekly to worship the Lord in Gurung. Please, can you come and help us do it again?"

We had actually met with Bhim on an earlier visit to Pokhara at a gathering of Gurung believers and evangelists held in the home of an American couple. The couple were focussing their ministry on the Gurung. On that visit to Pokhara, we had located a trunk of Gurung literature that we had left long before with Ras Kumari, one of the Ghachok believers, for her to use and distribute. We now passed the trunk of materials on to the American couple.

Bhim's reference to district varieties of Gurung was significant. We had understood from the survey of Gurung dialects that Warren did with Dr John Landon in 1975 that there are at least two mutually unintelligible dialects of Gurung – east, spoken in Lamjung and Gorkha districts, and west in Kaski, Syangja and Parbat districts. But Warren had a hope and dream that there might be a central variety, in western Lamjung or eastern Kaski, that would be adequately understood across the whole Gurung-speaking area.

In February 2009, Warren spent three weeks back with the Gurungs. He met Bhim and other Gurung believers from some of the many churches now in Pokhara. They were meeting in a mid-week Gurung language house fellowship. Some, including Bhim, came from the big village of Yangjakot in eastern Kaski district. Was this the "central Gurung" of Warren's hope and dream in the 1975 survey?

Over the three weeks, he worked with one of the fellowship leaders in keyboarding 120 songs into an expanded Gurung hymn book – songs written over the years by Tirtha Kumari (most of them) and several other Gurung believers. Working with Bhim, he translated six discipleship lessons for a program set up to train village evangelists. And they started work on revising the Gospel of Luke to the more central dialect of Gurung that Bhim spoke, plus adding Bible study questions throughout.

At each of the three weekly meetings, the fellowship asked Warren to share from the Word. He chose passages from Mark's Gospel in Gurung, since he had found several copies of Mark in the storage trunk. We heard, with delight and thanksgiving, that the subsequent fellowship meetings included regular singing from the new songbook and reading from the Gospel in Gurung. For many folk there it was the first time to see their language in print and therefore challenging to read, as Bhim had forewarned us in his letter.

That first visit in 2009 began a partnership with that small group of believers for the re-translation of the New Testament into their central dialect, as they had requested. Although they themselves are completely bilingual in Nepali and spiritually fed via their Nepali Bibles, the group stressed that their relatives and friends still living in the mountain villages needed a translation in their mother tongue, one that represented the way they spoke.

In our visits in 2010 we encouraged the Gurung team to practise reading their own language so that they could record the revised Gospel of Luke in order to share it in audio format with their friends and relatives.

We felt the project would take only two to three years since we still had, from SIL's archives, an electronic copy of the 1982 version of the New

Gurung readers, practising in February for recording Luke

Testament and could make use of the Adapt-It program, written by Dr Bruce Waters. It enables a person fluent in both dialects to make a quick first draft from one dialect to the other. Bhim's wife, Nani Ganga, was the ideal person for this project. She grew up in Ghachok village (many years after our departure from that village) and spoke that dialect as her mother tongue. After marrying Bhim, she had learned his central dialect. She is very intelligent and quickly learned the principles of meaningful translation, and how to use the Adapt-It software. We were quickly able to print a Gospel adapted to the central Gurung dialect. We thought they would welcome this output to fulfil their request. They did, but that wasn't the end of the story.

The Gurung elders felt that the 1982 Western Gurung version had used too many Nepali loanwords (which is actually how people speak). They wanted pure Gurung words – and the Gurung dictionary Warren had helped edit some ten years before became the principal source for digging up Gurung words, often archaic ones, to replace the Nepali loans. They used these words whether they were currently understood or not!

The picture significantly muddied in 2011 when most of the group left their different churches to form a separate monoethnic Gurung church. The broader fellowship of churches in Pokhara strongly opposed this development. They believed that meeting separately as ethnic groups contradicts the Gospel truth that "there is neither Jew nor Greek [but we] are all one in Christ Jesus" (Galatians 3:28 KJV). Ethnic identities are a complex, very divisive issue across South Asia, and elsewhere.

We could certainly understand these concerns, but also knew from the history of the church in many parts of South Asia that where ethnic churches were formed, the church grew exponentially. (See *Ethnic Realities and the Church* by Donald A McGavran, 1979.) Subsequently, we have seen the Gurung church grow from the little home group of 20 people, to a flourishing community of about 100 adults, youth and children worshipping together. It is the only place in Pokhara where Gurungs can come and relearn their heritage language, and it is the only church committed to the translation project. Could this be a fresh approach God was opening before us?

As we did checks of the draft books from Nani Ganga's computer with the team, further problems surfaced. They became increasingly sensitive to the "looseness" of the translation style in the 1982 version. That version had amplified the text in various ways to give untaught readers some Biblical background so they could grasp the meaning intended by the original authors. For example, the clarification of why Peter thought he was a sinful man in Luke 5, that I referred to in chapter 17, "What is sin?" But the new team wanted their version to match completely their Nepali Bibles – in grammar and in the choice of many key biblical words. So, rather than being a version that their village relatives could easily understand, it was becoming a version that urban Gurung believers would accept and hopefully use. We wondered if our friends were hoping in this way to win back those who had opposed the formation of the monoethnic Gurung church and hence the Gurung translation.

With external funding support from America and technical support from an English brother Alastair (who also provided office space in his rented home in Pokhara), the translation project continued for over ten years. The publication of the Gurung mini-Bible took place 25 February 2020, less than a month before the worldwide lockdown due to the COVID-19 pandemic.

The Gurung church celebrates the launch of their mini-Bible

Later, in October 2021. Warren was happily surprised to be invited to participate in an International Tamu (Gurung) Conference on Zoom. There were 100 participants from 24 countries, expertly facilitated by a committee in Nepal! International scholars and Gurung academics from many parts of the world shared their insights. Warren contributed on the history of Gurung language development – particularly writing systems and literacy. It was so encouraging to see the level of activism and concern by the current generation of Gurungs, particularly the diaspora, for their culture and language.

For us, the ten years involved two trips a year, usually about four months in total, in our "retirement" years. We often despaired as to how viable or necessary the project really was. Was this work being done for another dying language? For what purpose? But on each visit many relevant Scripture passages, such as Isaiah 42:16 (in *The Message*), deeply encouraged us:

> I'll take the hand of those who don't know the way, who can't see where they're going. I'll be a personal guide to them, directing them through unknown country. I'll be right there to show them what roads to take, make sure they don't fall into a ditch. These are the things I'll be doing for them – sticking with them, not leaving them for a minute.

We had a team of about 50 praying supporters who stood with us week by week as we sent home endless SOS letters expressing our concerns and disappointments. We could also share the miracles of grace that kept assuring us that the smile of God was indeed on this project. The translation team included our dearly beloved sister Lakshmi, the writer of many songs and the translator of the Psalms. She told us how she had been encouraged by a vision of the Lord standing in front of her translation desk. He smiled at her and told her she was doing His work. The team's faithfulness kept us committed to seeing the project completed. And the promise of Isaiah 55:11 kept us mindful of God's perspective: "It is the same with my word. I will send it out, and it always produces fruit." The LORD is the producer of the fruit; our job is to be faithful in helping prepare it.

The dedication of the Gurung mini-Bible on 25 February 2020 was a day of grand celebration and rejoicing. The Gurung church rented an event facility in the city so that they could invite both secular and Christian communities to celebrate with them. I analyse the opportunities and challenges facing this publication in Appendix D, "Will this Bible ever be used?"

It delighted us all that Mark and Merryn had flown in from opposite ends of the globe to celebrate with us the culmination of our service with the Gurung people – people with whom they themselves had spent their childhood years.

As cream on the cake, we had some other significant closures. Mark and Merryn joined us to revisit Ghachok, this time only a 90-minute trip by bus! We all marvelled at the construction of a motorable road up to the high plateau. In their childhood, the trip had taken five hours on foot. In our two days there we visited around the village, including several favourite childhood picnic spots and the three houses where we used to live. Although many people have left Ghachok over the years for education and employment, we discovered a goodly number of former neighbours with whom we could reconnect. One was a believing man who was the son of perhaps the very first believers in Ghachok. We remembered him as just a little toddler 50 years ago. His parents were among the relatively few poor Gurung families in the village.

Amazingly, on returning to Pokhara, we could gather with the extended family of our former landlord, Ram Phal. They had come from far and wide to honour him at his post-funeral event, a big ceremony held 49 days after a Gurung's death. There we met so many people who had been in Ghachok, and played with our kids, 50 years earlier. It was a big challenge to put names to much more mature faces! But they of course remembered us, and fed us like royalty.

The Lord had truly woven our personal Gurung story into a completed circle. But surely the story of the impact of the Word of God upon the Gurung peoples is not complete. They live not only in the mountains of Nepal, but these days in many cities throughout the world, including Melbourne. That story is in the hands of the One who gave them their beautiful mother tongue.

47 You feed them

But we have only five loaves of bread and two fish. (Luke 9:13)

Another unexpected and bewildering email came to us in 2008: "Dear Uncle and Aunty Glover. I am Bijay*, the son of your former employee, Hal*. My Dad, Mum and I now live in Kathmandu. We three have all taken baptism and belong to Jesus' family now. If you come to Nepal. please come and see us."

I was amazed. The last news I'd had of Hal was of a very disappointing event 13 years before, at the end of my work with the Gorkha Women's' Literacy project. A year after my official farewell in January 1994, I was invited to make a return visit to all the classes once more in order to present the certificates to the newly literate learners of the 1995 year. I looked forward very much to revisiting the project, and especially to reconnecting with my staff team from the previous three years. I wondered much whether Hal, in particular, had progressed in his spiritual search. During my time in the project, he had joined our daily pre-work staff prayer times regularly.

But on my return visit the project director, Rudra, told me of Hal's dismissal and transfer to another project because he had taken as a second wife one of the class facilitators only a few months before. That class had stormed Rudra's office with the complaint that his own staff, Hal, had one week talked with them about the social ills of joint wives and then in the very next week had taken their own class facilitator as his second wife! I was devastated. What would this professional and personal downfall do in Hal's life? How had these events impacted his search for Jesus? I felt it as a cruel blow and personal failure, since Hal had been a focus of our prayers and teaching ministry over our three years in the project. He belonged to the highest caste in the Hindu system, so I recognised that to become a Christian would be an immense loss of status – to join the "cow-eating" religion. But far from doing that, this moral lapse had brought great shame on himself, on the project, and on his family.

Now, looking at this email from his son, I wondered, "Could the Lord have turned Hal's life around for good, forgiven him for his adultery, and blessed them both with redemption?" But which "Mum" was Bijay referring to? His birth mother, or Hal's second wife?

We replied to Bijay, arranged a rendezvous for our next trip to Nepal, and were amazed and once again baffled to find wife #2 full of joy in the Lord, along with Hal and Bijay (his son by wife #1). Hal explained that his first wife still lived on the family farm back in Gorkha district with their daughter and she was well provided for there. Why was I baffled? This clear blessing of God was outside my assumption of how God's mercy should work. I had much to learn.

Wife #2, a stunningly beautiful and vivacious woman, shared how she had come to faith in Jesus and trusted Him to forgive her sin. But in the ten years of their marriage she could not conceive. At first, she wondered if this was a punishment from the Lord, but one day in her scripture reading the Lord had given her a promise from Psalm 113:9, "He gives the childless woman a family, making her a happy mother." She felt the Lord would now help her conceive, but when that didn't happen, she and Hal prayed through the issue. Maybe the Lord wanted them to give a home to the multitude of orphans and devastated children whose lives had been so impacted by the ten-year civil war that had been raging throughout the country and also by the HIV AIDS scourge. They asked if we might help them in setting up such a home!

For some time, I resisted this call on our compassion and resources. Perhaps I was still struggling with the paradox of God blessing family #2 while I wondered how wife #1 and the daughter were faring. We counselled Hal that such a project would need a guiding board, a separate bank account with board signatories, and a clearly defined accountability system. This prerequisite should stall proceedings for a time, I thought. But on our next visit to Nepal, we found these structures in place. The board chairman himself had been nurtured from the age of eight in a loving Christian home. Hal and his wife had already taken into their tiny home three girls recommended to them by village authorities for compassionate care – little ones from badly impacted families.

Soon after this, back in Australia, I attended a prayer retreat where I was part of a prayer triplet. In that group, one person facilitates the session, one silently prays for Holy Spirit guidance, and the third shares their current prayer issue. It was my turn to share a prayer need. I told them of the conflict in my spirit about getting involved in the children's home ministry. "This is not our primary calling or skill. I feel that getting involved would drain our own resources and energy when we are still struggling with the Gurung project in Nepal."

"Well, let's just lay these issues before the Lord," the facilitator said. "Let's be still before Him and trust Him to show you what His thoughts are."

It wasn't long before the Gospel narrative of the feeding of the five thousand (Luke 9:10–17) came to my mind. The disciples, like me, complained to Jesus, "Send the crowds away to the nearby village and farms, so they can find food and lodging." But Jesus responded, "You feed them."

I knew, without a shadow of doubt, that this was a word from the Lord for me, and I needed to put away my prejudices and questions, and open my heart to help in whatever way we could. Warren, always generous, was already trying to figure out the best way to move forward. He wrote to our donor/prayer team, who had stood with us over many decades, with the story of the needy girls. Since then, the Lord has raised up a team of donors and supporters for Moonlight Children's Home (MCH). The team includes our personal contacts and friends in the UK and Europe.

Girls of the MCH family in school uniform—in July 2011 there were 12

Beginning with the first three girls in March 2009, the MCH family grew quickly as Hal and his wife responded to more calls of need. They had 12 girls in 2011 and 24 in 2019, and the MCH children in the household now number 26 (two of whom are Bijay's own daughters).

Not all the girls are full orphans, but all come from broken and dysfunctional families. In each case local village leaders had approached MCH to take in the girls for their future care and welfare. Three girls were brought to their attention by a Government children's welfare agency in Kathmandu. The agency had rescued three sisters (and an older brother) from the banks of the Bagmati River – really just a putrid sewer – which runs through Kathmandu. Their mother had deserted them some years before, and the father spent any money he got on drink. The children were destitute, surviving only on the rice grains left at the funeral pyres on the river bank. There was no girls' home to settle the children in and the agency begged MCH to take them in. (They placed the brother in another home.) The eldest of the three girls is now in Year 12 and has done very well in school. Just one of the transformations that Hal and family have seen over the past 12 years.

In 2019, 24 girls in their own MCH home

After renting a series of houses to accommodate the growing family, MCH received gifts to purchase land on the outskirts of Kathmandu. On this land they have a custom-built three-storey home and have planted an extensive orchard and vegetable garden to help with their daily food needs. Exceedingly above all that they could have asked or thought (Ephesians 3:20)!

The longer-term sustainability of the home is a continuing concern for us and for the MCH leadership. The financial challenge has increased as the eldest three girls, now young women, graduate from Year 12 and look towards tertiary education in medicine, teaching and commerce. And their younger "sisters" are coming along in succeeding classes.

For some years MCH kept a large chicken farm, which helped them in paying off some outstanding loans for the building of the house. Then the local municipality rezoned their area as "urban" and banned chicken farms, for fear of bringing in bird flu and because of complaints from neighbours about the smell. Now they are seeking to establish a goat farm on a hillside on Hal's rural village in Gorkha district. They hope that the sale of young goats will provide a significant sustainable income stream into the future. We hope so too.

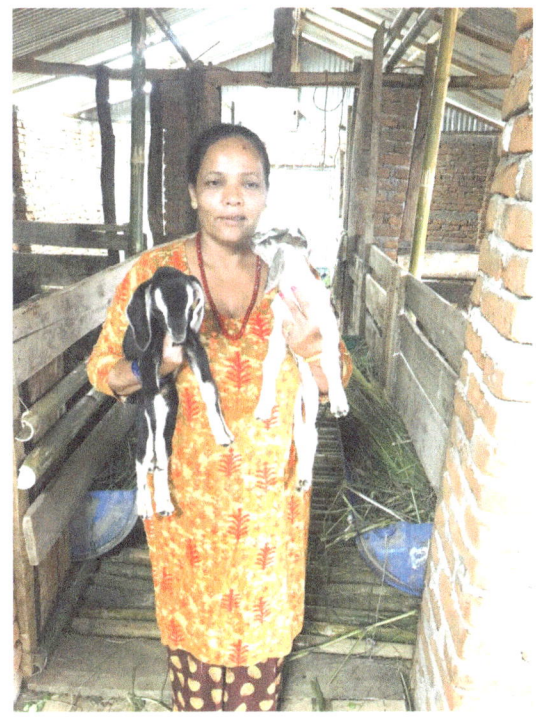

Hal's wife with two kids, as the flock multiplies!

48 Epilogue

What does retirement really look like? – for a follower of Jesus.

Warren and I are now in our 80s. God has abundantly blessed us, enabling us to live full and incredibly purposeful lives amongst some of His "other sheep", mostly in South Asia. We've had excellent health (apart from Warren's malaria, hepatitis, heart attacks, diarrhea of many varieties, and hip and knee replacements, and my polymyalgia rheumatica and a thyroidectomy) and an incredible band of prayer warriors, financially supporting individuals and churches standing with us in our going out and coming in. The integrity and support of our Wycliffe family have all helped to make that journey happen. Our good health continues, for which we are daily thankful. Energy and strength are definitely more limited, but like Caleb of old, we are still up to some further climbing (or claiming?) of mountains.

Our twice-yearly trips to Nepal are now history, although there is a passion in my heart to be on site when the Faith Comes By Hearing (FCBH) team eventually gets to Nepal for recording the Gurung New Testament. COVID-19 restrictions on border closures between India and Nepal make the timing of that visit highly uncertain. That visit aside, we are asking the Lord to show us, as His followers, where He would have us prioritize whatever energy we still have.

In a recent pastoral letter (June 2020) the vicar of our local church here in Melbourne, Revd Bruce Bickerdike, raised a challenge: "Might the Lord be leading us as a church to begin a journey toward reconciliation with our indigenous peoples?"

Warren and I put up our hands to help with our parish's Reconciliation Action Plan because Bruce's challenge resonated with earlier concerns we have had for our First Nations peoples: Warren's involvement with the Aboriginal Scholarship group at Melbourne University; his distress at the conditions he saw on a central Australian bus trip in the 1960s; our expectation that when we had to leave Nepal in 1976 we would work with the Australian Aborigines Branch of SIL; and our grandson Joshua's inspiration, challenge, and guidance to us in reconciliation steps.

This challenge began for me in 2019 on a bus in Nepal with Joshua. He learned that one of my forebears had settled at Appin, NSW, and read to me from his mobile phone about the Appin massacre (April 1816). It happened on the Cataract River where more than a century later I had enjoyed swimming. "Was he involved in the massacre?" Josh asked. I was relieved to discover that my ancestor John Percival only arrived in Australia, and Appin, in 1833, aged 18. He certainly had no part in the 1816 massacre! But the shocking facts of history continue to distress me.

Is this our family story coming full circle, with not only our son (see chapter 25, "Stirring up the nest"), but now our grandson being our youthful counsellors? We expect to discover again that God is good, however difficult the trail may be. And so I conclude with the final portion from our daughter's poem "My Mother's Hands":

My mother's hands are older
than her memory,
and will outlive it,
holding on, till all else is forgotten
and fallen,
till a greater, older hand
takes hold,
and her fingers trace
its wound
and her own name carved beside.

In January 2015, the family joined us for our 50th wedding anniversary. In the photo Mark's family is on the left, and Merryn's on the right.

A Child of Two/Three Families

Birth family—SEGAL

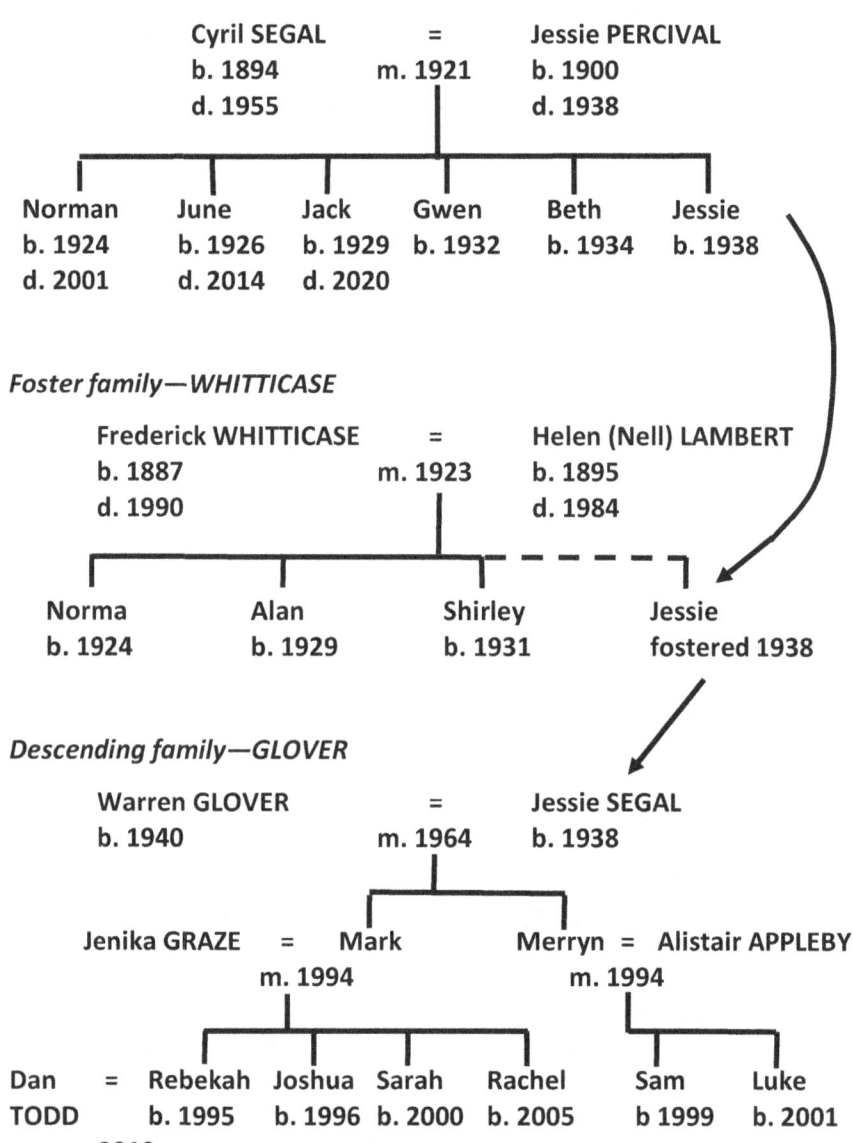

Cyril SEGAL = Jessie PERCIVAL
b. 1894   m. 1921   b. 1900
d. 1955   d. 1938

Norman   June   Jack   Gwen   Beth   Jessie
b. 1924   b. 1926   b. 1929   b. 1932   b. 1934   b. 1938
d. 2001   d. 2014   d. 2020

Foster family—WHITTICASE

Frederick WHITTICASE = Helen (Nell) LAMBERT
b. 1887   m. 1923   b. 1895
d. 1990   d. 1984

Norma   Alan   Shirley   Jessie
b. 1924   b. 1929   b. 1931   fostered 1938

Descending family—GLOVER

Warren GLOVER = Jessie SEGAL
b. 1940   m. 1964   b. 1938

Jenika GRAZE = Mark   Merryn = Alistair APPLEBY
m. 1994   m. 1994

Dan = Rebekah Joshua Sarah Rachel   Sam   Luke
TODD   b. 1995   b. 1996 b. 2000 b. 2005   b 1999   b. 2001
m. 2019

Appendix. Timeline of significant events

Abbreviations used in the Appendix:

ANU	Australian National University, Canberra	OZ	Australia
		PEO	Principal Executive Officer
FCBH	Faith Comes By Hearing (a recording ministry)	PKR	Pokhara, Nepal
		PNG	Papua New Guinea
IICCC	Indian Institute for Cross-Cultural Communication	SAG	South Asia Group of SIL
		SIL	Summer Institute of Linguistics Inc.
INF	International Nepal Fellowship		
		SMBC	Sydney Missionary and Bible College
KTM	Kathmandu		
MCH	Moonlight Children's Home, KTMPNG Education	SPSIL	South Pacific Summer Institute of Linguistics
MRRV	Ministry Renewal Retreats Victoria	SU	Scripture Union
		TCDW	Translation Consultant Development Workshop
MUT	Missionary Upholders Trust, Odanchattram, Tamil Nadu		
		TSC	The Seed Company
MTCN	Mother Tongue Centre Nepal	TU	Tribhuvan University, Kirtipur, Nepal
NCGGC	Nepal Christian Grace Gurung Church, Pokhara		
		UBS	United Bible Societies
NRS	New Reader Scriptures	WBT	Wycliffe Bible Translators
NT	New Testament		

Date	Event	Comment
The First Miles **1938-1963**		
1938	6 January: my birth, sixth child of Jessie and Cyril Segal, orchardists in Wilton, NSW	My mother dies some weeks afterward, and I am fostered by Fred and Nell Whitticase, friends of the family just down the road.
1949	Closure of Wilton Public School.	Severe dissonance between Cyril Segal and Fred Whitticase. Conflict is never resolved.

Date	Event	Comment
1951	7 February: **death of brother Alan** in a motorcycle accident.	Awareness of the Lord's comfort in grief and pain.
1952-54	Allan Laing joins the local parish staff (and our family).	I come to a greater understanding of salvation through Christ's work on the cross.
1955-56	Wagga Wagga Teachers College.	Grow in faith thanks to Allan's urging to join the Christian group in college.
1957	Full commitment to Christ. Begin teaching, Hammondville Public School.	Through the break-up of a close relationship I receive an overwhelming infilling of the Holy Spirit.
	First missionary convention facilitated by St Mark's, Picton.	At the convention I respond to a challenge towards overseas mission.
1957-61	Five years of teaching at Hammondville	Involve with CMS League of Youth, lead a young people's group at St. Anne's, Hammondville, and attend SU camps/missions
1962	Transfer to teach at West Wollongong Primary School	Begin a League of Youth group in Wollongong and meet Warren.
1963	6 October: Engaged to Warren	After courtship and the challenge to join him in WBT. No longer "on the shelf"!

Beginning the Long Partnership 1964–65

Date	Event	Comment
1964	At SMBC. Joined WBT (March).	Warren studies at Ridley College, Melbourne.
	28 November: **married at St Mark's, Picton.**	Glover family travels from Melbourne and Canberra for the event
1965	August–December: Jungle Camp in PNG `	Return to Wollongong late 1965

Date	Event	Comment
	Distant Horizons 1966–70	
1966	10 March: sail for India on *Galileo Galilei*.	Study Hindi in Poona, with several other new assignees in SIL's new India advance.
	6 October: **Mark Warren born in Poona.**	Hot days for a thirsty baby!
	22 December: flew to Nepal	Into the chill of a Himalayan winter.
1967	Initial study of Nepali in KTM.	Helped by having some Hindi from Pune.
	5 May: moved to Gurung village Ghachok	Called back into KTM in July when the administrator and family return to UK.
1968	May: Hales arrive to help us fulfil professional expectations of Tribhuvan University.	Tribhuvan University Journal (Special Linguistic Number) is published with five articles by the SIL team. Hence TU contract is renewed for five years to 1974.
1969	January–February: India holiday.	Return to Nepal and succumbed to Asian flu, whole month of March.
	12 April: **Merryn Suzanne is born .**	A very delayed arrival—born in a former Rana palace in Kathmandu!
	June–August: Ken and Evelyn Pike's visit.	Workshop on tone systems in languages of Nepal
1970	1 October: Warren begins PhD at ANU	Mark joined pre-school playgroup, became fluent in English.
	Translators' Tales 1971–79	
1971	February: to Nepal for Warren's field trip.	I begin home schooling children in Ghachok.

Date	Event	Comment
1972	April: Mark's Gospel consultant checked .	Transformation in Baje Baidera, the first village convert. Returned to Canberra late April.
1974	March: return to Nepal.	Field testing of the Gurung literacy primer.
1976	18 August: banished from Nepal!	Intense Scripture production in Kathmandu, 51 portions in 21 languages.
1977	March: to Pokhara, Nepal on tourist visas.	Progress on translation and Scripture engagement. Children in Pokhara Study Centre.
	late July: Mark and Chris Meyer join Woodstock School.	Mark threatens to run away from school!
1978	March: rented a house in Landour.	Merryn joins Woodstock as a day scholar.
	August: "Last and Exit" 7-day visas, left Nepal,	Final consultant check of Gurung NT with Kent Gordon in Mussoorie..
1979	In Canberra – Warren back at ANU..	Children in Canberra schools. Mark not happy, longing to get back to Woodstock.

**Give Me This Mountain
1980–82**

1980	March: house move to India.	Imported 21 boxes of course materials for IICCC. Settled into Lower Bethany.
	May–August: first IICCC course	Children in boarding at Woodstock.
	August: Dallas for New Testament typesetting	Difficult transition to US, with separation from Mark and Merryn.
1981	Lower Bethany, for the 1980–81 winter.	Snowed in! Warren to Dallas for another semester of editing and typesetting.
	November: return to OZ for SPSIL.	Children helped us in processing the Pakistan decision.

Date	Event	Comment
	Heading West **1982–87**	
1982	17 July: Dedication of Gurung NT in two Pokhara churches.	Only 36 NTs were purchased.
	8 December: Arrived in Hyderabad, Pakistan.	Children helped in orientation and child care.
1984	26 January: phone call from OZ – my Mum broken her hip.	Flight to Lahore-Karachi-Bangkok-Sydney was disrupted by missing flight out of Karachi!
	7 March: **Mum dies in hospital**.	I stayed with Dad till after Mum's funeral and returned to Hyderabad late March.
	June: **Mark graduates from Woodstock.**	Family round the world trip back to OZ.
1985	January: return to Pakistan.	Warren stayed a while to get Mark settled in Uni and student hostel at Kew Baptist.
1987	April: UBS translation workshop (Genesis).	Translated Genesis New Reader Scriptures into Gurung.
	1 May: leave Pakistan.	
	June: **Merryn graduates from Woodstock.**	Exhausting hot overland journey to Nepal.
	July–August: checking, printing Genesis NRS.	INF housing in Pokhara.
	August: Return to OZ.	Merryn's transition after Woodstock.
	29 October: **Dad's 100th birthday.**	Family celebration at Wilton.
	27 November: Become "first home owners".	Amazing financial provision when we had but $1,000 to start the process.

Date	Event	Comment
	Heights to Conquer 1988–93	
1988-89	Together in 31 Oban Road, Ringwood.	Family all involved in tertiary study.
	21 July 1988: **Warren's dad dies.**	We are in Ringwood, and can attend the funeral and spend time with Mother Glover.
1990	April: Return to Nepal Good Friday.	"Open door to serve with UMN (and to work on literacy and translation in the eastern (Gorkha) dialect of Gurung).
	July–December: Asia SIL school in Singapore.	Teaching literacy
	8 August: **my Dad dies**	I flew from Singapore for the funeral
1991	February: Begin three-year NFE consultancy in Gorkha project.	Impact in 60 villages; at least 1000 women become literate.
	November 1991: two month visit by Merryn.	She meets Alistair in Amp Pipal.
1992	February: **death of Roy Wark (Brother-in-law)**.	Pancreatic cancer – very sudden.
1993	October: Mark and Jenika visit.	To acquaint Jen with South Asia
	Roy and Janet Gwyther-Jones visit.	Popular craft workshops for third year literacy classes.
	Family Joins the Journey 1994–2001	
1994	26 February: **Mark marries Jenika.**	Community Church of St Mark, Clifton Hill.
	26 March: **Merryn marries Alistair.**	Wycliffe centre, Kangaroo Ground. Five of Al's family members come from UK.
	1 July: Warren begins as Principal of SPSIL.	Move to Buangvillea at Kangaroo Ground.

Date	Event	Comment
1995	25 March: **Rebekah Trudi Glover born in Melbourne.**	Our first grandchild
1996	2 October: Director of South Asia Group.	Living in Bakhundol, near both Mark and Merryn and families in KTM.
	15 December: **Joshua Mark Glover born in Melbourne.**	
1998	4 April: **Mother Glover's 90th birthday.**	Trip back from Nepal for the celebration, and for the marriage of Philip Glover and Liza.
	12 August: Warren's heart attack!	Alistair's triage training of Patan hospital staff contributes to good recovery for Warren.
1999	13 April: **Mother Glover dies in Melbourne.**	
	May: SIL international conference.	Round-the-world trip to Waxhaw, NC. .
	23 June: **Samuel James Appleby born.**	Visited him in Stirling, Scotland, at the end of our trip!
2000	22 January: Family reunion in memory of the four Evans siblings.	Merryn and baby Sam with us for the memorial, plus myriad rellies.
	05 March: **Sarah Jenika Glover born in Melbourne.**	
	March: Central Australia holiday	Travelled to Alice Springs by bus with the Wycliffe Associates work party
2001	10 August: **Luke Thomas Appleby born in Stirling, Scotland**	
	December: I finish up as SAG director.	Term of 5+ years .

Date	Event	Comment
	Retirement Triathlon 2002–	During 2002–2015 I spent four or five months each year in literacy consulting and training workshops, largely in Nepal and NE India.
2002	May–June: Holiday with Applebys in UK.	Visit Oban, Tobermory, and Iona.
	July: Coordinator for SIL teams in India.	Bangalore. Warren secures business visas for his work in training Indian translators.
2003	May: Gurung-Nepali-English dictionary.	It becomes a major source for the team in their language preservation efforts ten years later.
	May: Visit to Melbourne to consult a surgeon on Warren's knee replacement.	Warren gets sciatica, which goes with him to India. He works from bed, or flat on the floor, with a *tummy top* computer. Healed six months later by lying prone for 36 hours on a train trip, first class, from Bangalore–Delhi!
	October: Release of Gurung *Jesus* film in Pokhara.	Warren can not leave India because of passport problems – turned back at the departure gate in Calcutta!
2004	Extensive travels (mostly by Indian Railways!) for field visits in my role as personnel coordinator for India-based teams.	20–28 January: Palampur (UP), Delhi-with three teams February: Lamtaput (Odisha) – Holly Larson (US) Mancherial (Andhra Pradesh) – Pennys (NZ) May: Delhi – Sons (Korea) Poutalovs (Rus) Shimla – Arsenaults (Can), Neumans (US), Troy Bailey (US) Mussoorie – Evy (Can) June: Delhi – Steve Lilley (Oz), Liza (Russian) Jodhpur – Daileys (USA) Rajpur – Eatons (US) in Pahari Macro Team, Neumans (US), Irene van Riezen (Neth) Bangalore – Busemans (US), Troy Bailey (US) August, Hyderabad – Pennys, Troy November, Leh (Ladakh) – Steve Lilley
	October: Our 40th wedding anniversary celebration.	With our 1964 wedding attendants (Pam and Ray) plus SIL friends, and Applebys who from Scotland. Family revisited Ghachok.

Date	Event	Comment
2004 (ctd)	December: Beach holiday in South India. Boxing Day tsunami	Miraculously spared, but difficult to contact our worried family because of broken communications.
2005	March: two trips to family in Scotland.	Before and after MLE seminar at Horsleys Green.
	June: Closure of our KTM flat and many farewells.	Housemate Mary Morgan also leaving.
	October: resuming occupancy of 31 Oban Road, Ringwood .	Mark meets me at airport, and helped me get unpacked, utilities reconnected, etc. Garden and house a mess.
2006	14 March: Warren's hip replacement.	Marvellous recovery and relief of pain.
	May–June: thank-you trip to NSW and QLD.	Great time catching up with Townsville relatives.
	July–November: EQUIP at Kangaroo Ground	Teaching Literacy.
	November-January: visiting Nepal, Pakistan, UK, NEI, Thailand (13 weeks)	Project evaluation (Pakistan), MLE teaching (NEI), family visits (UK), R&P training (Bangkok).
2007	May–June: Round Australia trip with Ray Christmas.	Broome, Mt Tom Price, Darwin, Kakadu, Mt Isa, Longreach, etc. – good contact with Townsville relatives again.
	November: Renewal and Prayer retreat in Chiangmai, Thailand.	Richly blessed time on staff – great fellowship, especially with Karen Block.
	7 December: theft of our computers and backup drive!	No break-in. Must have been former tenants who still had a key.

Date	Event	Comment
2008	1 April: Warren's left knee reconstruction	Excellent surgeon, John Bartlett. Good recovery after exhausting rehabilitation.
	July–August: Wonderful UK summer holiday.	Including Cornwall with Applebys and a week at Keswick.
	November: Reflection and Prayer retreat at Kangaroo Ground	Church friends Peter and Joan Latham were participants. Renewed fellowship with Evelyn Davis, Karen Block, Barry and Linda Proudlove.
2009	February: Central Gurung project begins	Warren works with Bhim and Om, and gets Luke's Gospel and song book printed.
	30 March: *Moonlight Children's Home (MCH) opens its doors*.	**Five (semi-)orphan girls** given a home.
	September–October: holiday with extended family.	Applebys arrive 21 September in Cairns for six weeks in OZ
2010	June–July: Scotland and Switzerland holiday.	Visited Hales (Wald), didiharu and Anne-Marie (Adelboden), Kym and Scott McKinnon (Basel).
	5–13 August: Nieces' daughters Michelle and Merryn's weddings.	A rare opportunity to reconnect with my Sydney relatives.
	23 September–11 October: Recording of Gurung Luke in PKR.	Rod Jones came to PKR from Wycliffe Australia.
2011	13 January: Brendan marries Lisa .	Another family round-up. In Sydney
	February-March: Nepal and NEI.	**MCH now has 14 girls**
	1 April: Warren begins as PEO of SIL Australia.	Warren exhausted from wrapup of TCDW workshop. No transition with previous PEO.
	16 May: death of Shah Bahadur Gurung.	**Shah was the main translator of the Gurung NT.** We met with his widow, Samjhana, in July.

Date	Event	Comment
2011 (ctd)	11–15 July: Reflection and Prayer retreat for Indian mission leaders.	Facilitated at MUT centre in Tamil Nadu by Evelyn Davis and MUT founder JJ Ratnakumar.
	November: Typesetting *On Trek with the Glovers*	Printed in time for Christmas gifts to family.
	23 December: Applebys arrive for Christmas	Extended family holiday at Lochsport and great celebration of my 74th birthday!
2012	March: Warren gets shingles, due to stress.	Quick diagnosis and treatment meant quick recovery, praise God!
	mid-May: Biblical By-ways tour of Turkey and Greece.	"In the footsteps of St Paul", led by Les and Kathy Bruce with an excellent Biblical consultant
	September: WA trip-with Ray Christmas.	Wildflower explorations north of Perth, plus southwest to Albany
	22 December: Applebys join us in Melbourne.	"Round the World in 80 wickets" – part of Al's Sabbatical break
2013	June–July: UK holiday – extensive visiting in England by train.	Celebrate with Merryn, signing the contract for publishing *A house called Askival*, her first published novel.
	August: Nepal visit.	TSC agrees to fund three translators for three years for Central Gurung NT.
2014	24 March: 50 years since joining Wycliffe.	All the way, God has led us!
	Early May: Ganga using Adapt-It from Western Gurung to Central.	Warren teaches her, with remote consultation from the software author, Australian Bruce Waters.
	18–31 May: Biblical Byways tour.	We meet Lathams and Wakefords in Bangkok and travelled together to Israel and Jordan.
	July: MCH family move to Taukhel.	Custom built three-storey home (A$250,000 at least). Financed via many Australian donors.

Date	Event	Comment
2014 (ctd)	July–August: Farewell to Guwahati.	Conclusion of 10 years of MLE facilitation workshops, seminars and consultations.
	September: Severe back pain after long hot walk in Pokhara.	Wheelchair needed at airports in travel back to OZ. Diagnosed as polymyalgia rheumatica. PTL for instant relief with prednisolone!
	28 November: 50 years married!	Celebration deferred to 6 January 2015
2015	6 January: Golden wedding celebration.	Great celebration at Kangaroo Ground with whole family and about 50 guests.
	25 April–15 May: Severe earthquakes in Nepal.	Widespread damage and loss of life from Gorkha eastward. Not so bad in Pokhara.

MCH now has 22 girls.

	First Translation Impact Committee meeting.	With 20 Gurung church leaders at Nepal Christian Grace Gurung Church (NCGGC), Pokhara .
	August: Sarah begins Year 10 at Woodstock..	The school where her Dad and Aunt Merryn had most of their school years.
2016	February: Escort Sarah to Woodstock for Semester 2.	Overnighted in Bethany, now completely renovated as an upmarket guest house!
	23–25 May: MRRV facilitator training, in Melbourne.	Great fellowship, and Bible teaching.
	Early June: SIL Nepal gathering in Pokhara.	Great to be with the whole gang, including Nepali staff.
	13 June–26 July: UK holiday	A week with Merryn on Scottish north coast, plus Yorkshire, and Northern Ireland.
	30 December: Dedication of the Gurung Mini-Bible.	Great celebration, at NCGGC: Genesis, four Gospels, and Acts.

Date	Event	Comment
2017	6 January: A birthday treat to Maling (Lamjung)!	A scary bus trip! Intelligibility of Central Gurung Bible was not good.
	24 January: Return visit to Amp Pipal.	Jeep from Dumre, with Ishwari, was much better than walking six hours!.
	January: Kathmandu and Pokhara.	Gurung orthography meeting at MTCN, and we visit MCH. **MCH now has 23 girls.**
	May: Gurung orthography and translation discussions.	A 40-year process revisited.
	1–17 July: South Australia and Top End trip, with extended family.	Great vacation, hired a campervan, celebrated three birthdays (Sam 18, Josh 21, and self 80) at Uluru.
	7 August: **Sister Norma's funeral.**	Sister Shirley looking very frail.
2018	July: Consultant check of three chapters of Exodus.	Dhan Tamang is a fluent Gurung speaker, mentored as trainee consultant by Warren!
	10 October: Translator-Lakshmi has a stroke.	Lakshmi translated Psslms and Proverbs and also had written and sung many hymns.
2019	February: Advanced Trauma Healing training, Sydney.	Stayed with Lucy Denley in Sydney, then Kath White in Albury on my return to Melbourne..
	Gurung teenage Sunday School class.	Using Genesis videos prepared over two years.
	23 March: **10th birthday of MCH.**	Party at Taukhel.
	March-April: UK for Merryn's 50th.	Also visited many UK friends and Hales and Didiharu in Switzerland.

Date	Event	Comment
2019 (ctd)	August: Minie checks Gurung Psalms.	Minie and Viji (a great computer support) staying with us in Nadipur.
	26 December: extended family holiday at Phillip Island.	Warren spends many hours on unexpected final editing for Gurung mini-Bible, becomes very ill, develops to pneumonia.
2020	25 February: Dedication of Central Gurung Mini-Bible in Pokhara.	Mark and Merryn join us. Mark miraculously makes it, after the date is preponed one day! Then a three-day foray back to Ghachok, travelling by bus!
	18 March: Return to Melbourne in time to escape COVID hotel quarantine, but self-isolating 14 days.	Coronavirus! Extended lockdown ensued, state and country wide. Praise the Lord the dedication was accomplished BEFORE the lockdown! But the visit of the FCBH team to record the Gurung NT was postponed, to January 2022.
	Begin writing my memoirs *All the Way*.	A great way to use the lockdown!
2021	1 January: Finished first draft of *All the Way*.	Warren spends all year in editing and typesetting it in preparation for self-publishing.

Bibliography

Askew, Eddie. 1985. *Many voices, one voice: meditations and prayers.* Brentford, UK: The Leprosy Mission International.

--- 1987. *No strange land: meditations and prayers.* Brentford, UK: The Leprosy Mission International.

Dye, T Wayne. 2009. The eight conditions of Scripture engagement, social and cultural factors necessary for vernacular Bible translation to achieve maximum effect. *International Journal of Frontier Missiology* 26.2:89-98.

Finlay, Everist, and Wheeler. 1996. *Nepal: a Lonely Planet travel survival kit.* Hawthorn: Lonely Planet Publications.

Glover, Warren. 2002. *Making a difference: training Bible translators in India.* Kangaroo Ground: Wycliffe Bible Translators.

Glover, Warren W., Jessie R. Glover and Deu Bahadur Gurung. 1977. *Gurung-Nepali-English dictionary with English-Gurung and Nepali-Gurung indexes.* Canberra: ANU Dept of Linguistics.

Glover, Warren W. and Ratna Bahadur Gurung. 2003. *Gurung-Nepali-English dictionary.* Kathmandu: Tamu Bauddha Sewa Samiti.

Hale, E. Austin and Kenneth L. Pike. 1970. *Tone systems of Tibeto-Burman languages of Nepal.* (Occasional Papers of the Wolfenden Society, ed. by F K Lehman, vol. 3.) Urbana: Department of Linguistics, University of Illinois.

Hale, Thomas B. 1993. *Living stones of the Himalayas.* Grand Rapids: Zondervan.

McGavran, Donald A. 1979. *Ethnic realities and the church: lessons from India.* Pasadena: William Carey Library.

Meyer, Carole. 2003. *Beyond the door.* Robina QLD: Faith Builders International).

Peterson, Eugene H. 2002. *The message: the Bible in contemporary language.* Colorado Springs: NavPress.

Swenson, Janel. 2015. A sociolinguistic study of Gurung in Nepal. *Linguistic Survey of Nepal.* Kathmandu: Central Department of Linguistics, Tribhuvan University and SIL International.

TEAR. 1994. *TEAR Target No. 13.* Melbourne: TEAR.

Made in the USA
Las Vegas, NV
16 February 2024